CLAMP

9

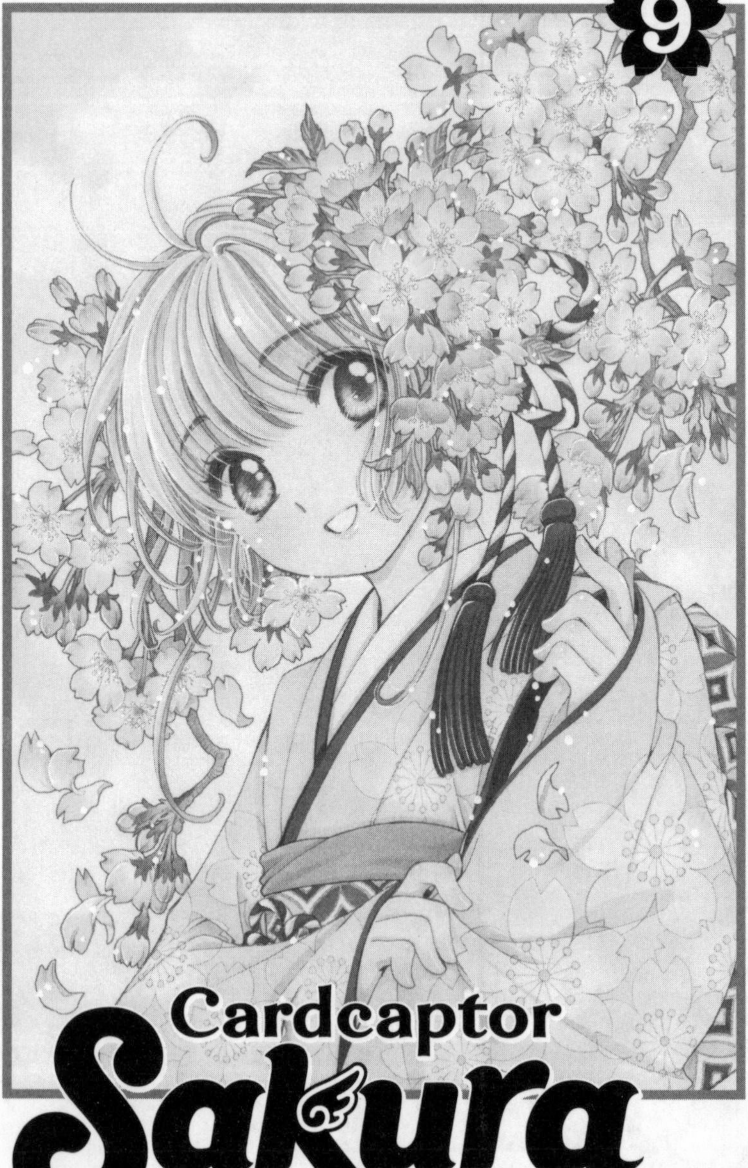

Cardcaptor Sakura

CLEAR CARD

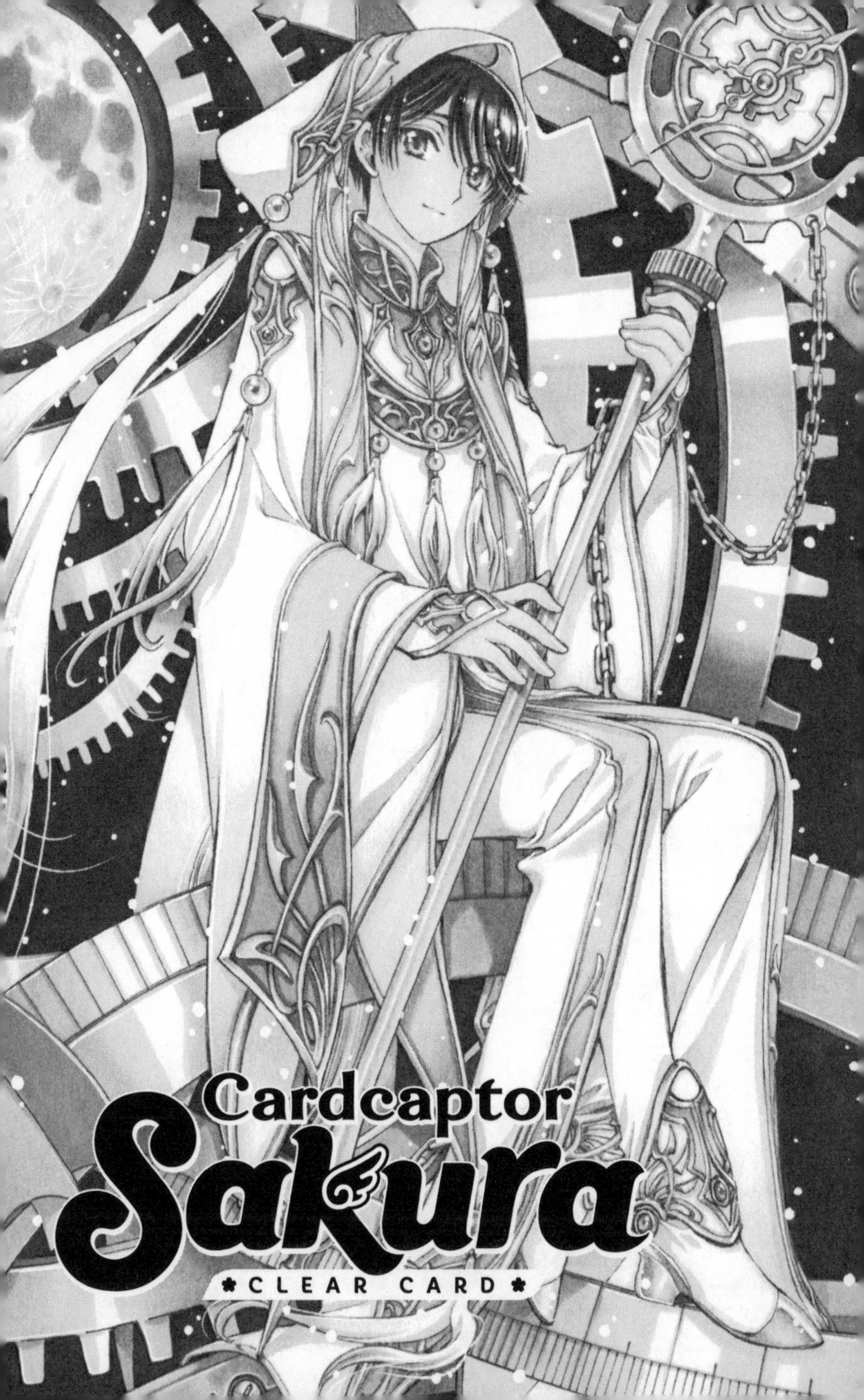
Cardcaptor
Sakura
CLEAR CARD

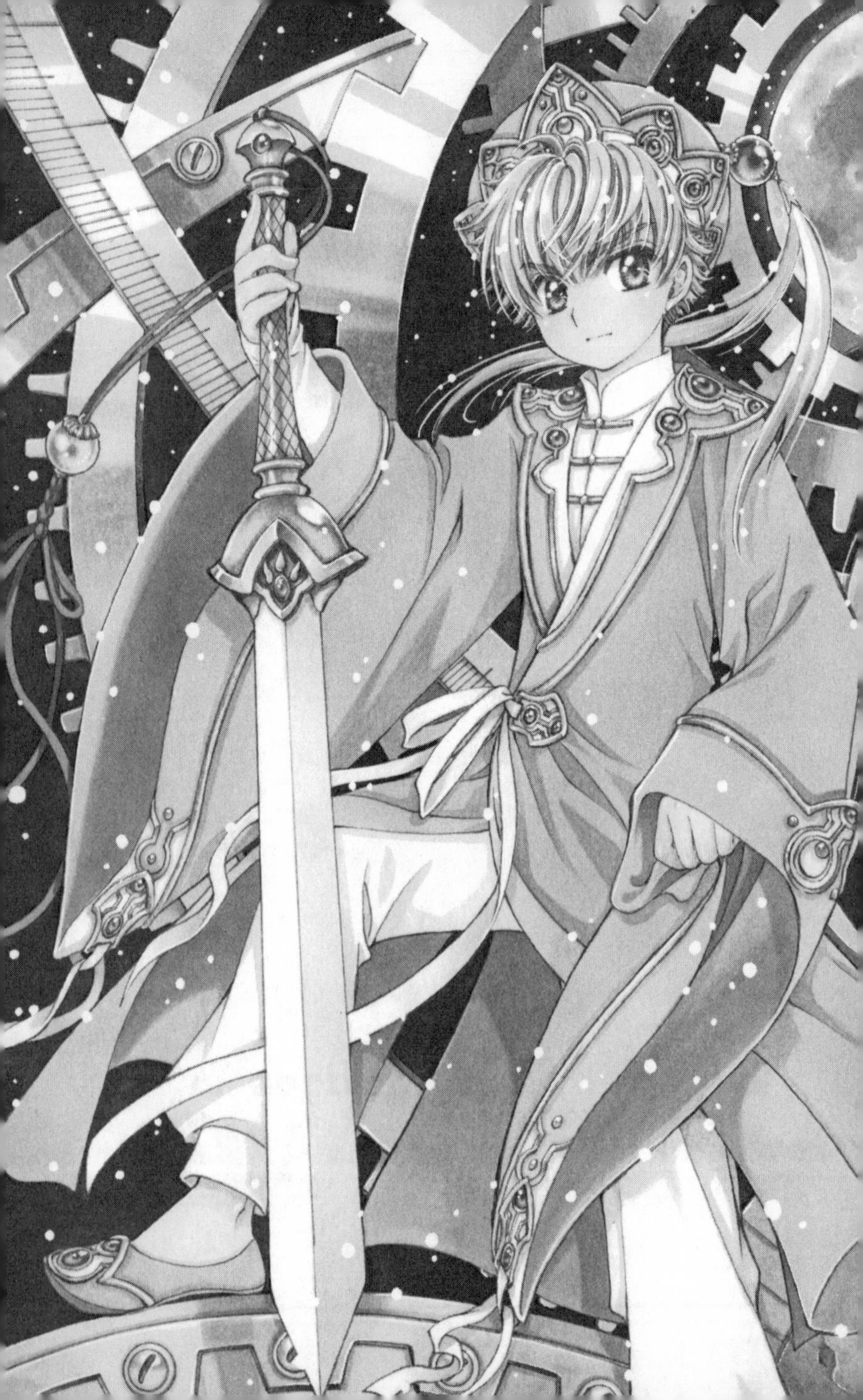

Cardcaptor
Sakura
CLEAR CARD

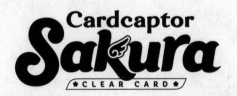

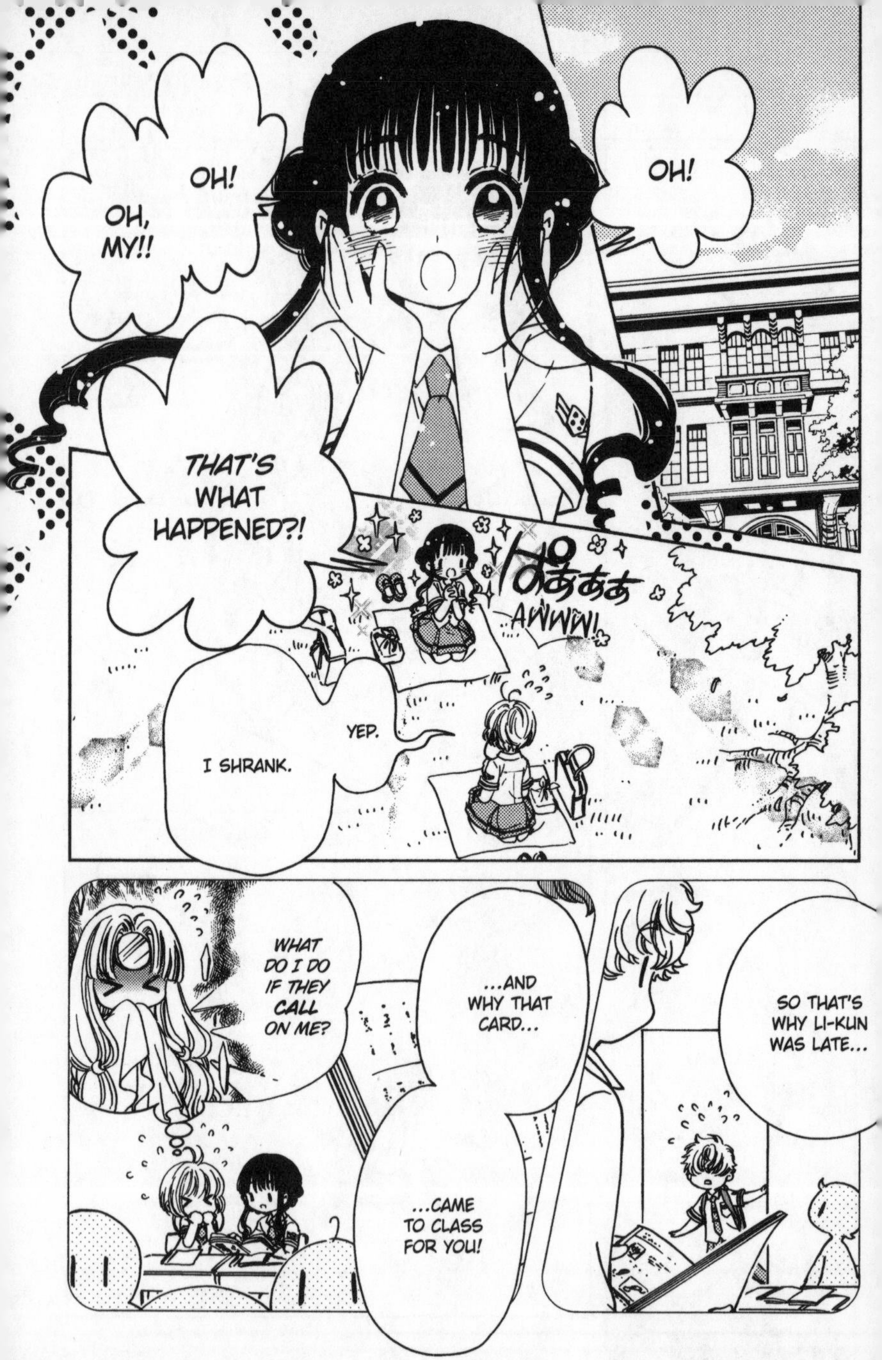
OH!
OH! OH, MY!!
THAT'S WHAT HAPPENED?!
ぱあああ
AWWW!
YEP. I SHRANK.
SO THAT'S WHY LI-KUN WAS LATE...
...AND WHY THAT CARD... ...CAME TO CLASS FOR YOU!
WHAT DO I DO IF THEY CALL ON ME?

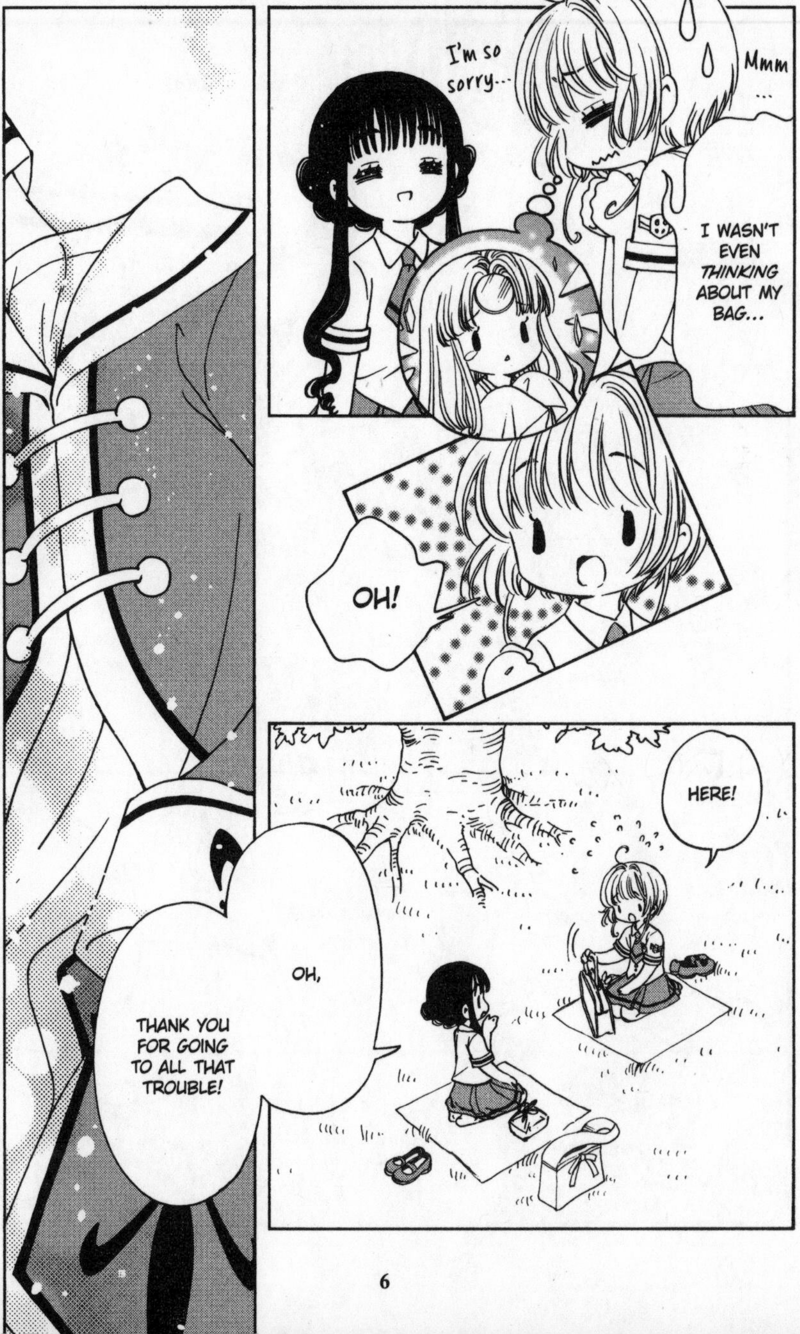
Mmm...
I'm so sorry...
I WASN'T EVEN *THINKING* ABOUT MY BAG...
OH!
HERE!
OH,
THANK YOU FOR GOING TO ALL THAT TROUBLE!

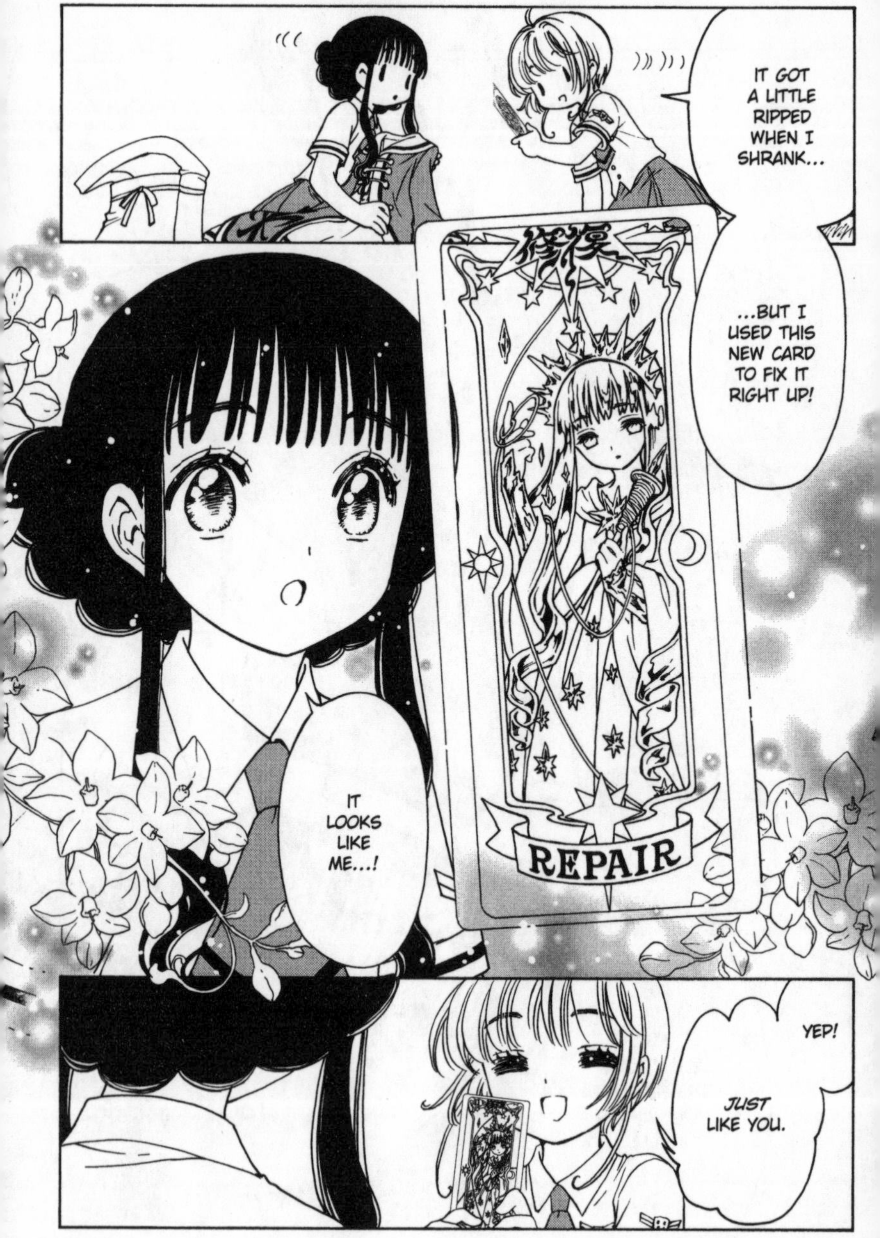
IT GOT A LITTLE RIPPED WHEN I SHRANK...
...BUT I USED THIS NEW CARD TO FIX IT RIGHT UP!
REPAIR
IT LOOKS LIKE ME...!
YEP!
JUST LIKE YOU.

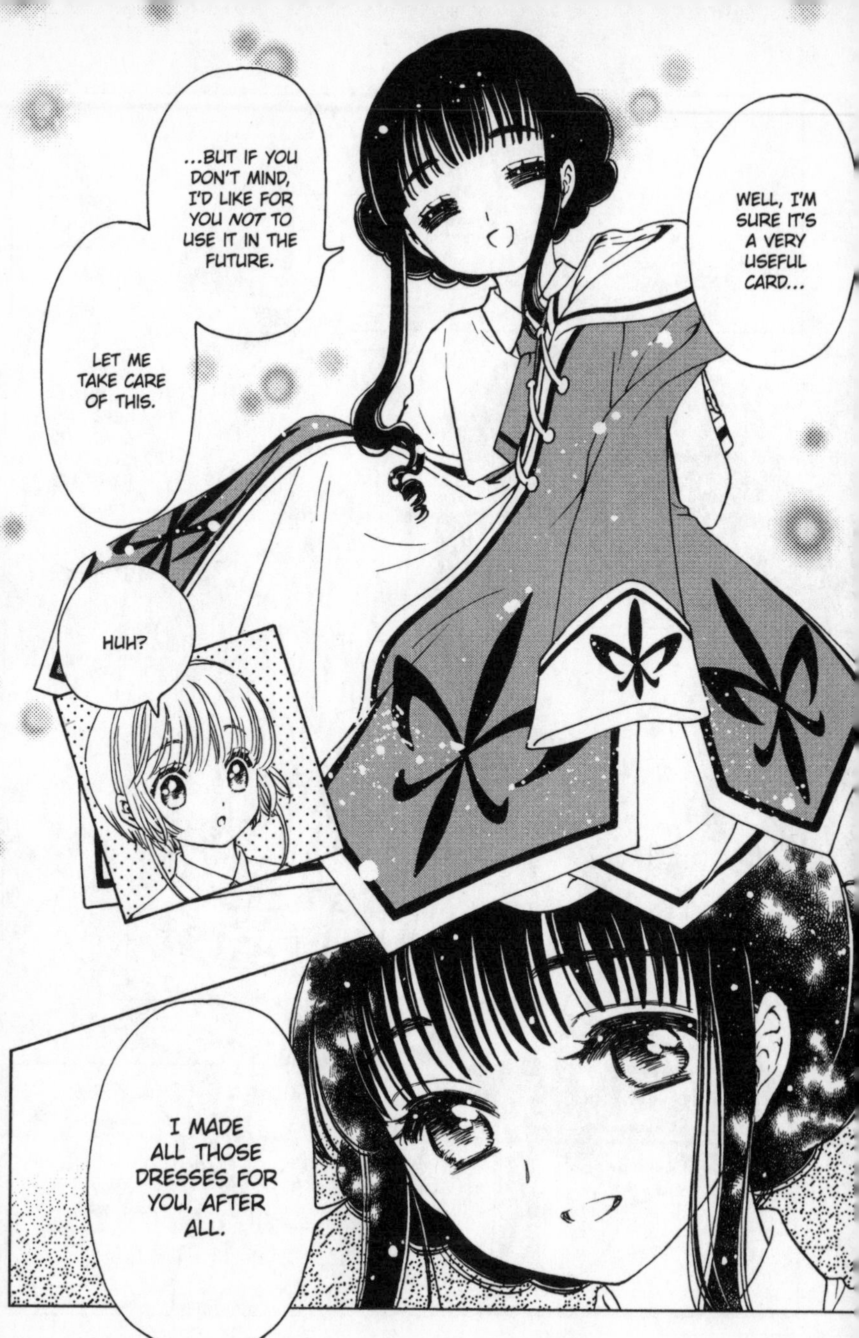
WELL, I'M SURE IT'S A VERY USEFUL CARD...
...BUT IF YOU DON'T MIND, I'D LIKE FOR YOU *NOT* TO USE IT IN THE FUTURE.
LET ME TAKE CARE OF THIS.
HUH?
I MADE ALL THOSE DRESSES FOR YOU, AFTER ALL.

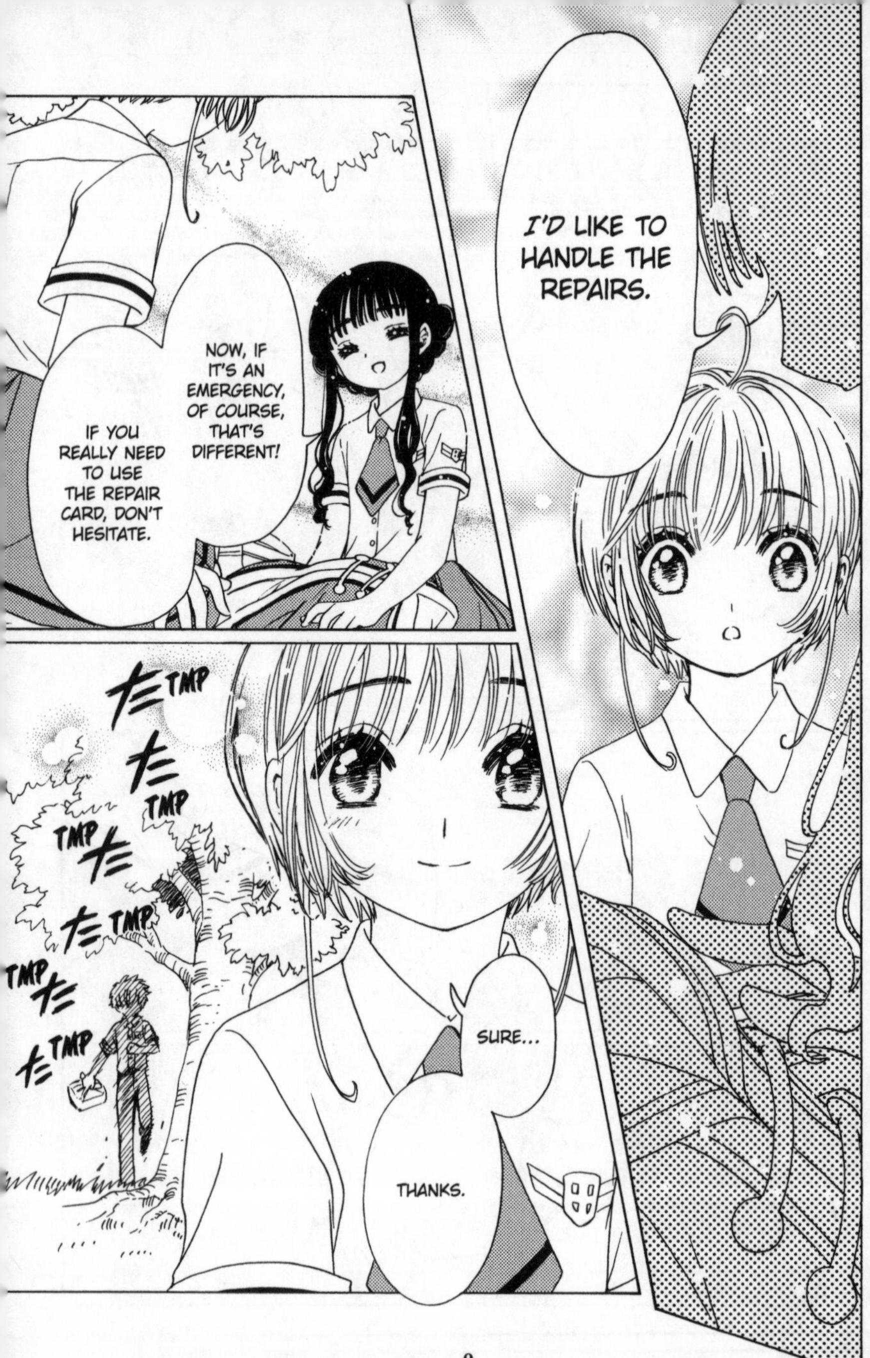
I'D LIKE TO HANDLE THE REPAIRS.
NOW, IF IT'S AN EMERGENCY, OF COURSE, THAT'S DIFFERENT!
IF YOU REALLY NEED TO USE THE REPAIR CARD, DON'T HESITATE.
TMP
TMP
TMP
TMP
TMP
TMP
SURE...
THANKS.

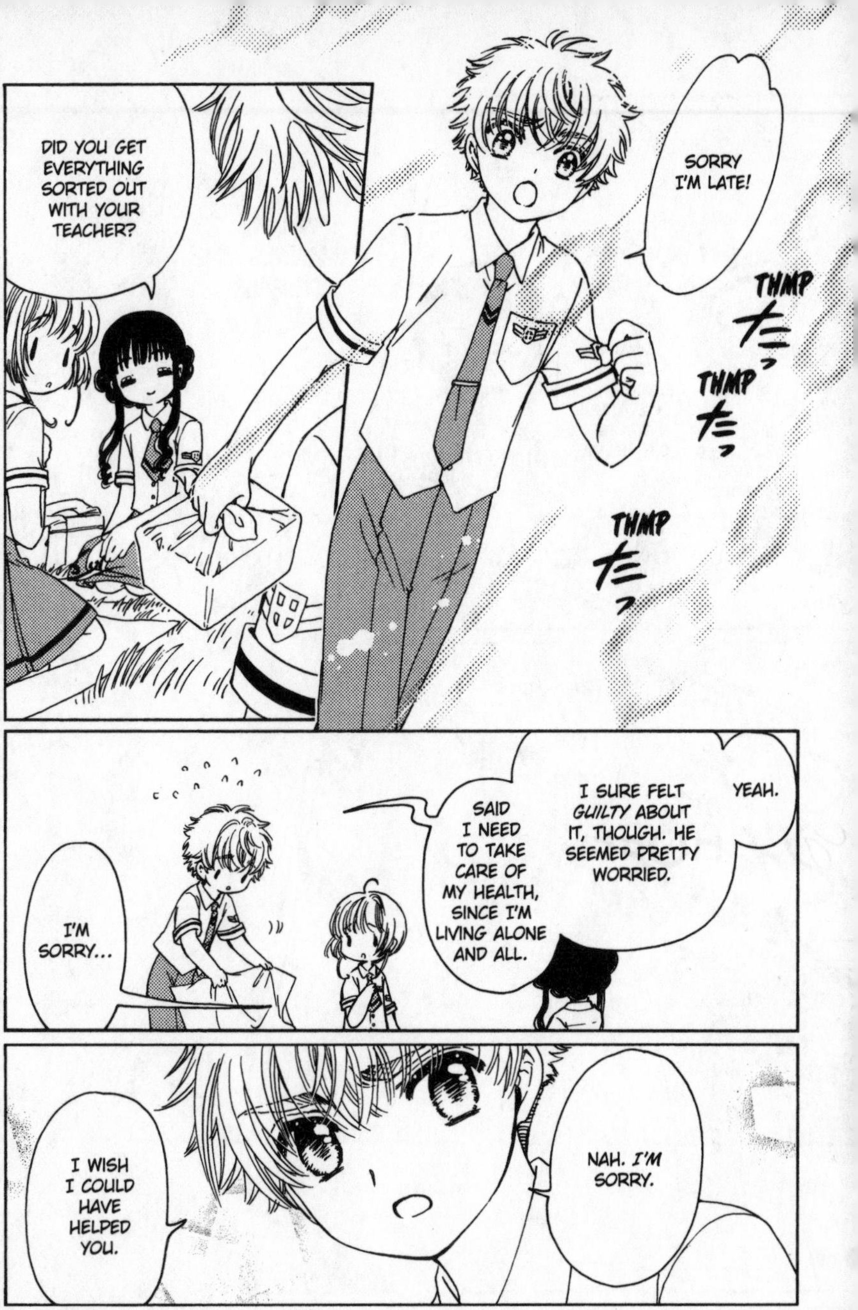
SORRY I'M LATE!
THMP
THMP
THMP
DID YOU GET EVERYTHING SORTED OUT WITH YOUR TEACHER?
YEAH.
I SURE FELT *GUILTY* ABOUT IT, THOUGH. HE SEEMED PRETTY WORRIED.
SAID I NEED TO TAKE CARE OF MY HEALTH, SINCE I'M LIVING ALONE AND ALL.
I'M SORRY...
NAH. *I'M* SORRY.
I WISH I COULD HAVE HELPED YOU.

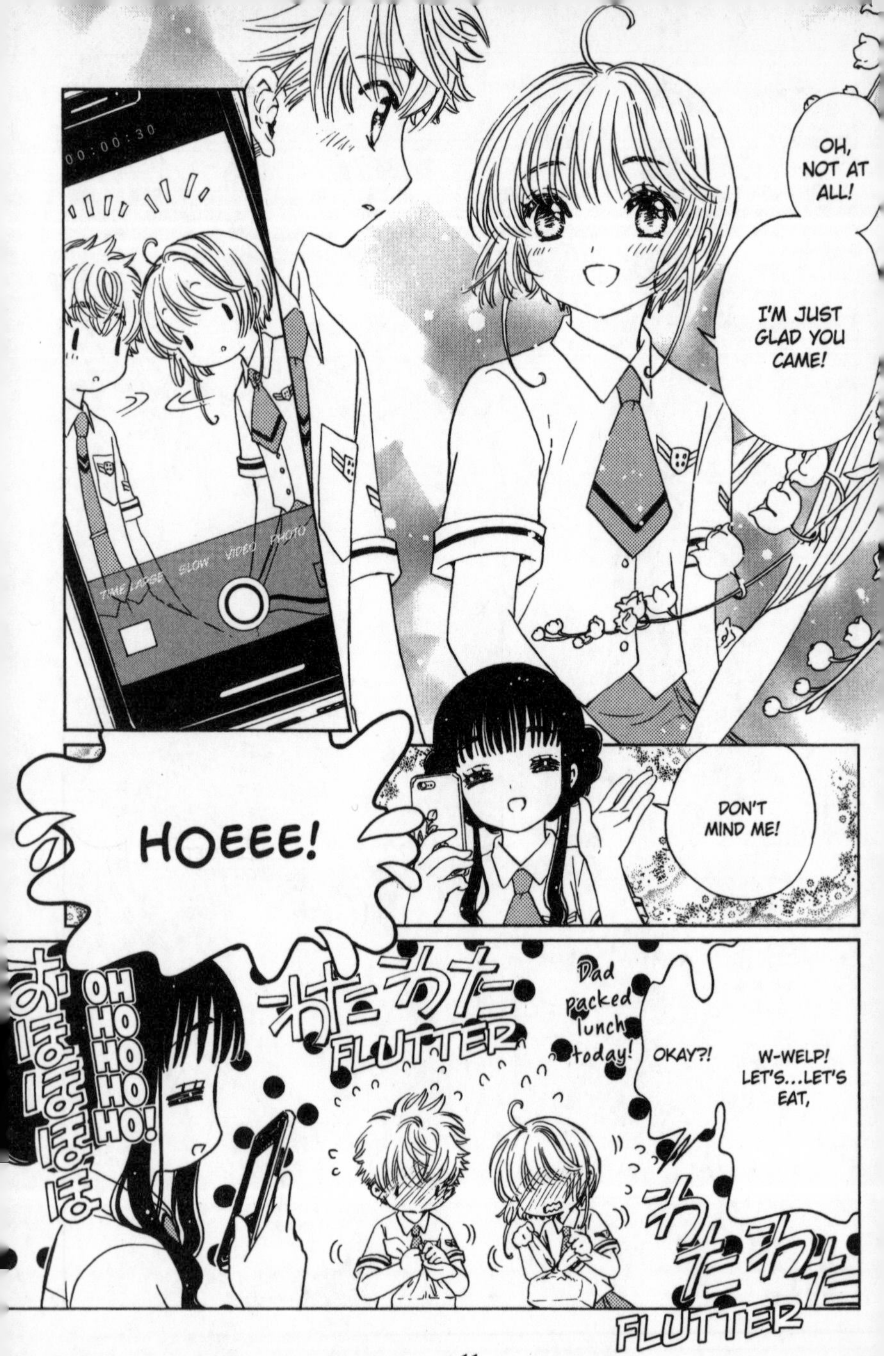
OH, NOT AT ALL!
I'M JUST GLAD YOU CAME!
00:00:30
TIME LAPSE
SLOW
VIDEO
PHOTO
DON'T MIND ME!
HOEEE!
W-WELP! LET'S...LET'S EAT,
OKAY?!
Dad packed lunch today!
わたわた
FLUTTER
わたわた
FLUTTER
おほほほほ
OH HO HO HO HO!

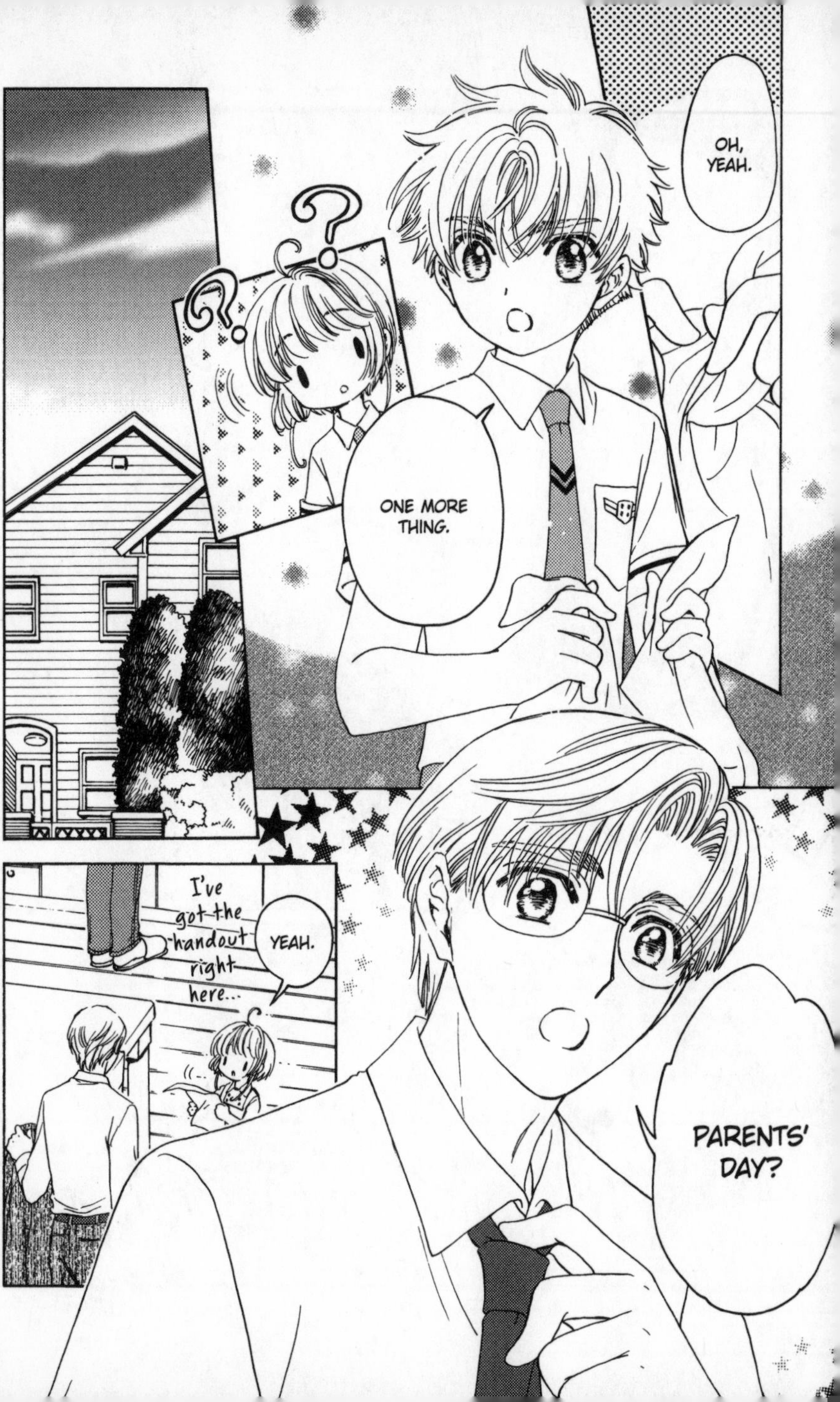
OH, YEAH.
ONE MORE THING.
PARENTS' DAY?
YEAH.
I've got the handout right here...

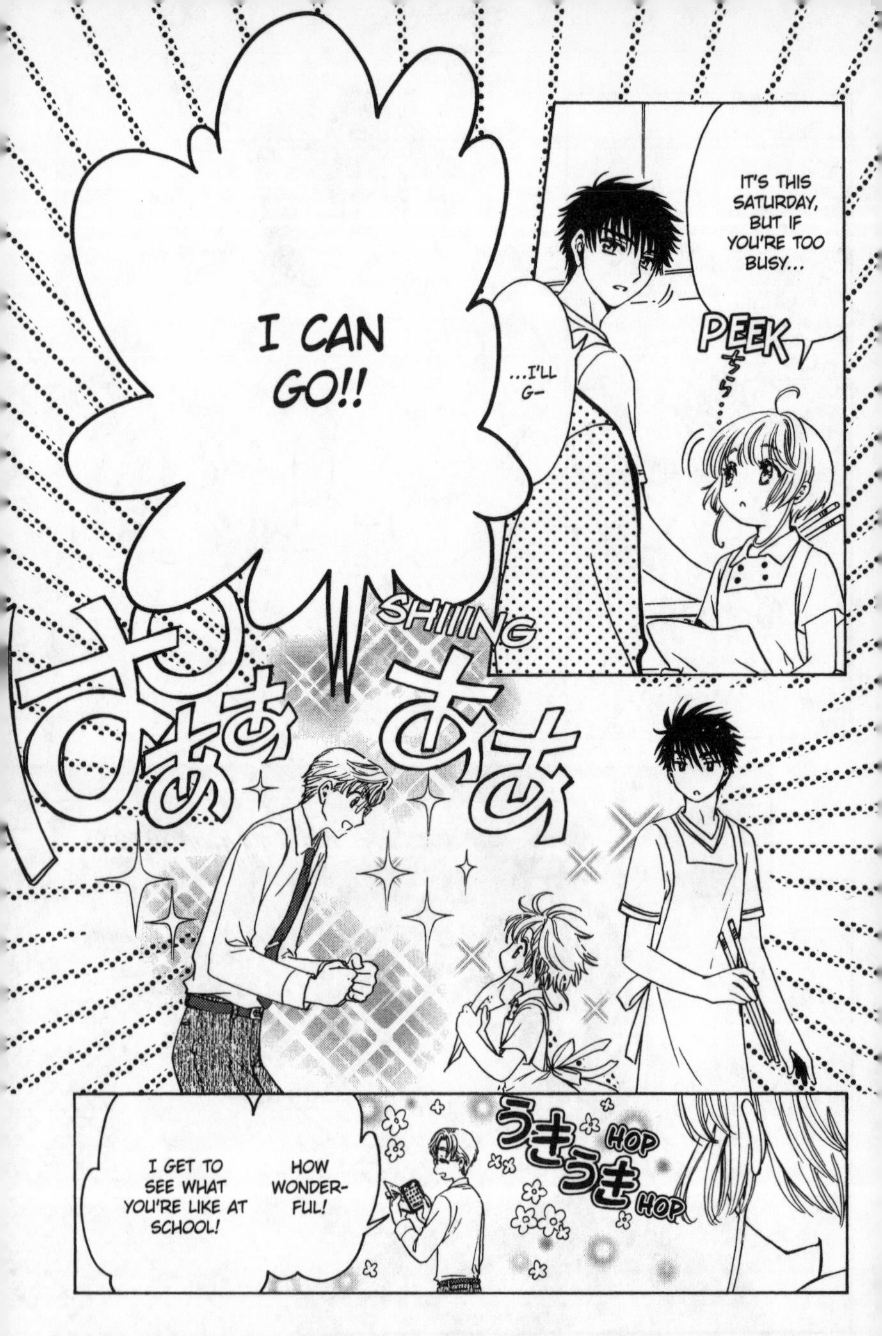
IT'S THIS SATURDAY, BUT IF YOU'RE TOO BUSY...
PEEK
...I'LL G–
I CAN GO!!
SHIIING
HOP
うきうき
HOP
HOW WONDER-FUL!
I GET TO SEE WHAT YOU'RE LIKE AT SCHOOL!

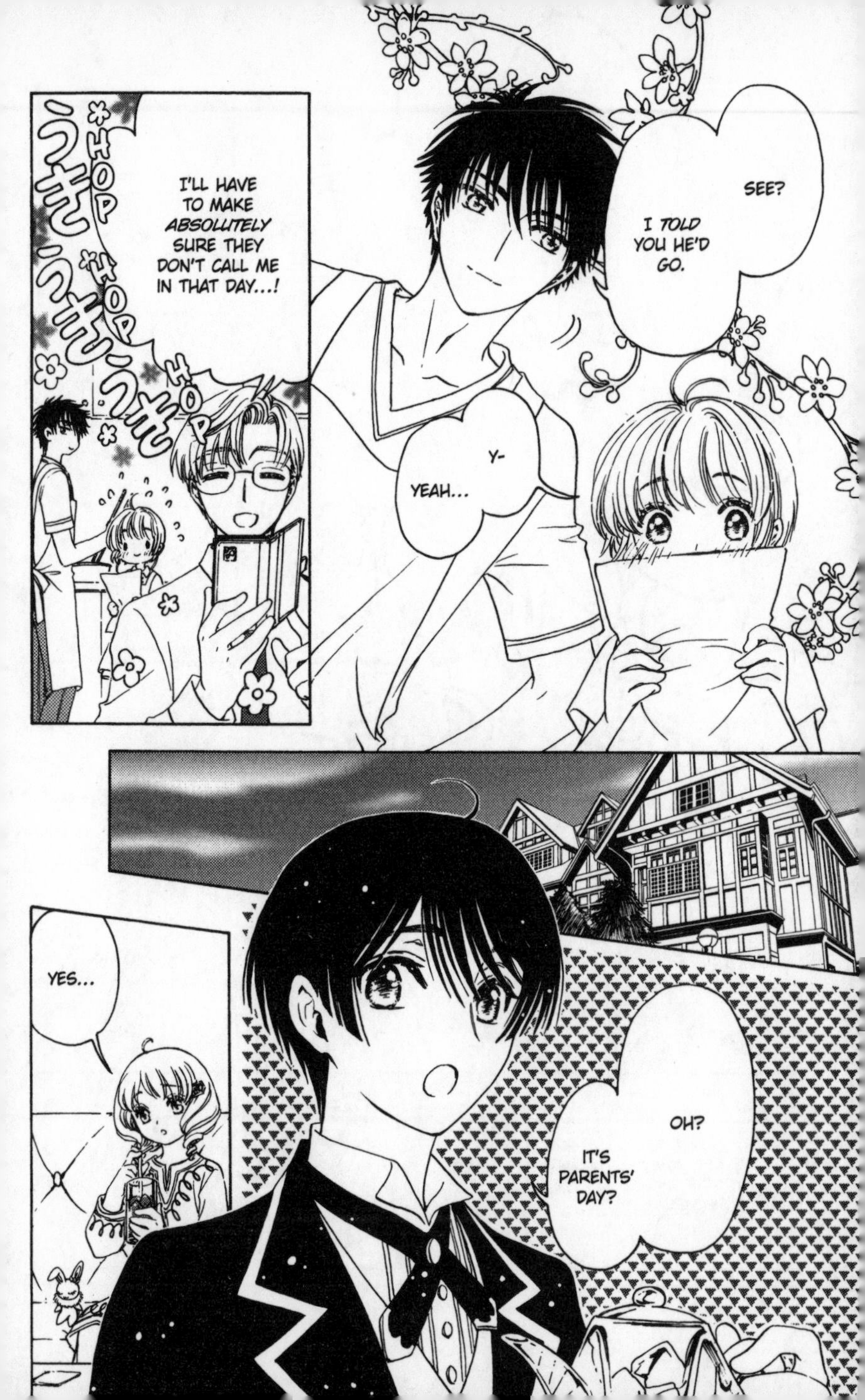
SEE? I TOLD YOU HE'D GO.
Y- YEAH...
I'LL HAVE TO MAKE *ABSOLUTELY* SURE THEY DON'T CALL ME IN THAT DAY...!
うきうきうき
HOP HOP HOP HOP
OH? IT'S PARENTS' DAY?
YES...

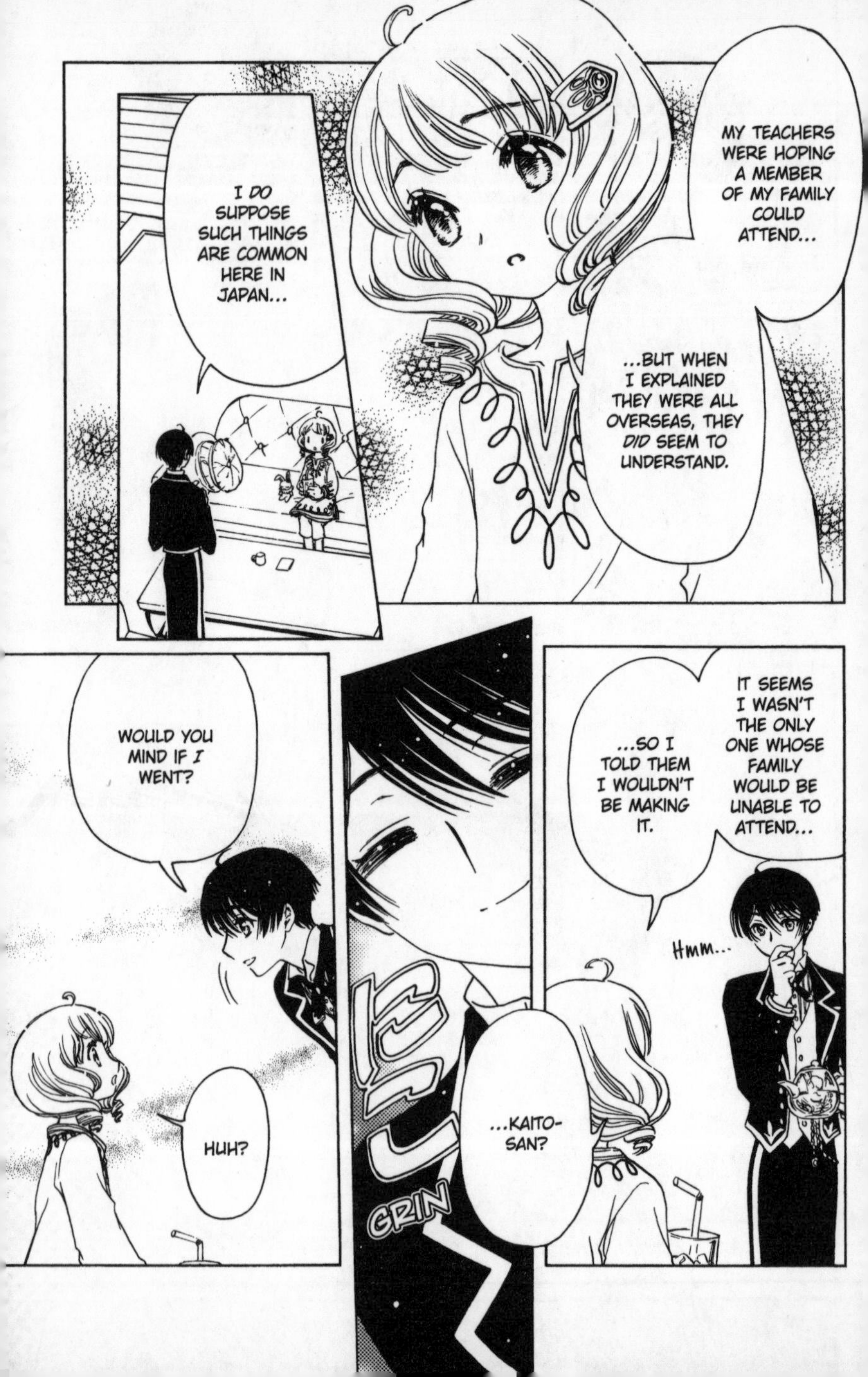
MY TEACHERS WERE HOPING A MEMBER OF MY FAMILY COULD ATTEND...
...BUT WHEN I EXPLAINED THEY WERE ALL OVERSEAS, THEY *DID* SEEM TO UNDERSTAND.
I *DO* SUPPOSE SUCH THINGS ARE COMMON HERE IN JAPAN...
IT SEEMS I WASN'T THE ONLY ONE WHOSE FAMILY WOULD BE UNABLE TO ATTEND...
...SO I TOLD THEM I WOULDN'T BE MAKING IT.
Hmm...
...KAITO-SAN?
GRIN
WOULD YOU MIND IF *I* WENT?
HUH?

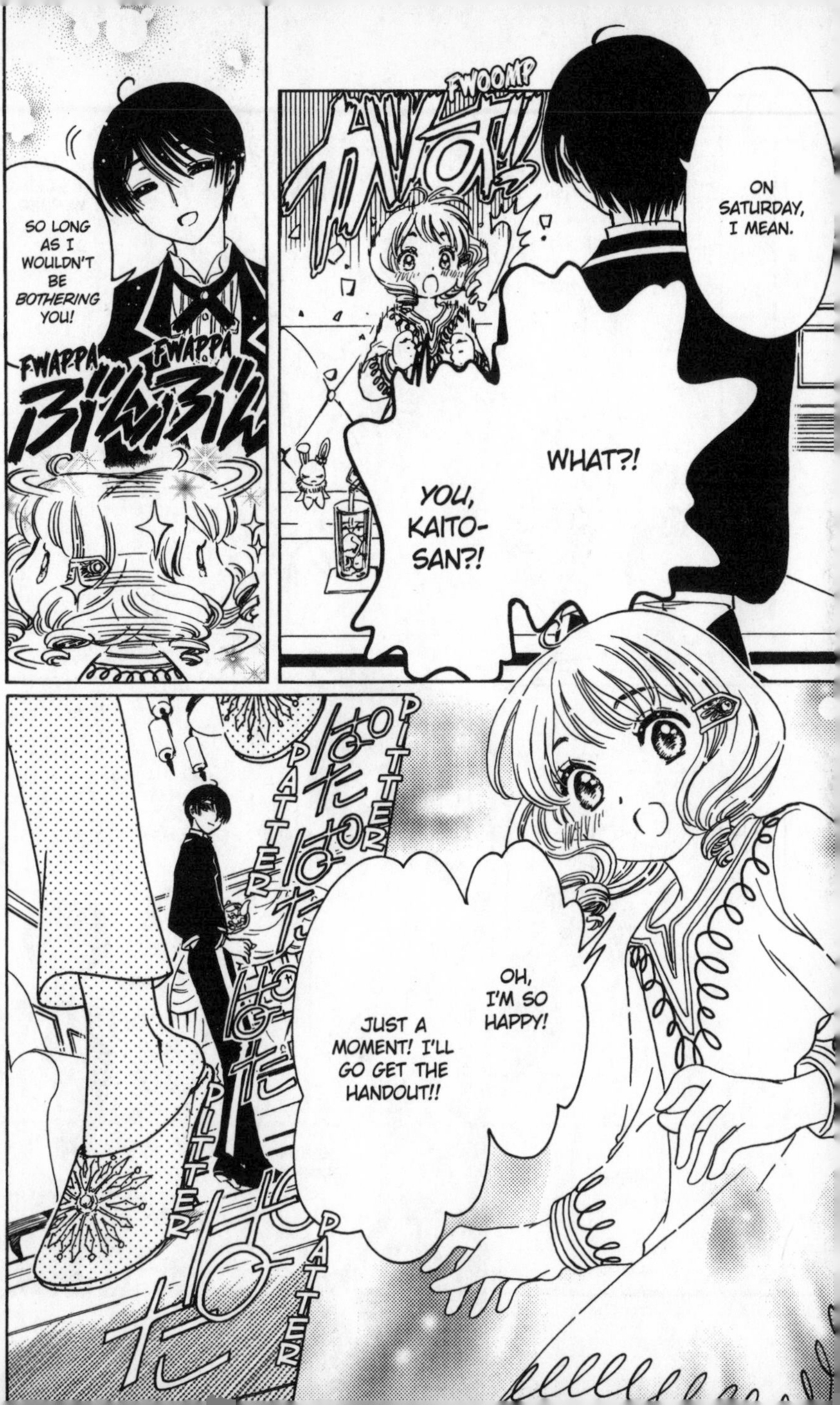
ON SATURDAY, I MEAN.
FWOOMP
WHAT?!
YOU, KAITO-SAN?!
SO LONG AS I WOULDN'T BE BOTHERING YOU!
FWAPPA
FWAPPA
OH, I'M SO HAPPY!
JUST A MOMENT! I'LL GO GET THE HANDOUT!!
PITTER
PATTER
PITTER
PATTER

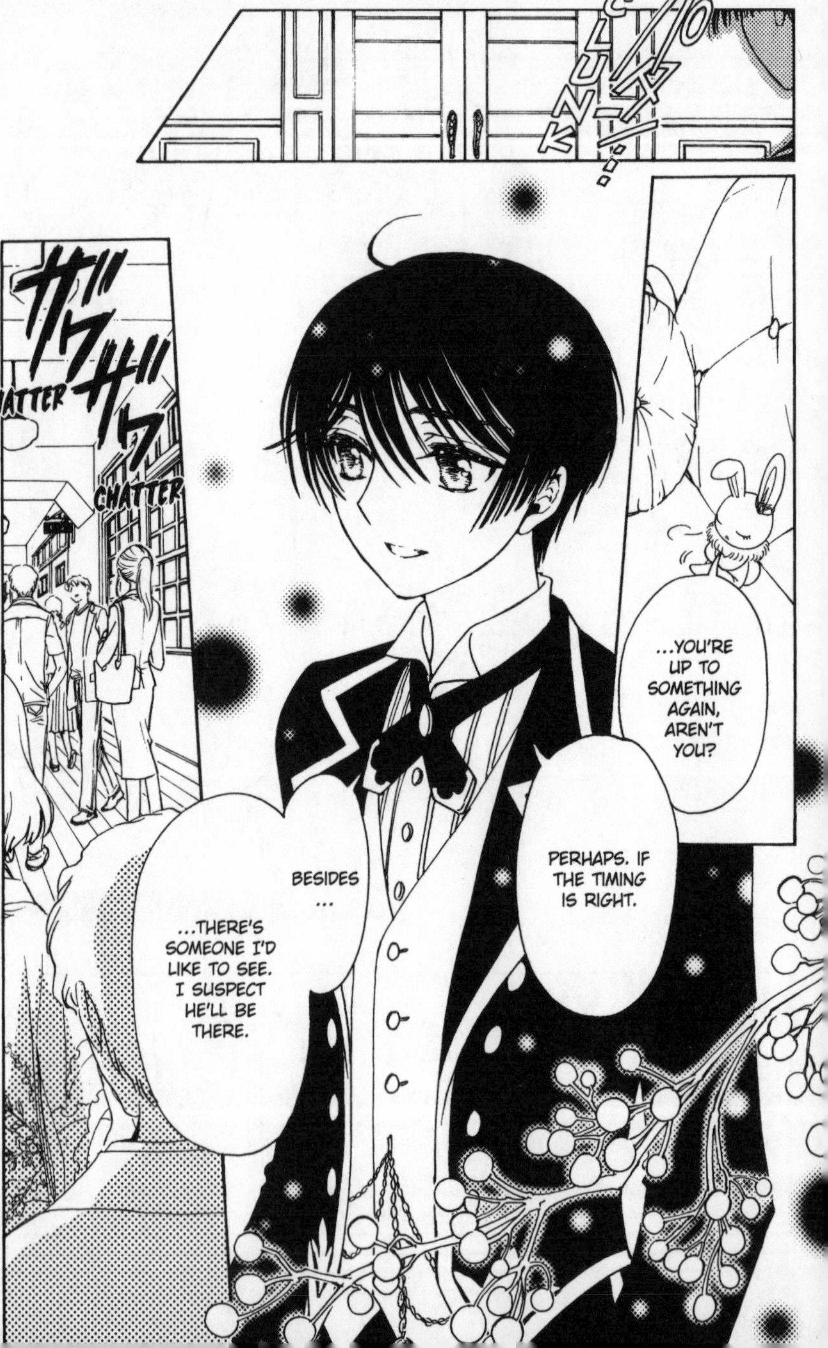
CLUNK—!
...YOU'RE UP TO SOMETHING AGAIN, AREN'T YOU?
PERHAPS. IF THE TIMING IS RIGHT.
BESIDES ...
...THERE'S SOMEONE I'D LIKE TO SEE. I SUSPECT HE'LL BE THERE.
CHATTER
CHATTER

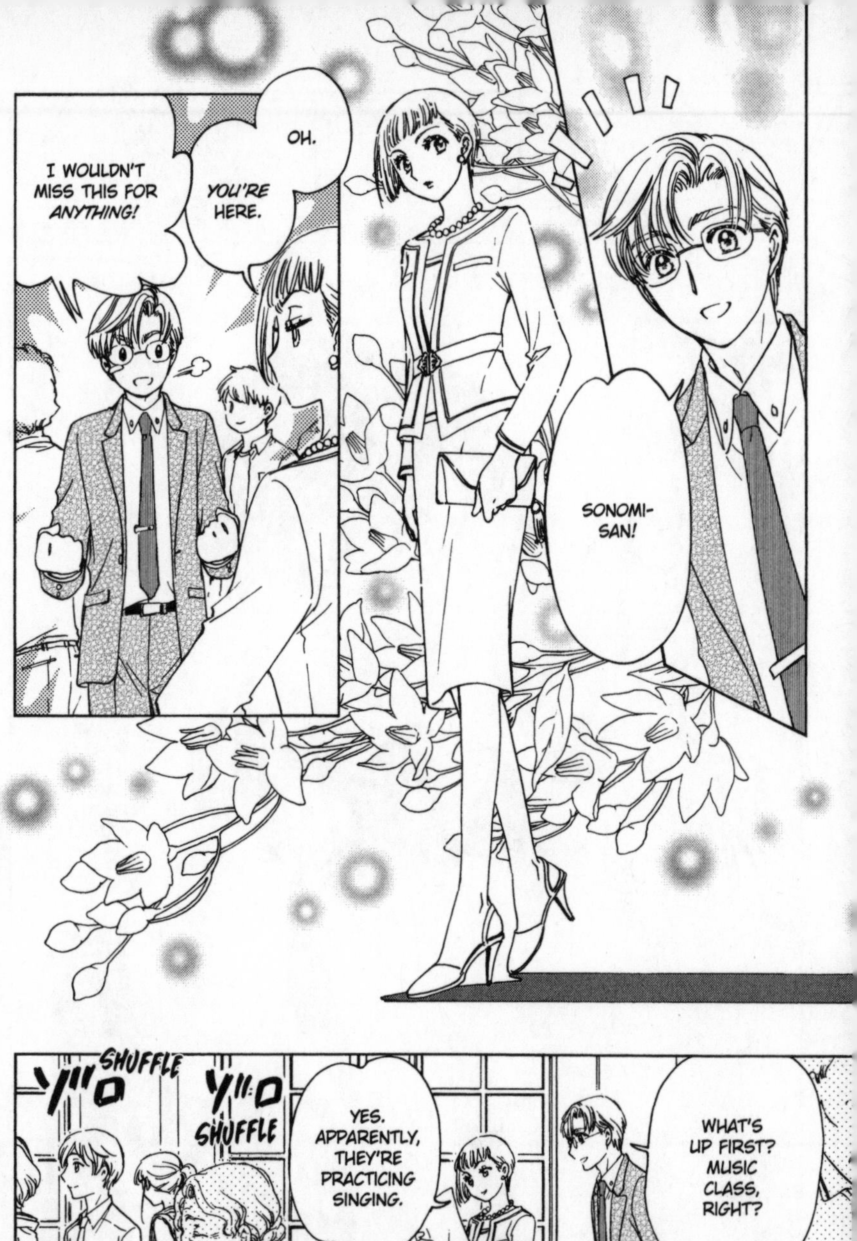
SONOMI-SAN!
OH. YOU'RE HERE.
I WOULDN'T MISS THIS FOR ANYTHING!
WHAT'S UP FIRST? MUSIC CLASS, RIGHT?
YES. APPARENTLY, THEY'RE PRACTICING SINGING.
SHUFFLE
SHUFFLE

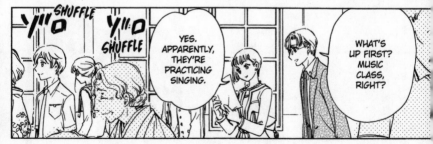

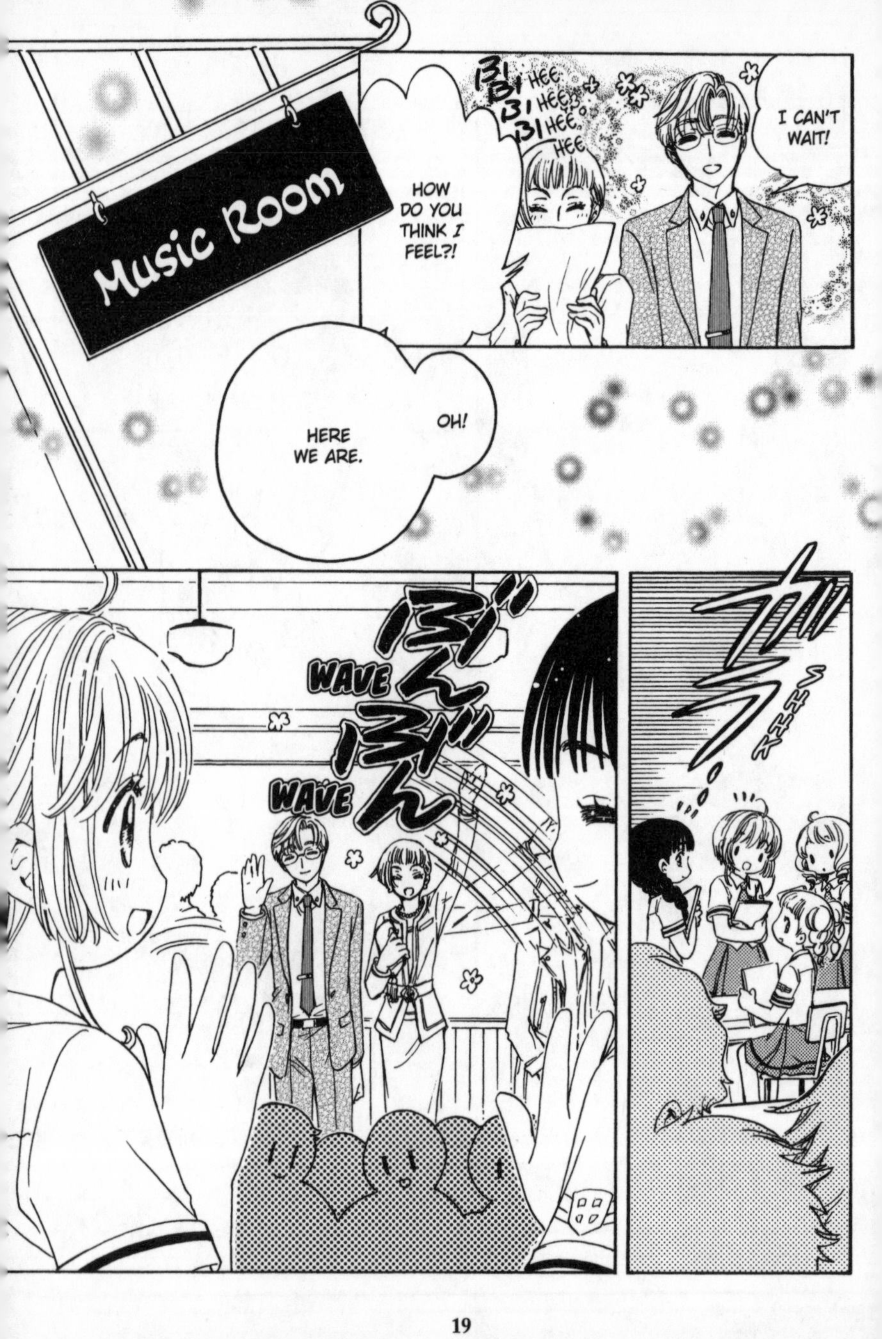
I CAN'T WAIT!
HEE HEE HEE HEE
HOW DO YOU THINK I FEEL?!
Music Room
OH!
HERE WE ARE.
SHHK
WAVE
WAVE

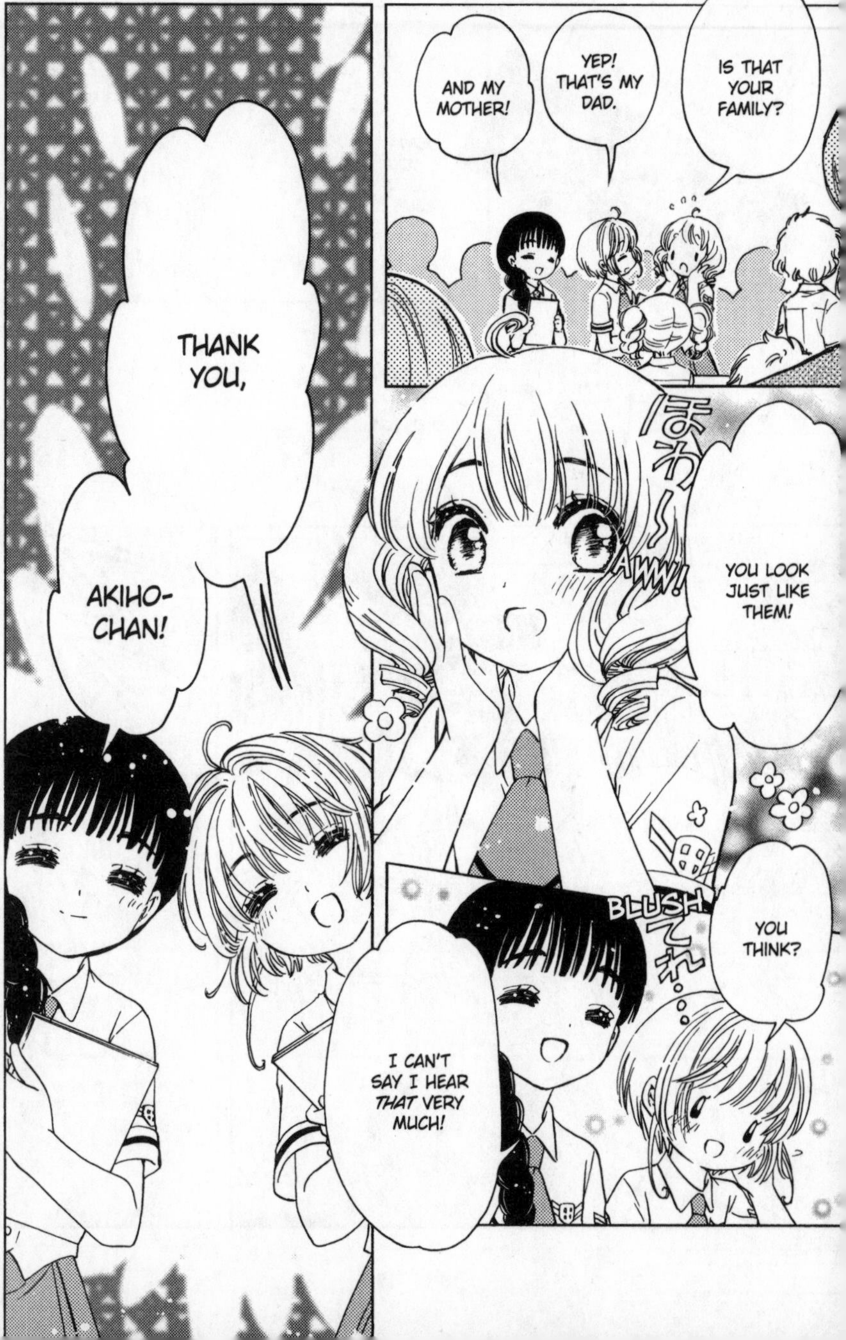
IS THAT YOUR FAMILY?
YEP! THAT'S MY DAD.
AND MY MOTHER!
ほわ～
AWW!
YOU LOOK JUST LIKE THEM!
YOU THINK?
BLUSH
てれ
I CAN'T SAY I HEAR *THAT* VERY MUCH!
THANK YOU,
AKIHO-CHAN!

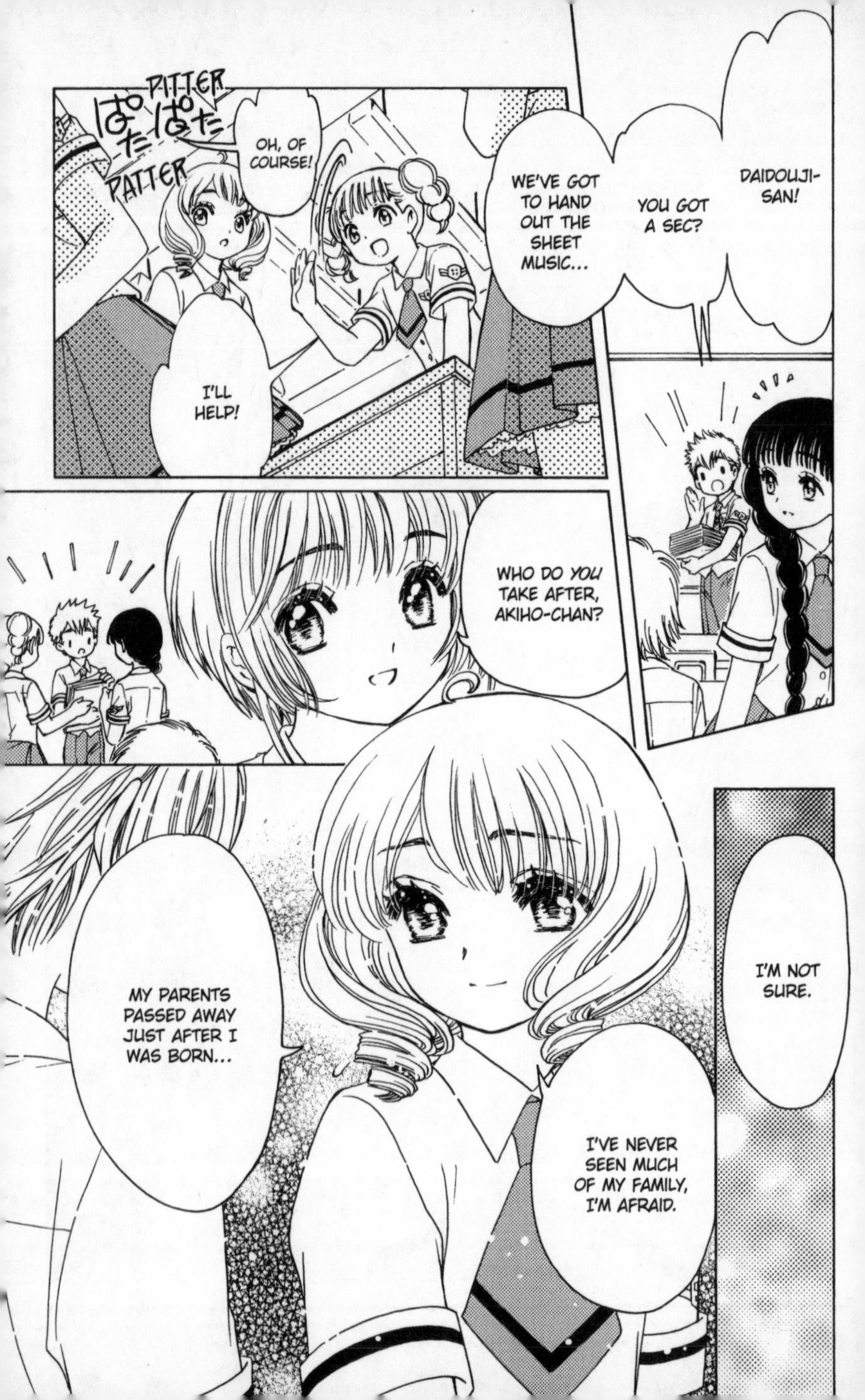
DAIDOUJI-SAN!
YOU GOT A SEC?
WE'VE GOT TO HAND OUT THE SHEET MUSIC...
OH, OF COURSE!
I'LL HELP!
ぱたぱた PITTER PATTER
WHO DO YOU TAKE AFTER, AKIHO-CHAN?
I'M NOT SURE.
I'VE NEVER SEEN MUCH OF MY FAMILY, I'M AFRAID.
MY PARENTS PASSED AWAY JUST AFTER I WAS BORN...

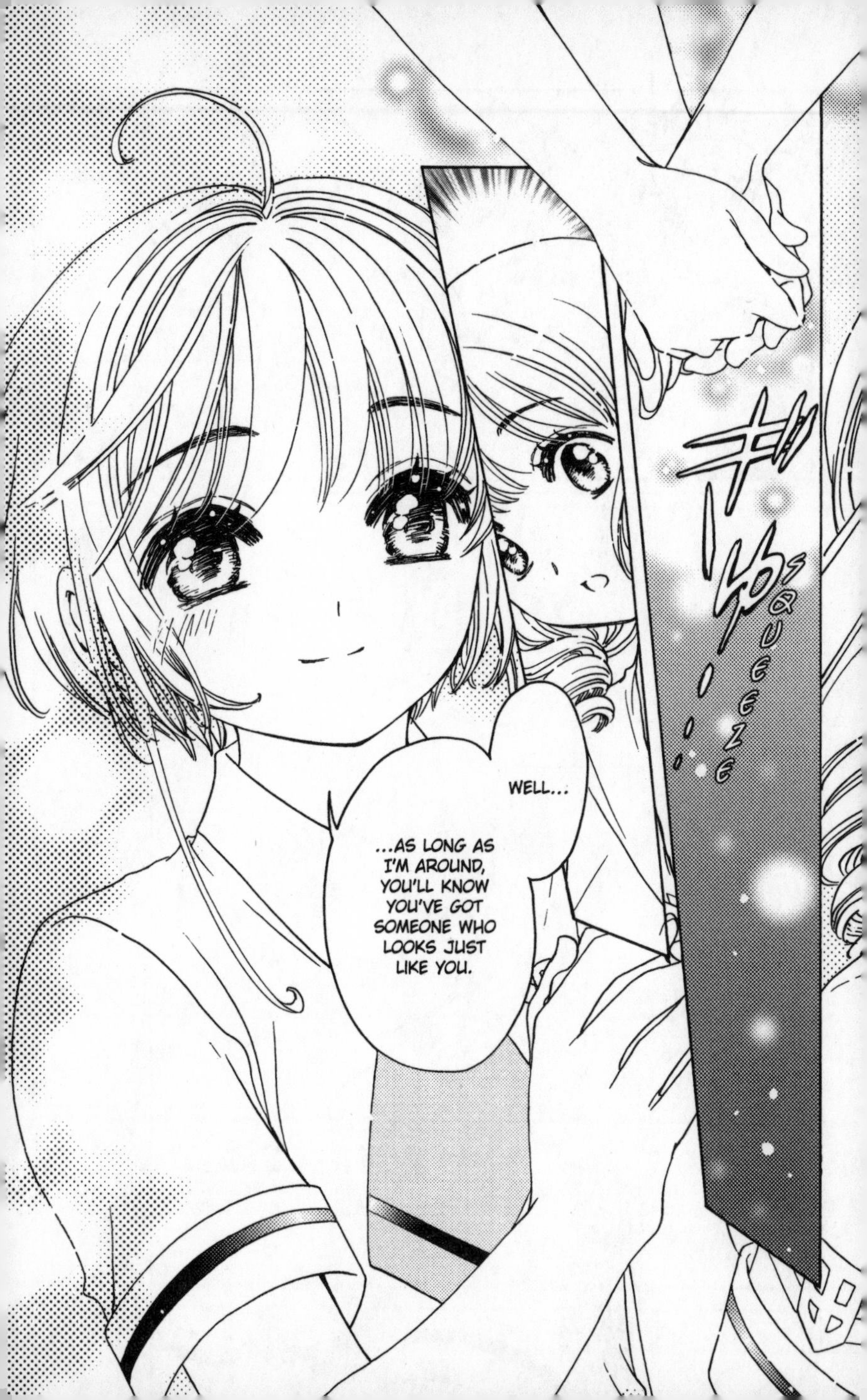
SQUEEZE
WELL...
...AS LONG AS I'M AROUND, YOU'LL KNOW YOU'VE GOT SOMEONE WHO LOOKS JUST LIKE YOU.

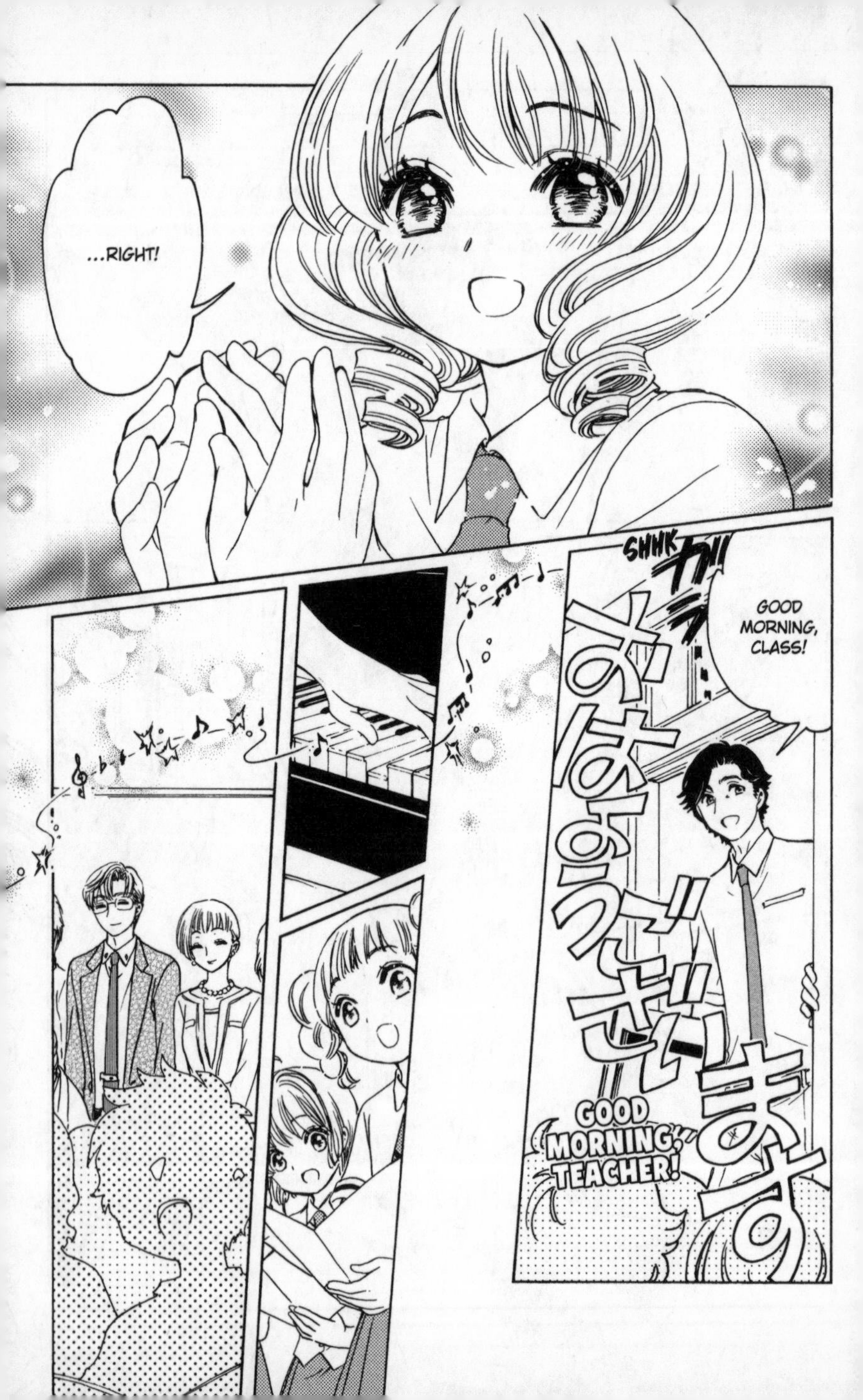
...RIGHT!
SHHK
GOOD MORNING, CLASS!
おはようございます
GOOD MORNING, TEACHER!

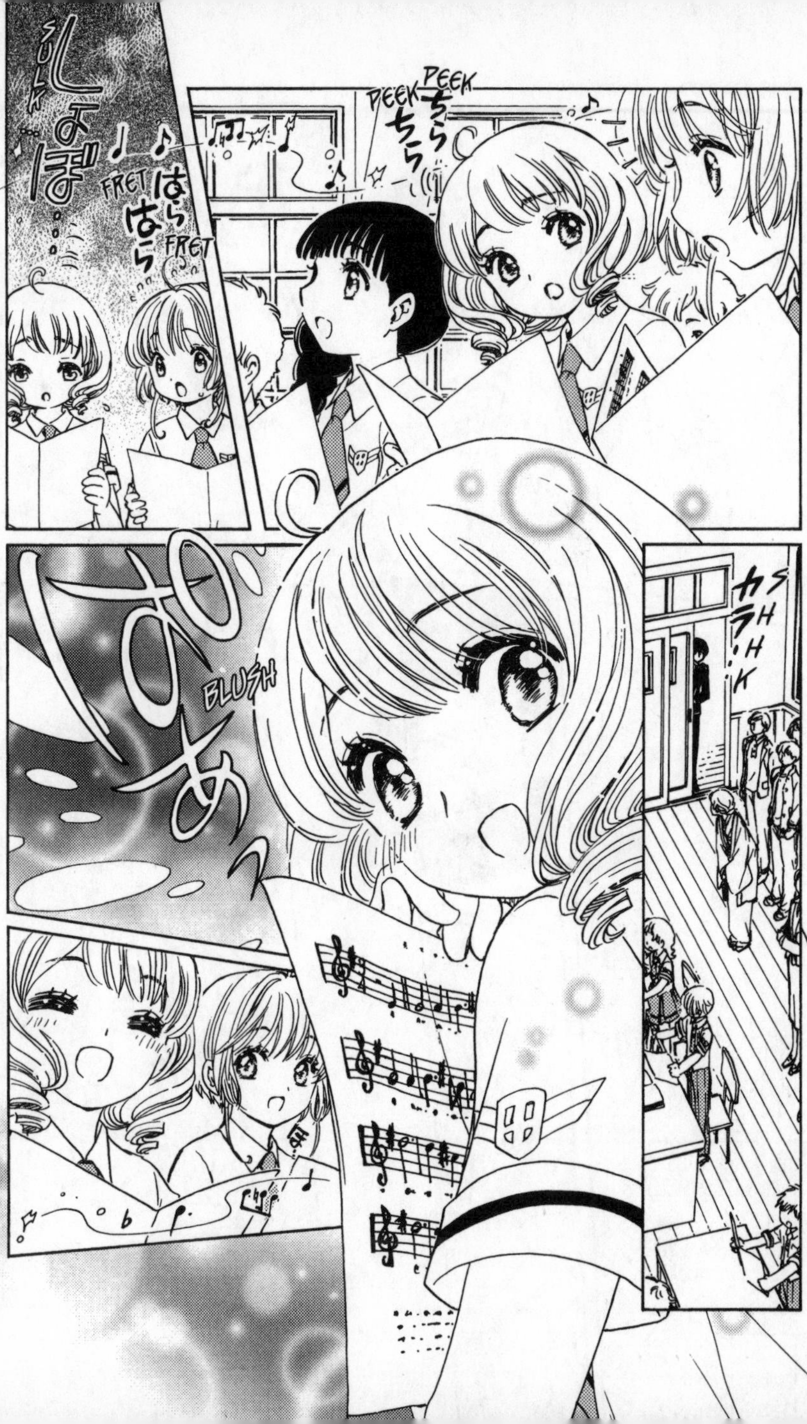

ちらちら
PEEK PEEK
しょぼ…
SULK…
はらはら
FRET FRET
カラ
SHHK
ぱあっ
BLUSH

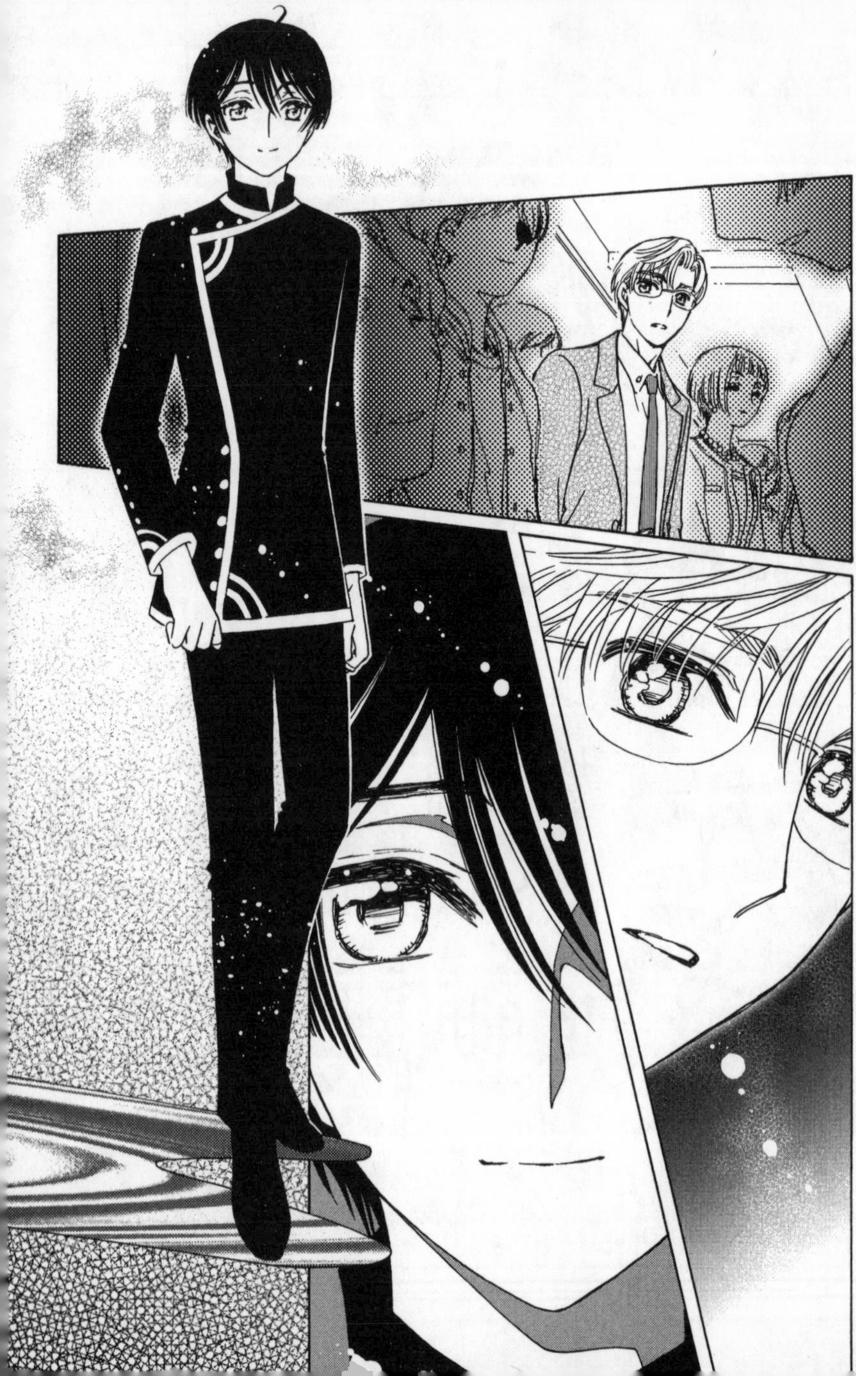

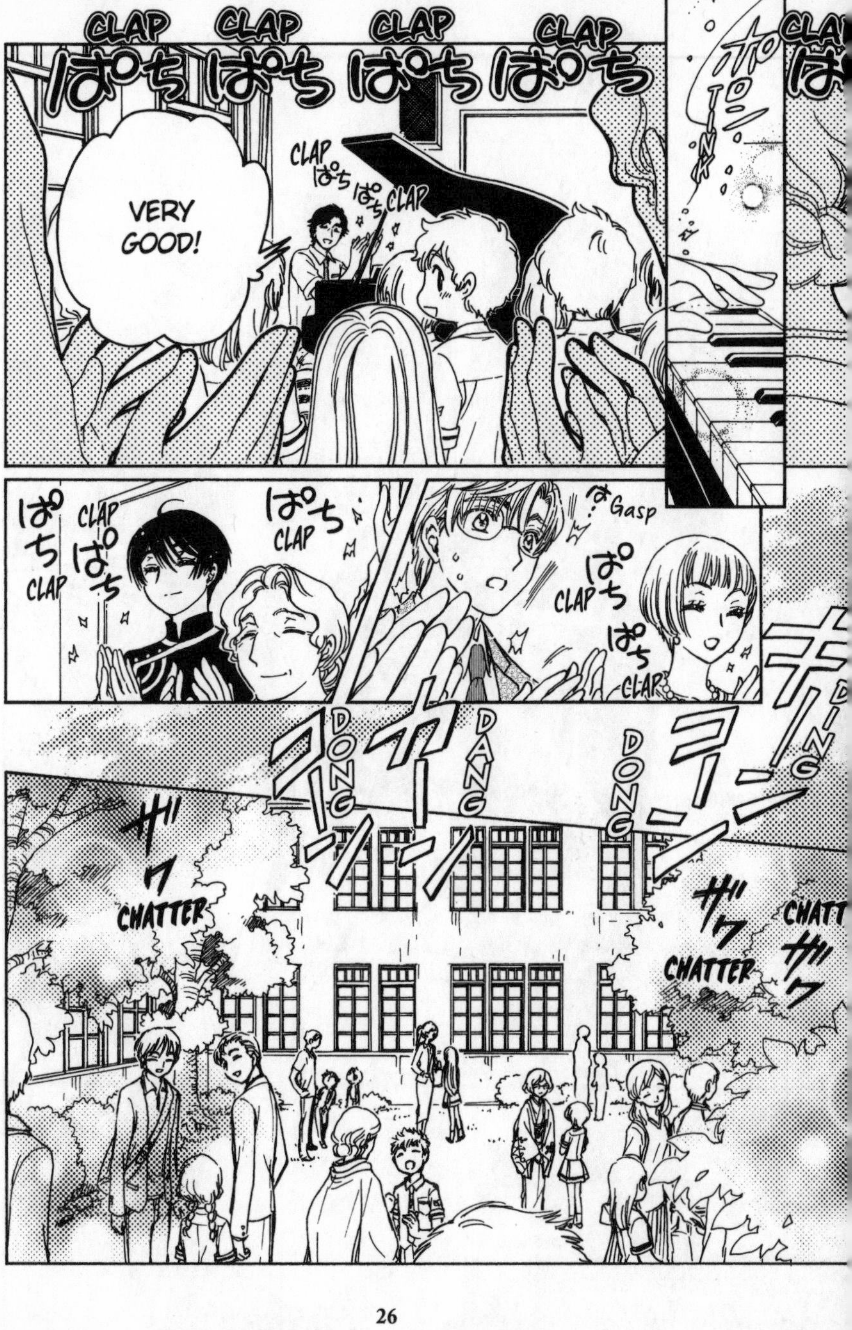
TINK
CLAP CLAP CLAP CLAP
ぱちぱちぱちぱち
VERY GOOD!
CLAP ぱち ぱち CLAP
Gasp
ぱち CLAP ぱち CLAP
ぱち CLAP
CLAP ぱち ぱち
ぱち CLAP
DING
DONG
DANG
DONG
CHATTER
CHATTER

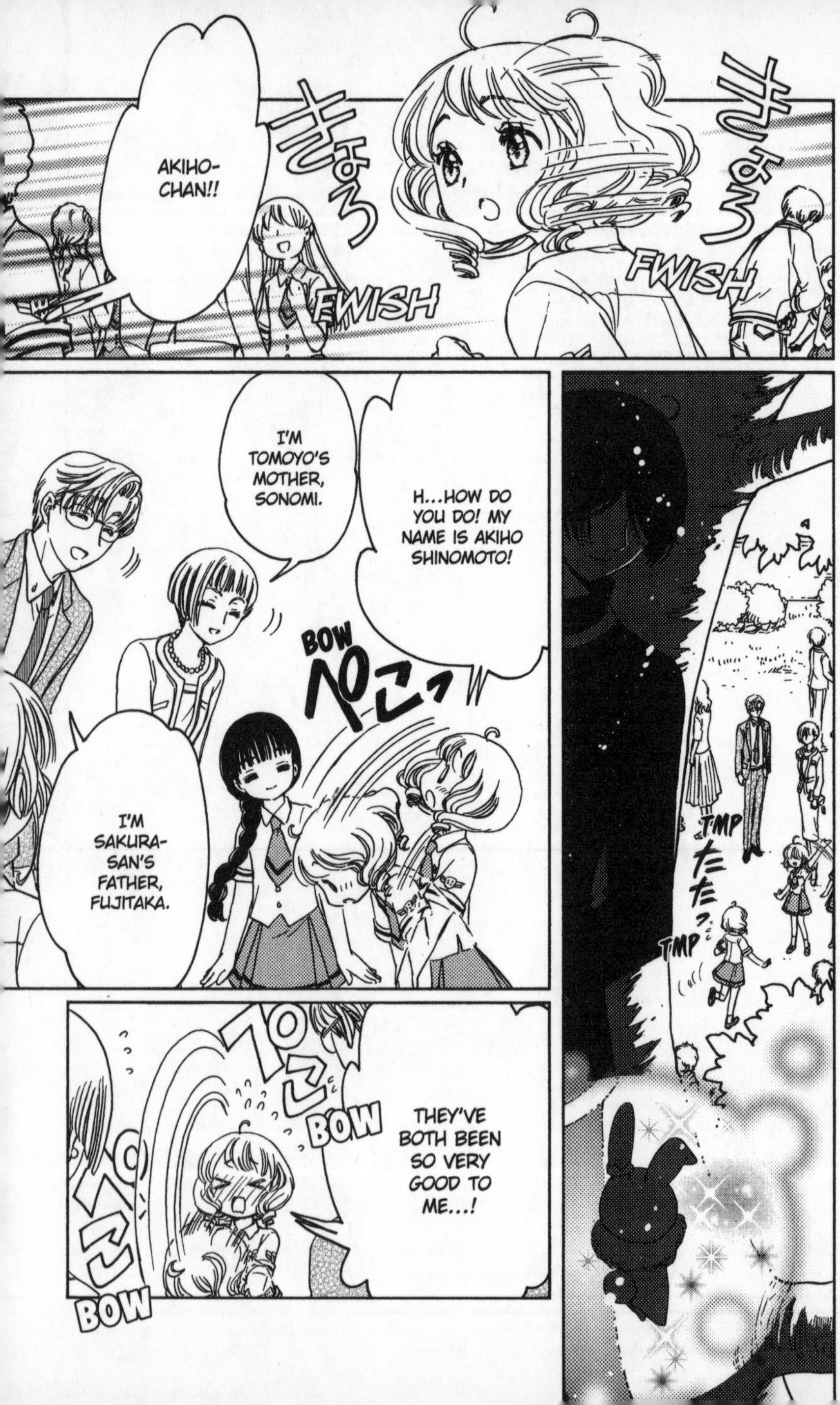
きょろ
FWISH
きょろ
FWISH
AKIHO-CHAN!!
TMP
たたっ
TMP
H...HOW DO YOU DO! MY NAME IS AKIHO SHINOMOTO!
BOW
ぺこっ
I'M TOMOYO'S MOTHER, SONOMI.
I'M SAKURA-SAN'S FATHER, FUJITAKA.
THEY'VE BOTH BEEN SO VERY GOOD TO ME...!
ぺこ
BOW
ぺこ
BOW

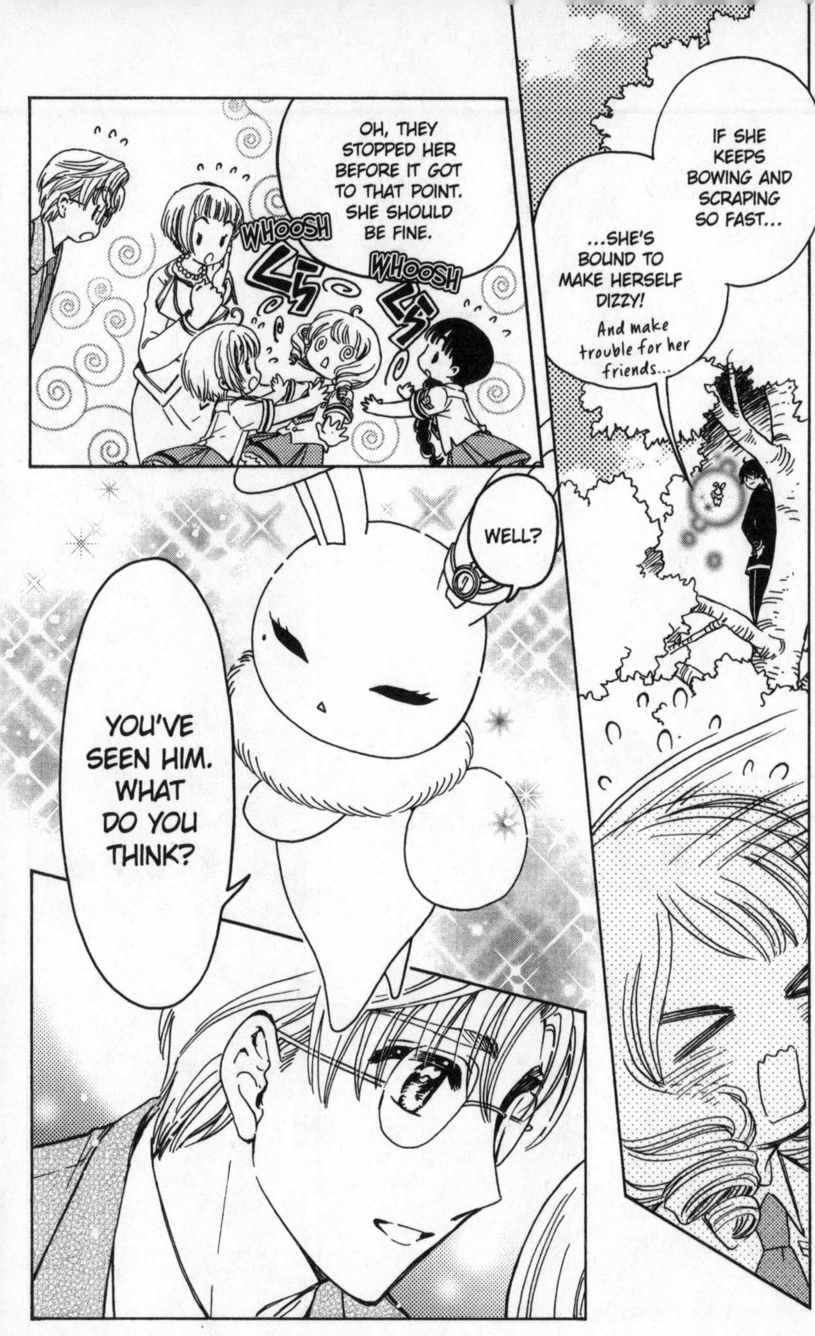
IF SHE KEEPS BOWING AND SCRAPING SO FAST...
...SHE'S BOUND TO MAKE HERSELF DIZZY!
And make trouble for her friends...
OH, THEY STOPPED HER BEFORE IT GOT TO THAT POINT. SHE SHOULD BE FINE.
WHOOSH
WHOOSH
WELL?
YOU'VE SEEN HIM. WHAT DO YOU THINK?

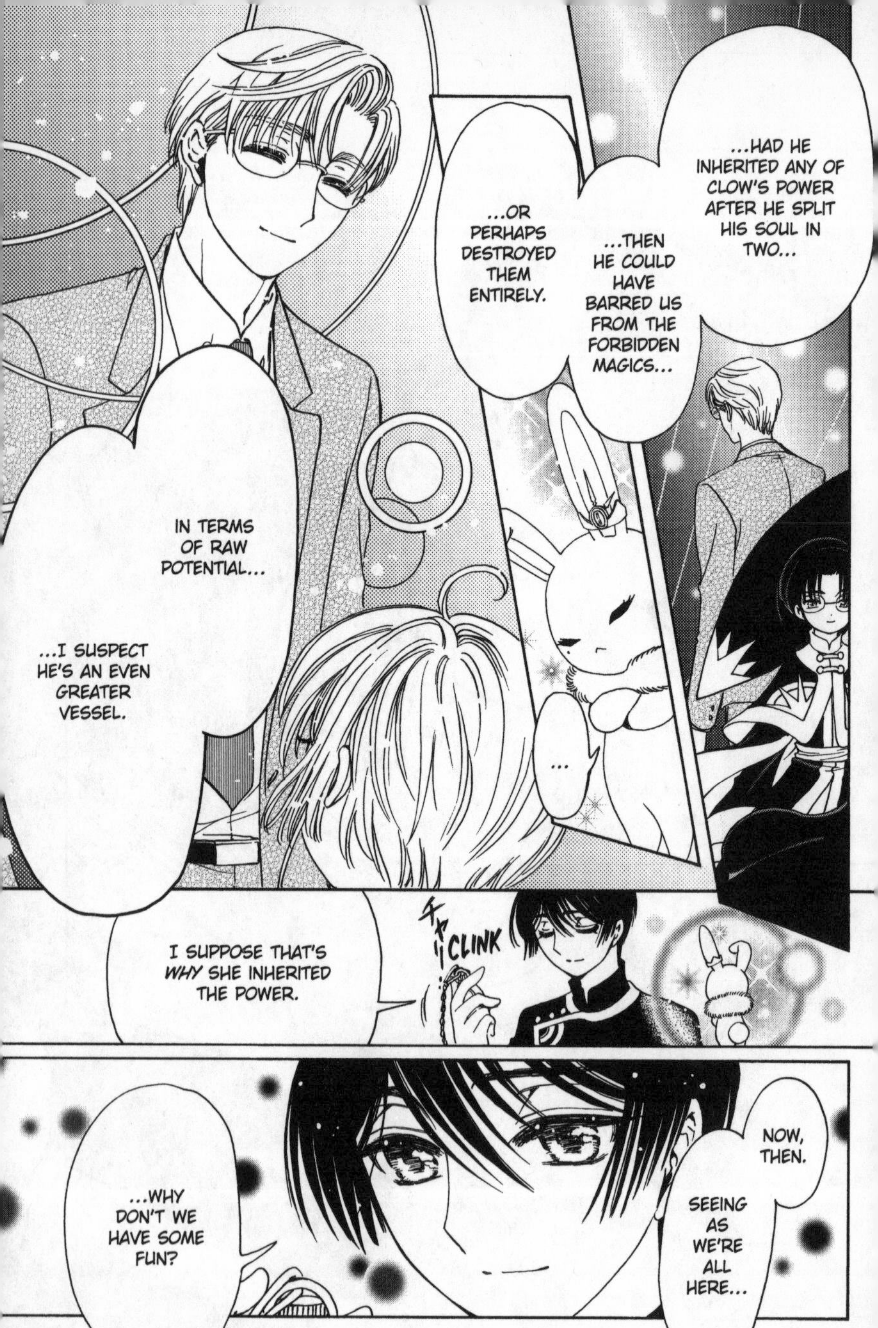
...HAD HE INHERITED ANY OF CLOW'S POWER AFTER HE SPLIT HIS SOUL IN TWO...
...THEN HE COULD HAVE BARRED US FROM THE FORBIDDEN MAGICS...
...OR PERHAPS DESTROYED THEM ENTIRELY.
...
IN TERMS OF RAW POTENTIAL...
...I SUSPECT HE'S AN EVEN GREATER VESSEL.
チャリ CLINK
I SUPPOSE THAT'S *WHY* SHE INHERITED THE POWER.
NOW, THEN.
SEEING AS WE'RE ALL HERE...
...WHY DON'T WE HAVE SOME FUN?

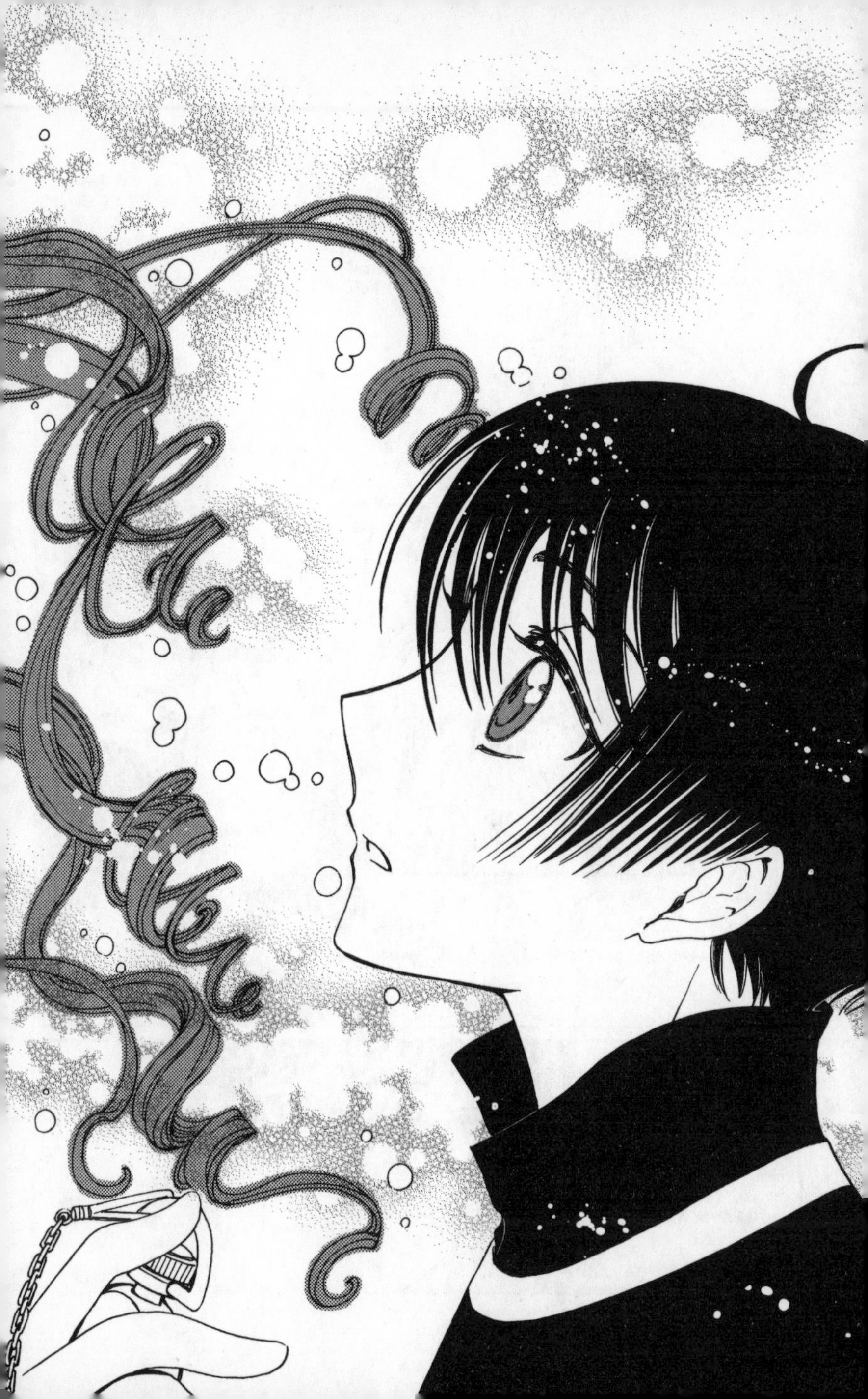

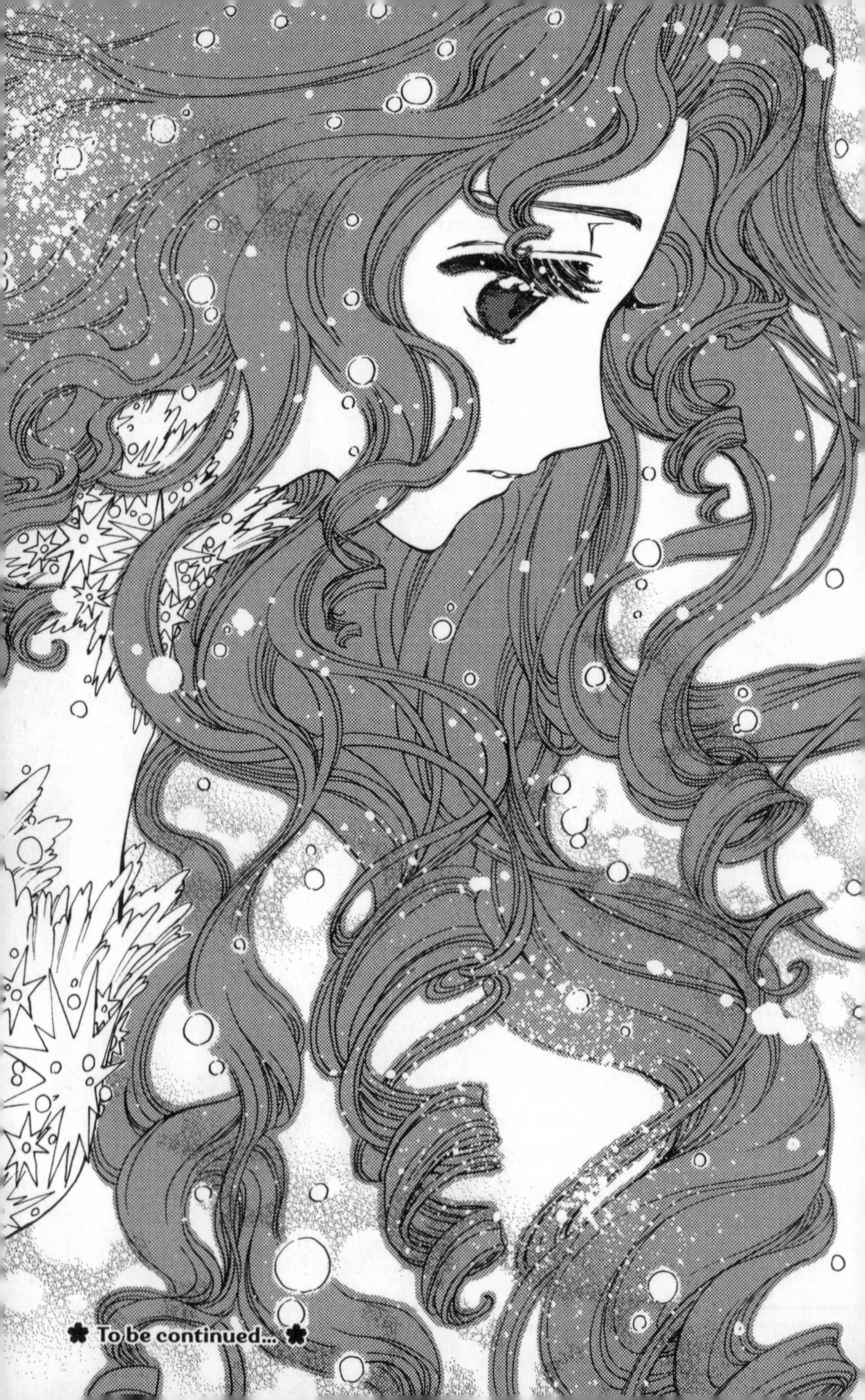
✿ To be continued... ✿

Cardcaptor
Sakura
CLEAR CARD

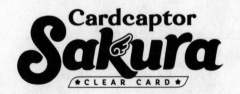

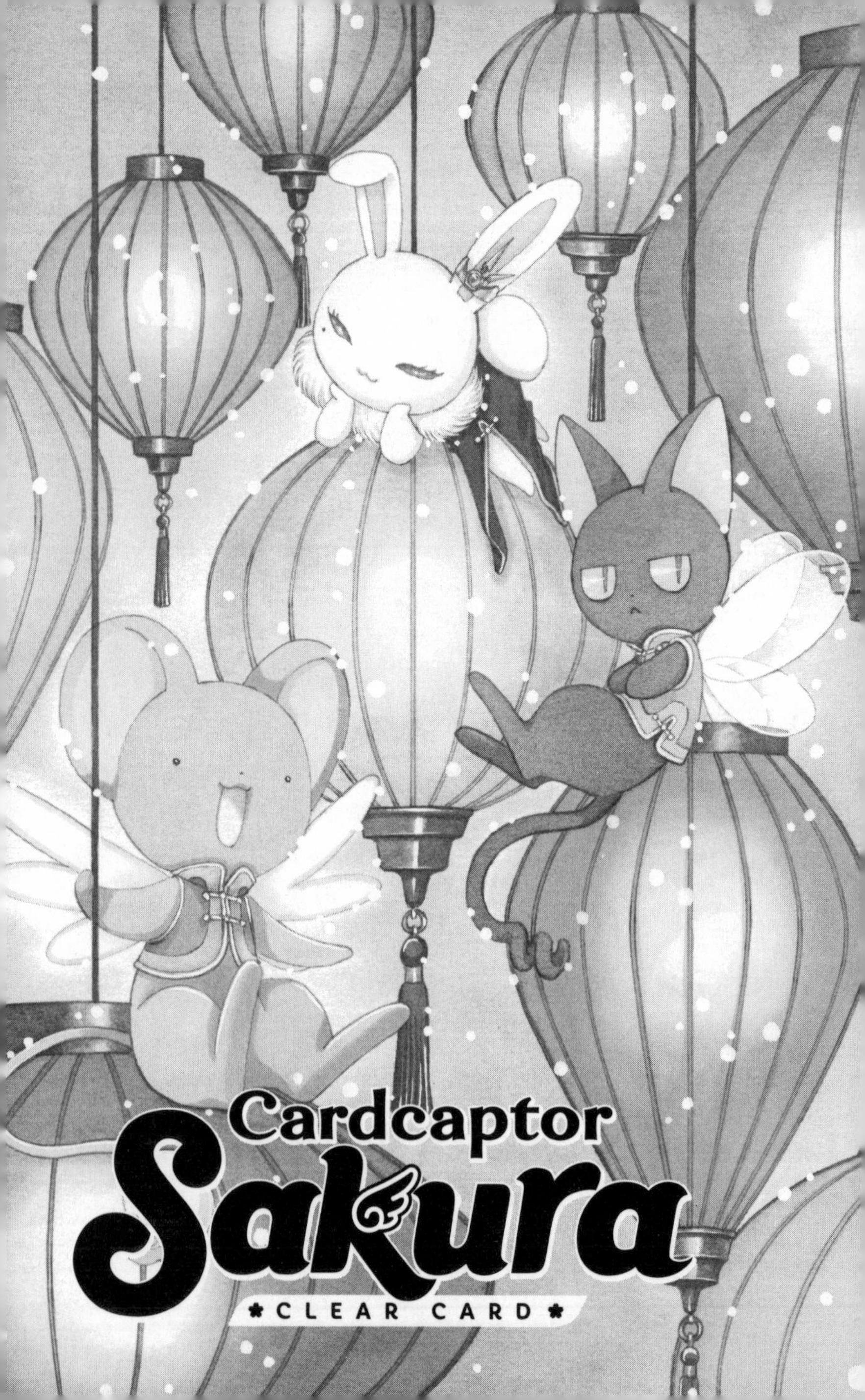
Cardcaptor
Sakura
CLEAR CARD

Cardcaptor Sakura
CLEAR CARD

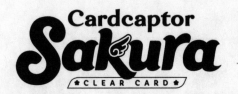

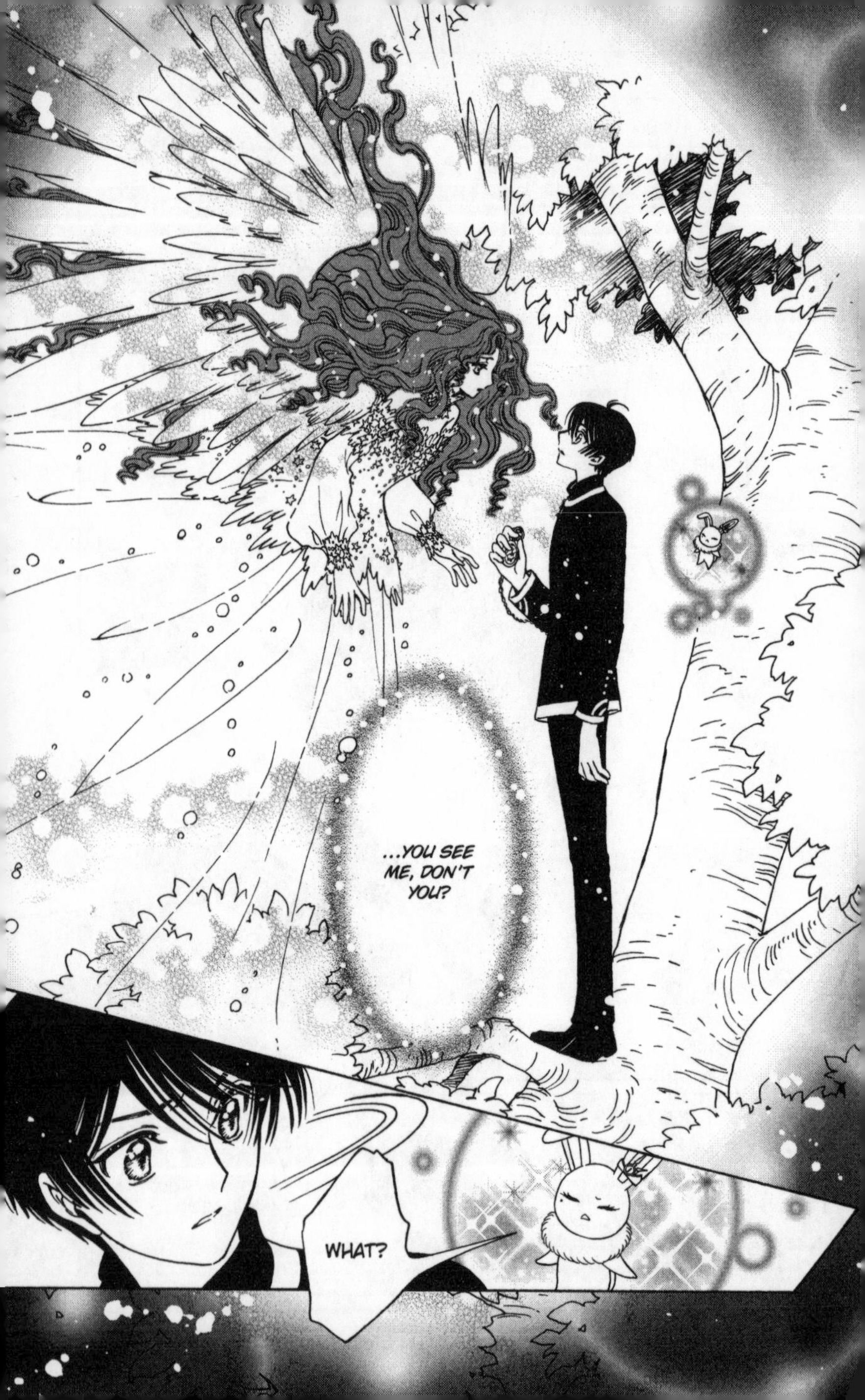
...YOU SEE ME, DON'T YOU?
WHAT?

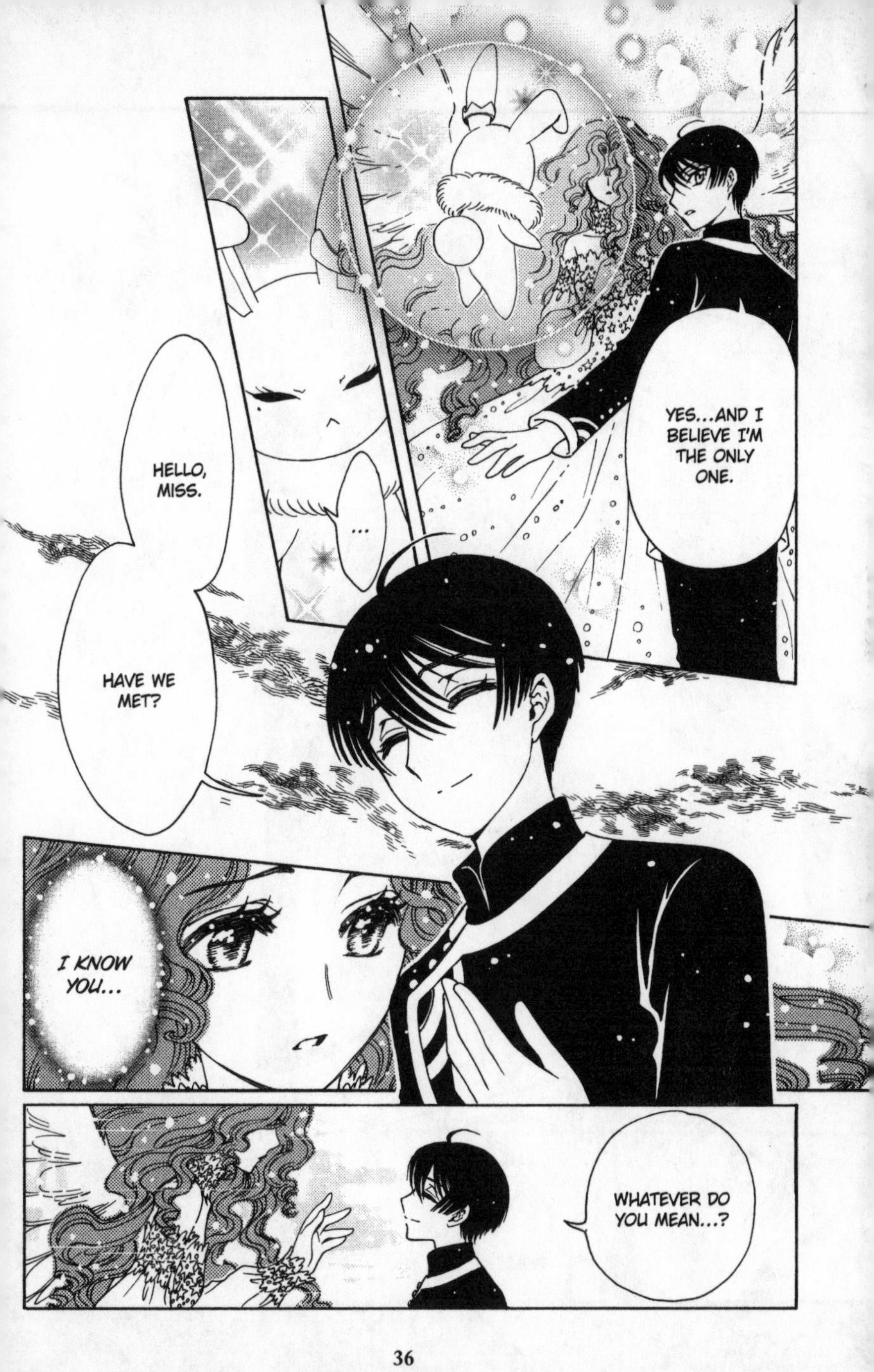
YES...AND I BELIEVE I'M THE ONLY ONE.
...
HELLO, MISS.
HAVE WE MET?
I KNOW YOU...
WHATEVER DO YOU MEAN...?

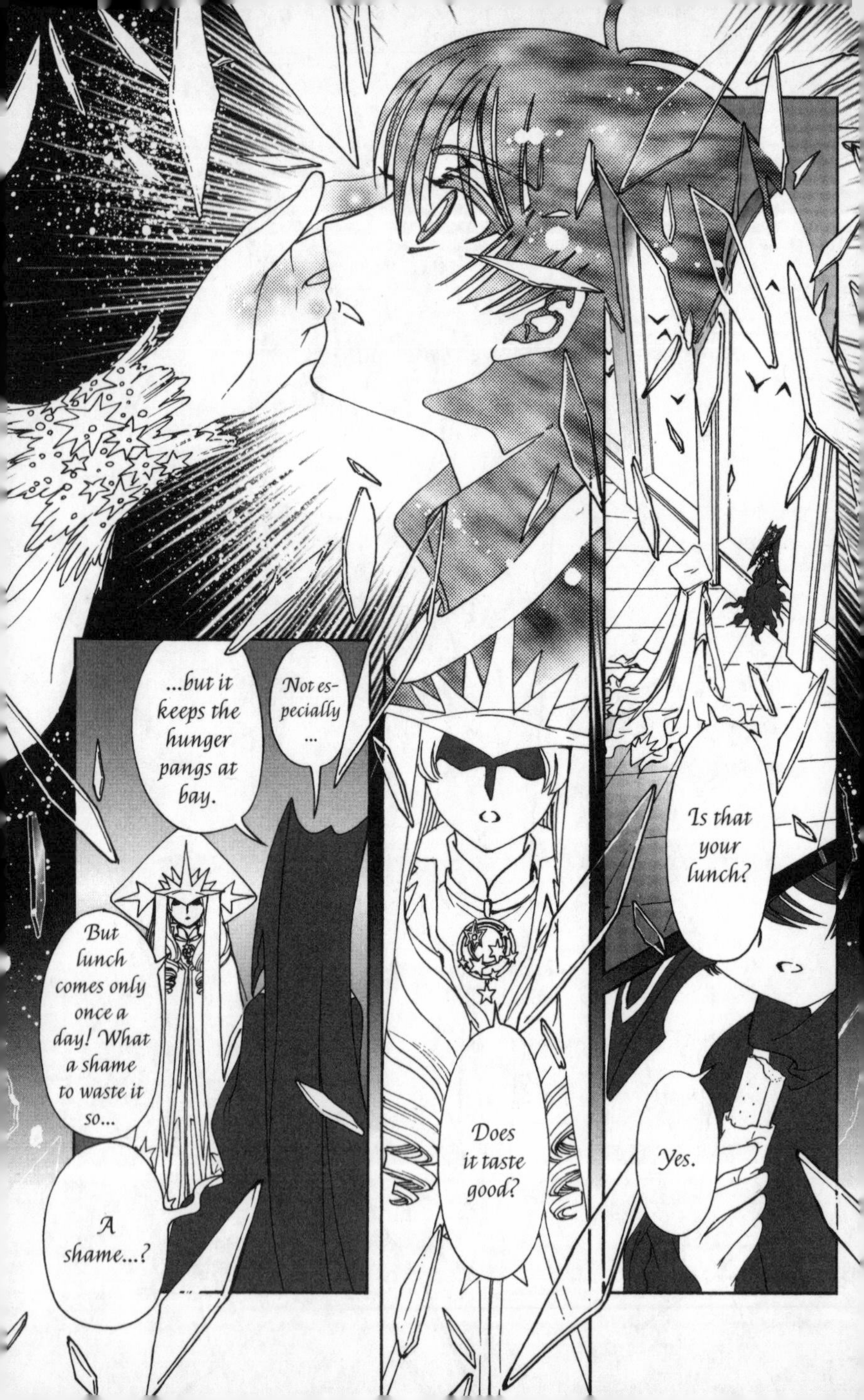
Is that your lunch?
Yes.
Does it taste good?
Not especially...
...but it keeps the hunger pangs at bay.
But lunch comes only once a day! What a shame to waste it so...
A shame...?

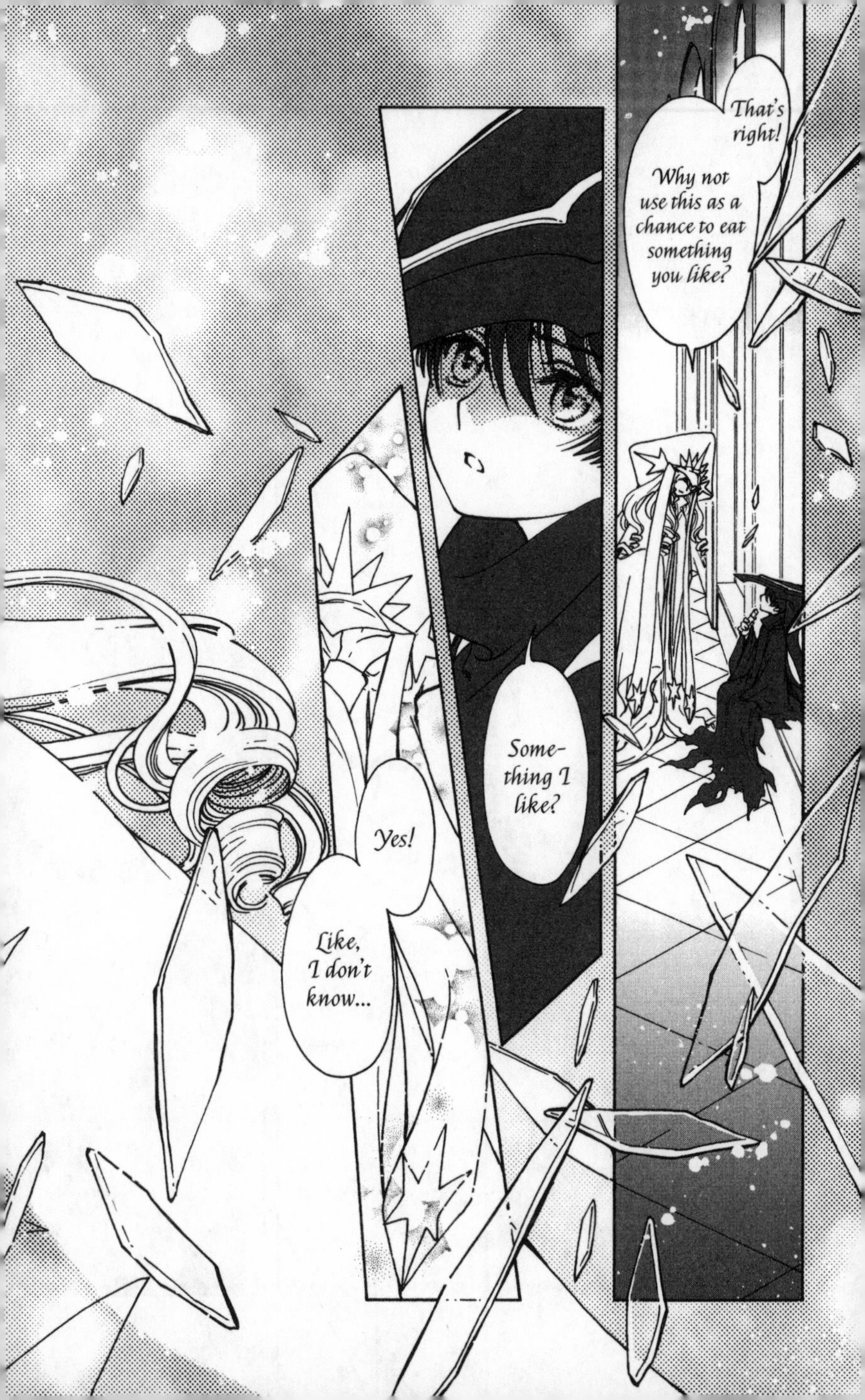
That's right!
Why not use this as a chance to eat something you like?
Something I like?
Yes!
Like, I don't know...

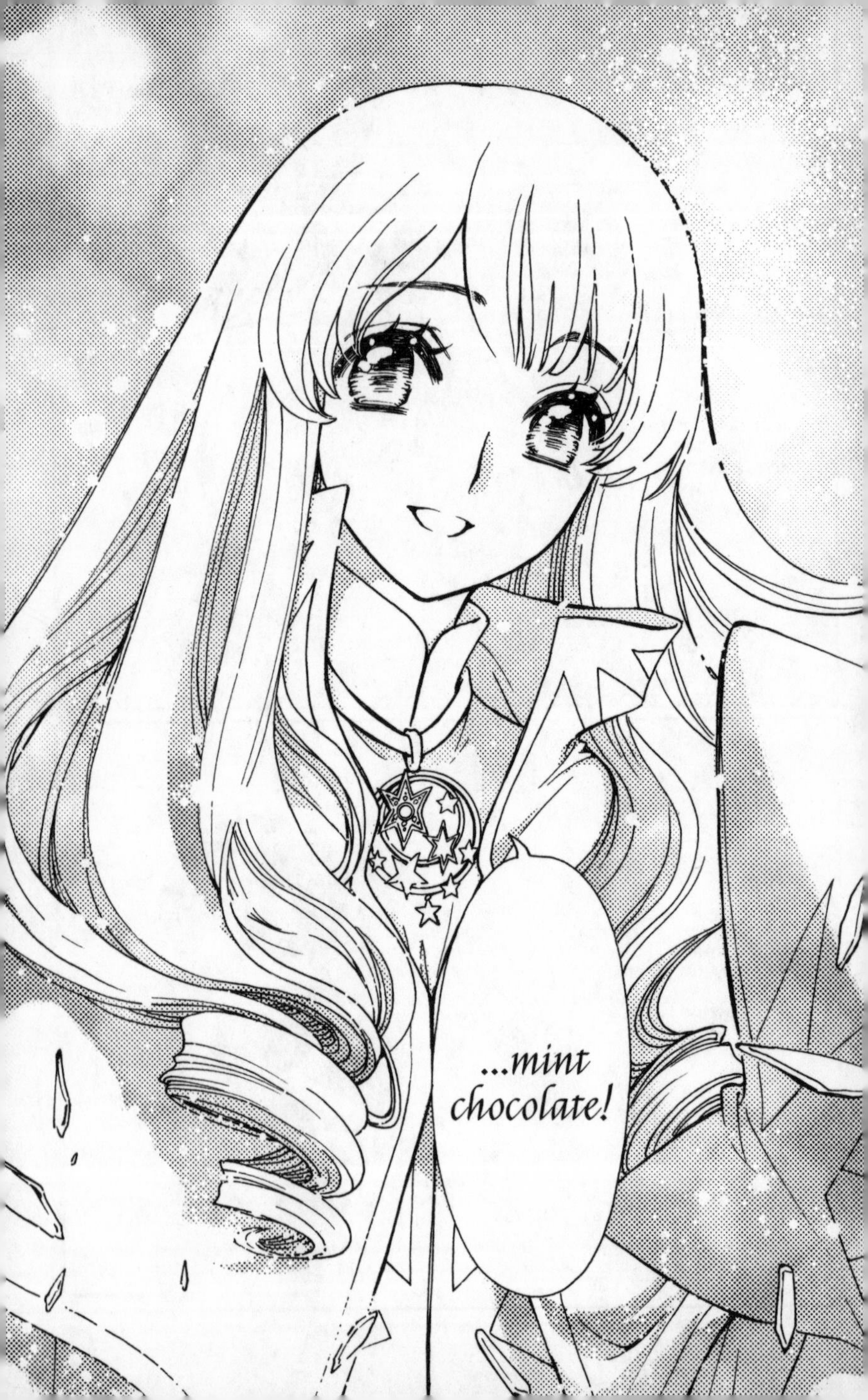
...mint chocolate!

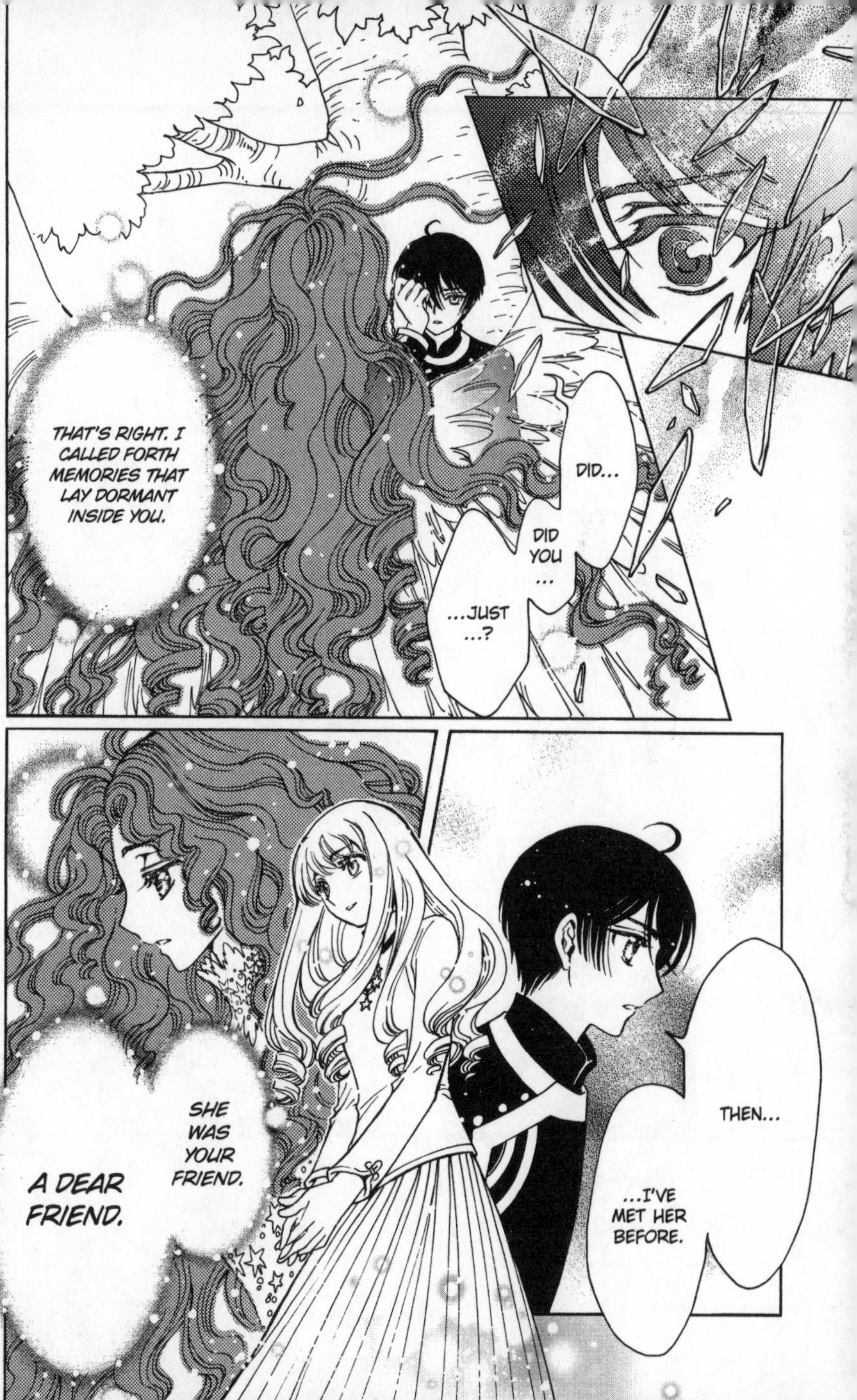
DID...
DID YOU ...
...JUST ...?
THAT'S RIGHT. I CALLED FORTH MEMORIES THAT LAY DORMANT INSIDE YOU.
THEN...
...I'VE MET HER BEFORE.
SHE WAS YOUR FRIEND.
A DEAR FRIEND.

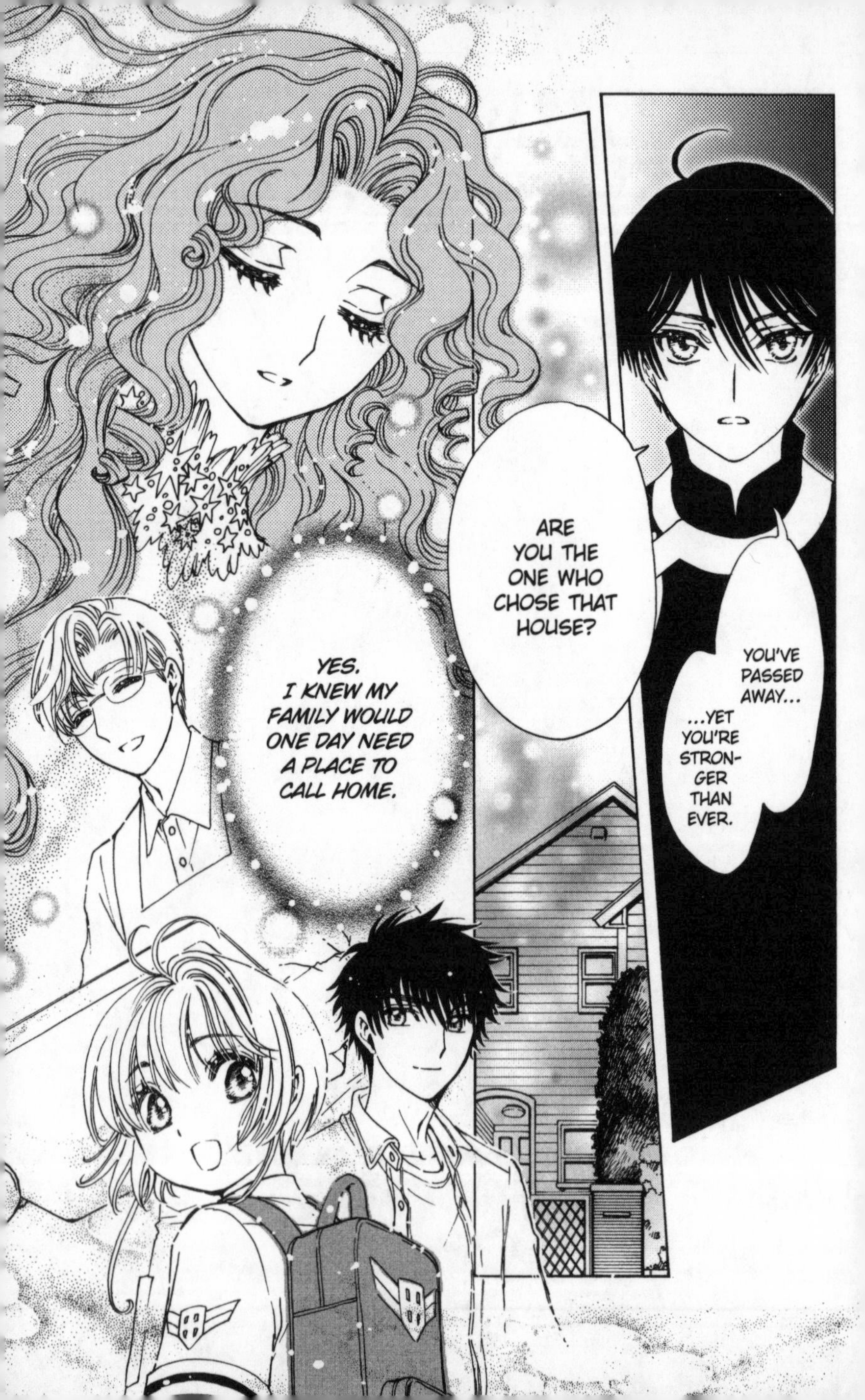
ARE YOU THE ONE WHO CHOSE THAT HOUSE?
YOU'VE PASSED AWAY...
...YET YOU'RE STRONGER THAN EVER.
YES. I KNEW MY FAMILY WOULD ONE DAY NEED A PLACE TO CALL HOME.

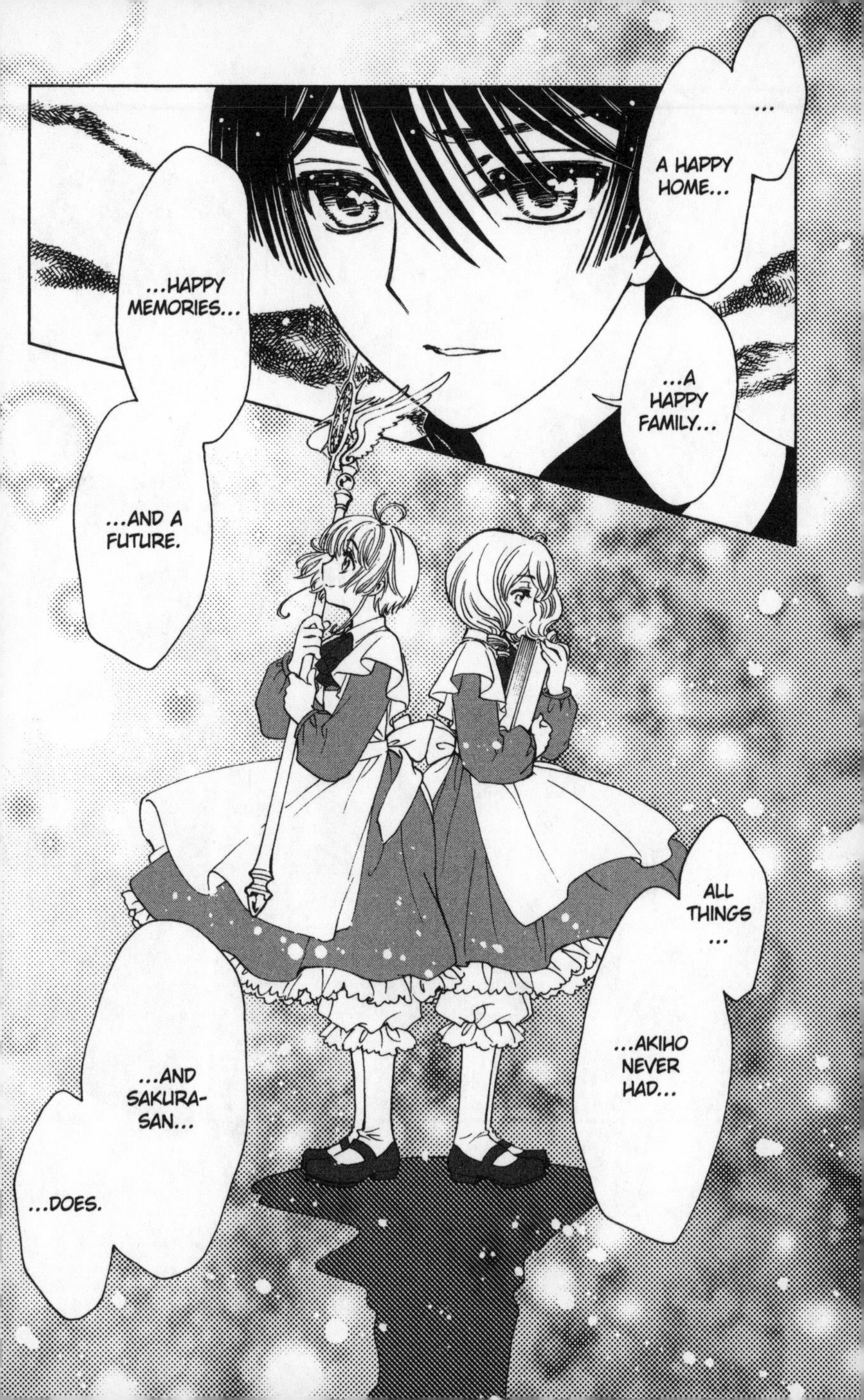
...
A HAPPY HOME...
...A HAPPY FAMILY...
...HAPPY MEMORIES...
...AND A FUTURE.
ALL THINGS ...
...AKIHO NEVER HAD...
...AND SAKURA-SAN...
...DOES.

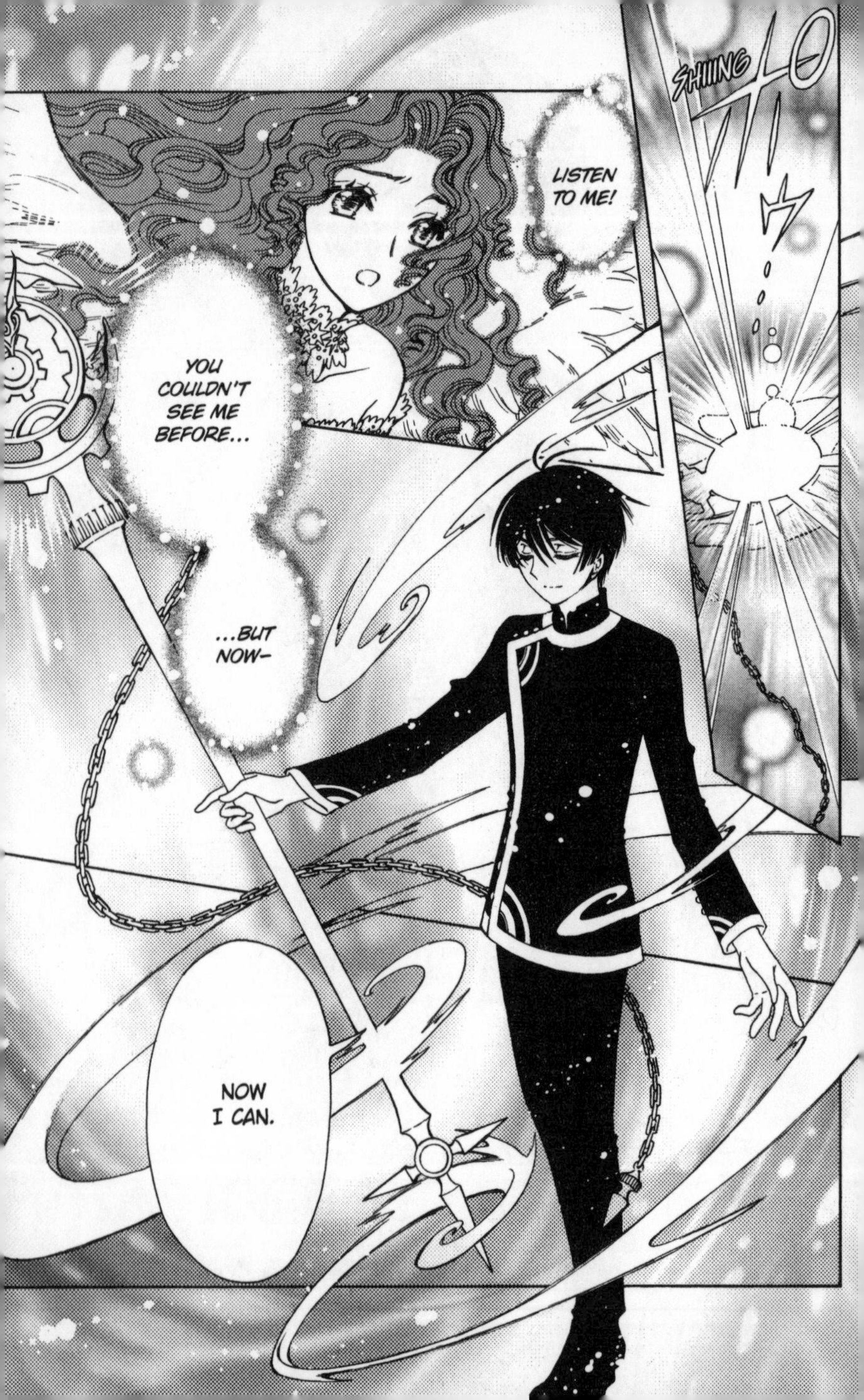
SHIIING
LISTEN TO ME!
YOU COULDN'T SEE ME BEFORE...
...BUT NOW-
NOW I CAN.

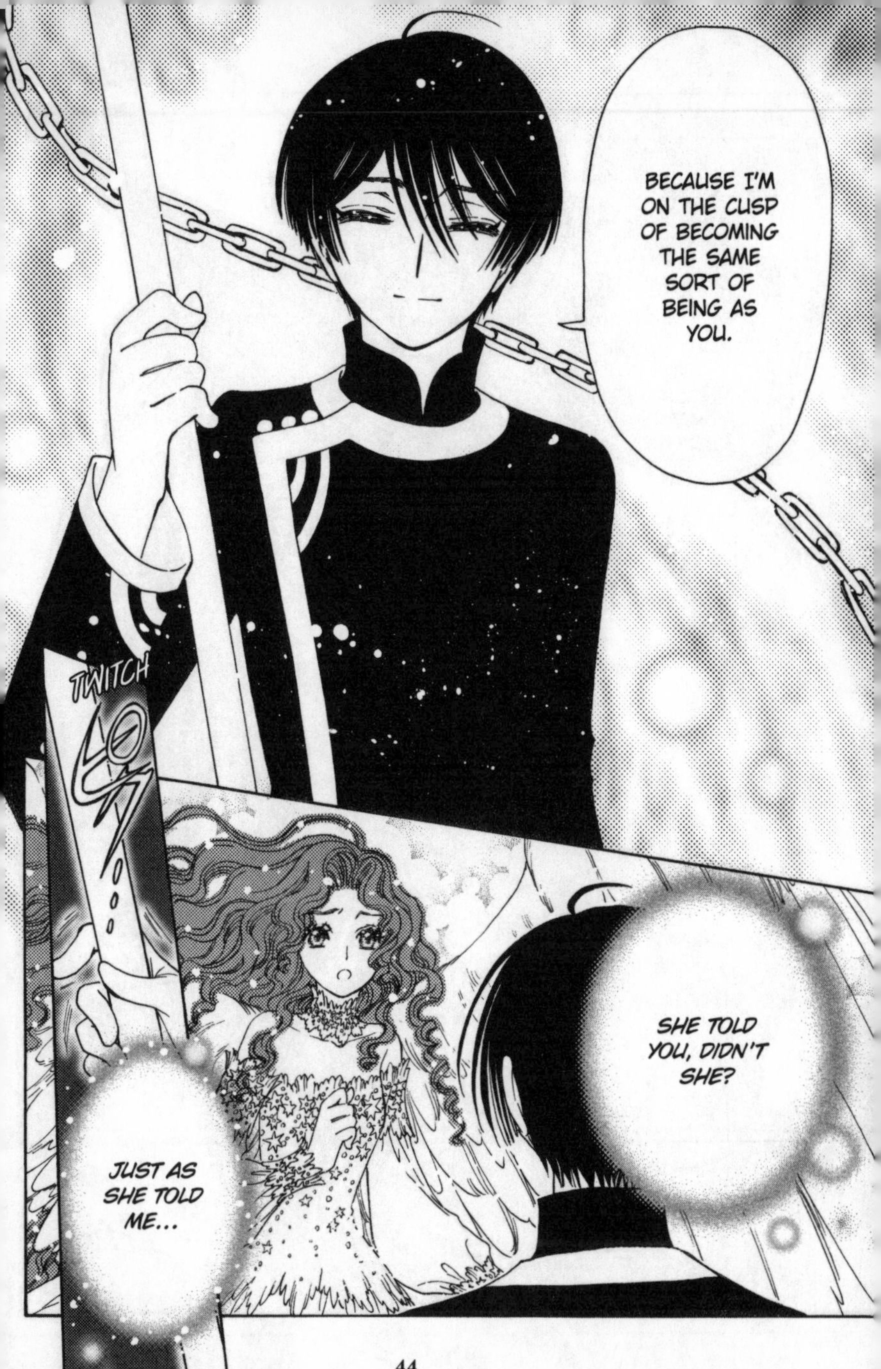
BECAUSE I'M ON THE CUSP OF BECOMING THE SAME SORT OF BEING AS YOU.
TWITCH
SHE TOLD YOU, DIDN'T SHE?
JUST AS SHE TOLD ME...

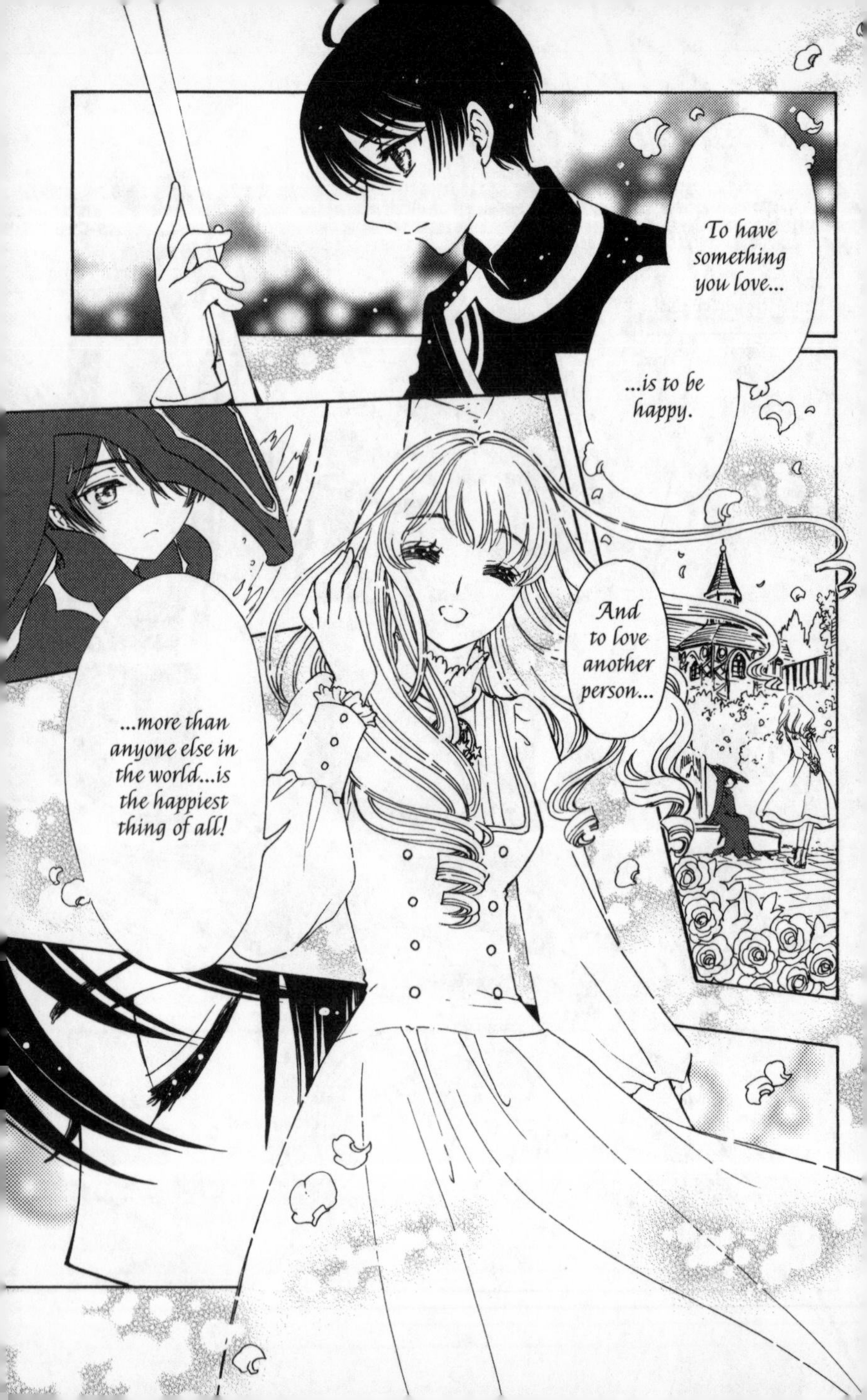
To have something you love...
...is to be happy.
And to love another person...
...more than anyone else in the world...is the happiest thing of all!

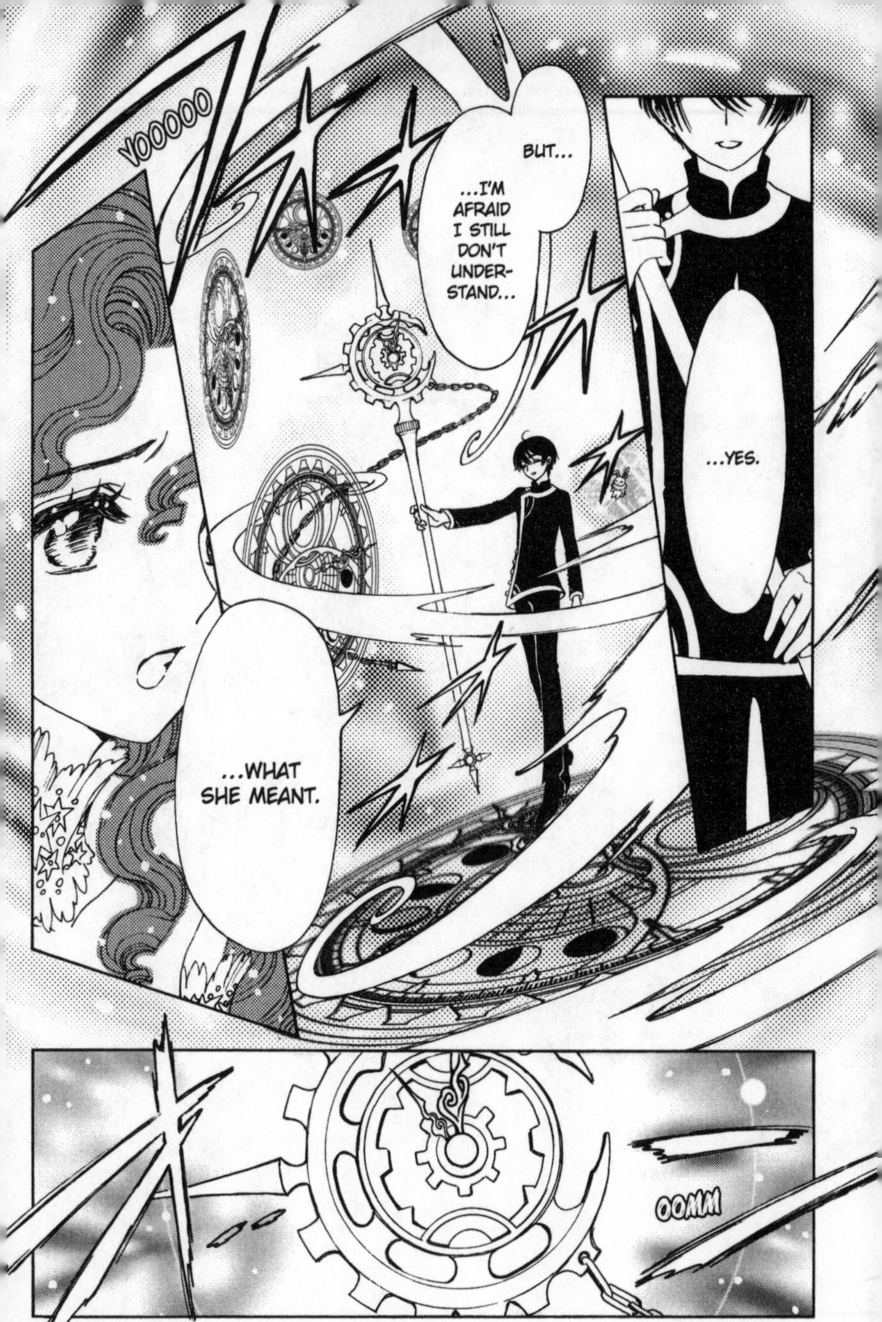
...YES.
BUT... ...I'M AFRAID I STILL DON'T UNDER-STAND...
YOOOOO
...WHAT SHE MEANT.
OOMM

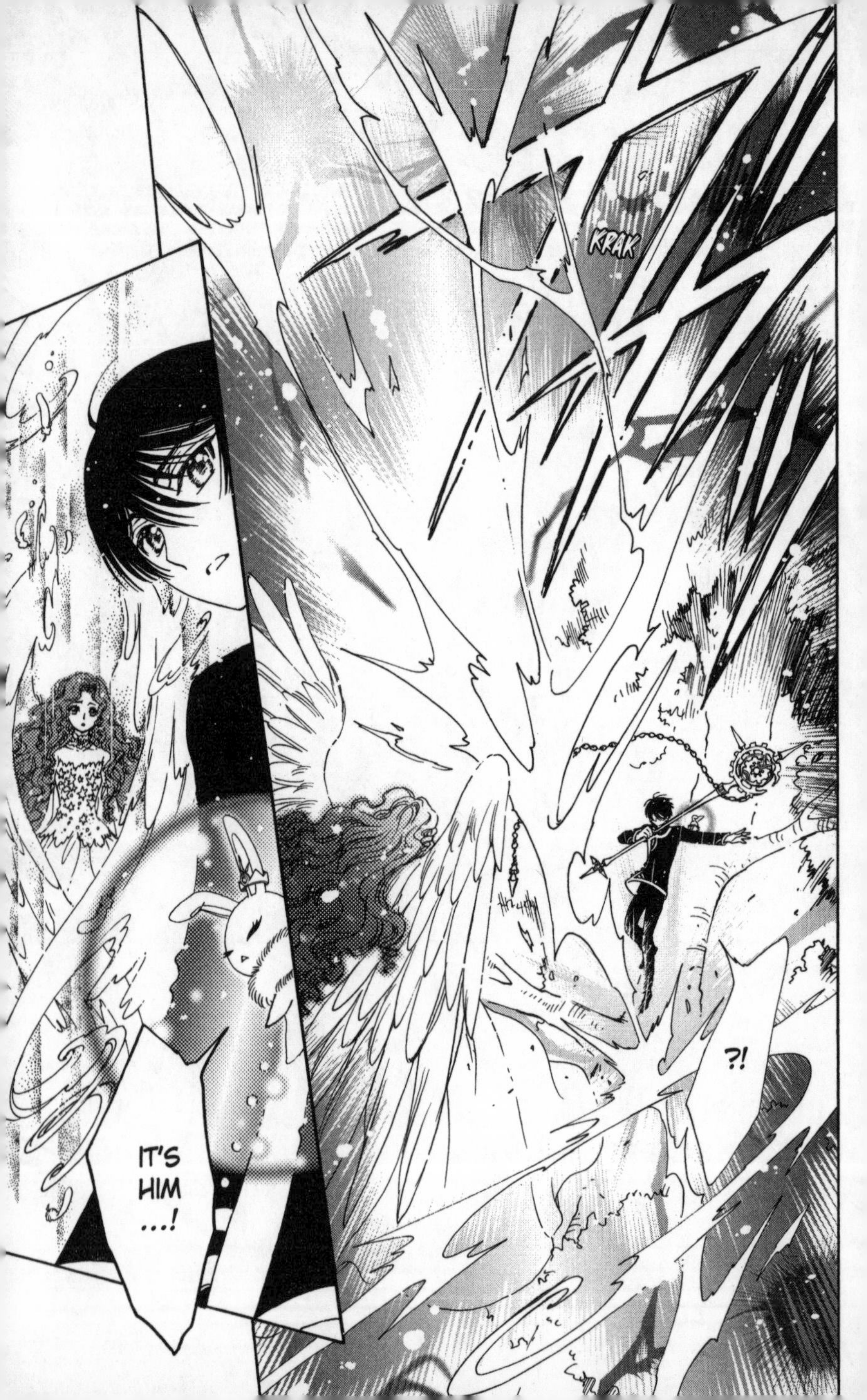
KRAK
?!
IT'S HIM ...!

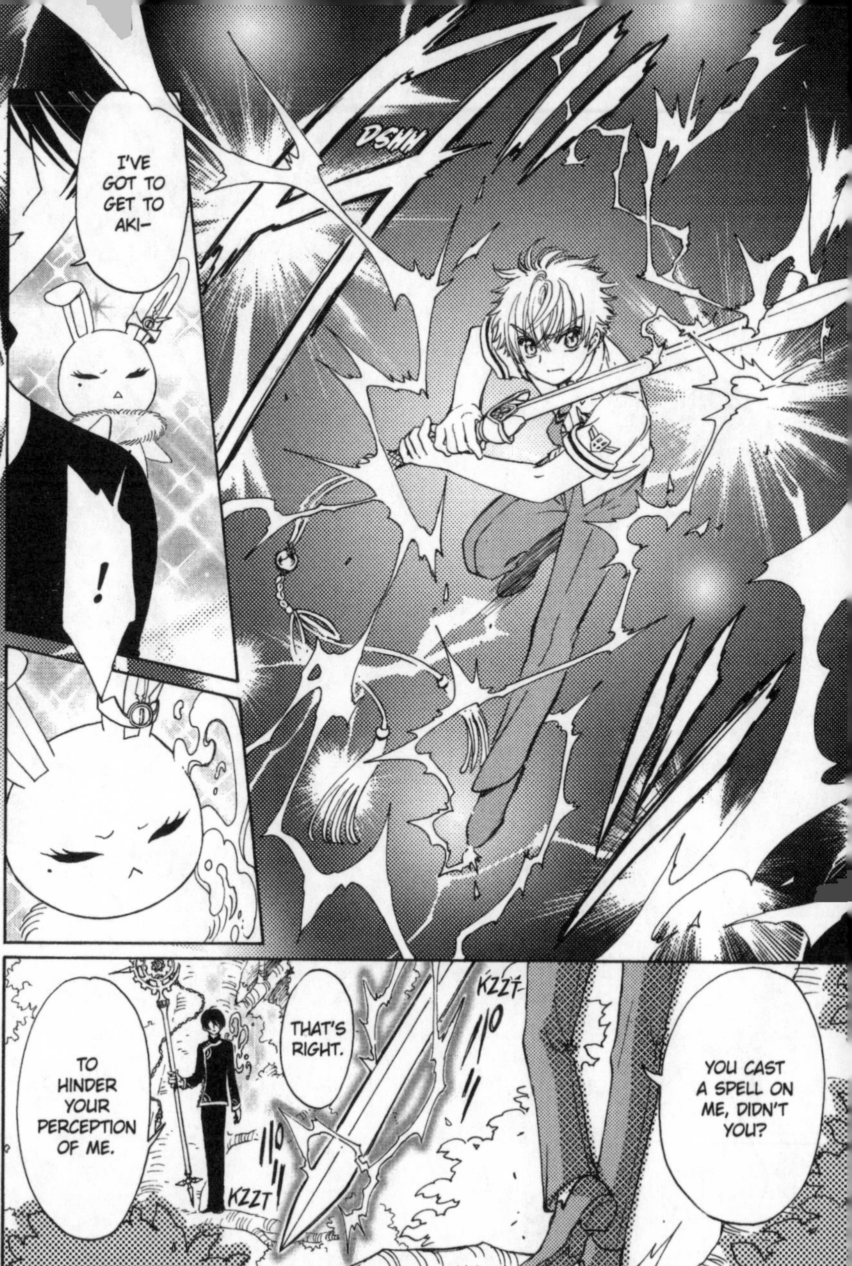

DSHH
I'VE GOT TO GET TO AKI–
!
YOU CAST A SPELL ON ME, DIDN'T YOU?
KZZT
THAT'S RIGHT.
TO HINDER YOUR PERCEPTION OF ME.
KZZT

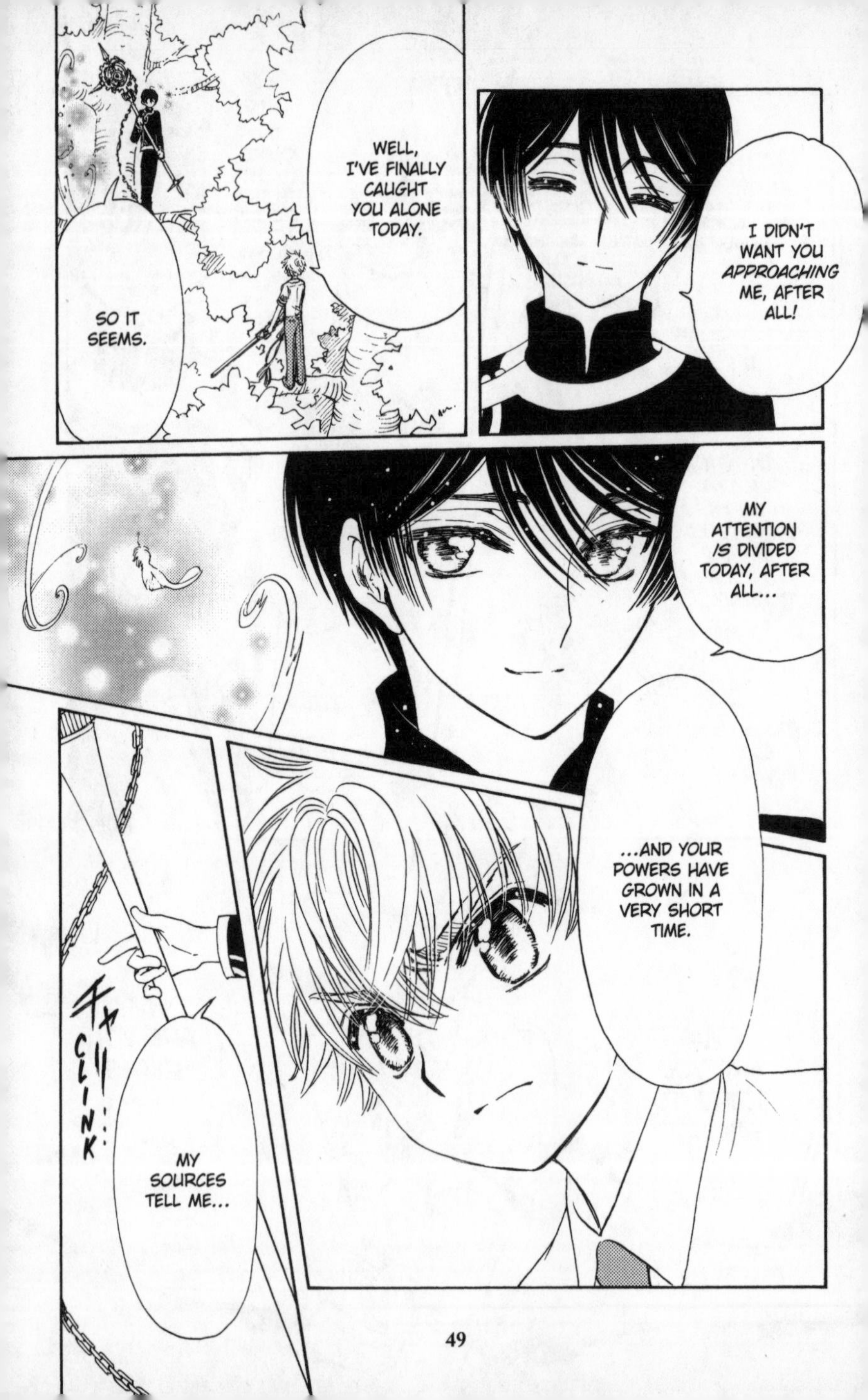
I DIDN'T WANT YOU *APPROACHING* ME, AFTER ALL!
WELL, I'VE FINALLY CAUGHT YOU ALONE TODAY.
SO IT SEEMS.
MY ATTENTION *IS* DIVIDED TODAY, AFTER ALL...
...AND YOUR POWERS HAVE GROWN IN A VERY SHORT TIME.
チャリ…
CLINK
MY SOURCES TELL ME...

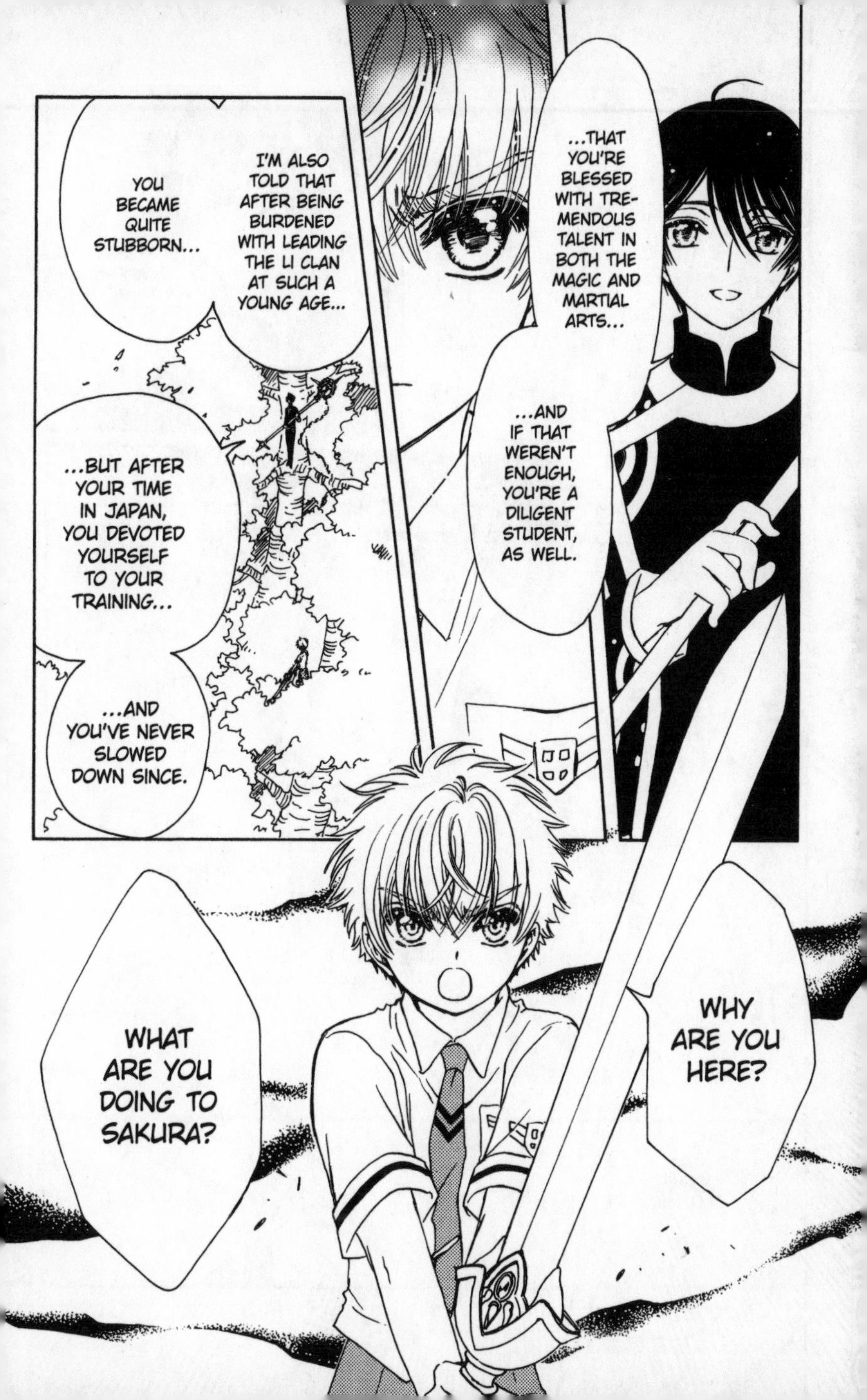
...THAT YOU'RE BLESSED WITH TRE-MENDOUS TALENT IN BOTH THE MAGIC AND MARTIAL ARTS...
...AND IF THAT WEREN'T ENOUGH, YOU'RE A DILIGENT STUDENT, AS WELL.
I'M ALSO TOLD THAT AFTER BEING BURDENED WITH LEADING THE LI CLAN AT SUCH A YOUNG AGE...
YOU BECAME QUITE STUBBORN...
...BUT AFTER YOUR TIME IN JAPAN, YOU DEVOTED YOURSELF TO YOUR TRAINING...
...AND YOU'VE NEVER SLOWED DOWN SINCE.
WHY ARE YOU HERE?
WHAT ARE YOU DOING TO SAKURA?

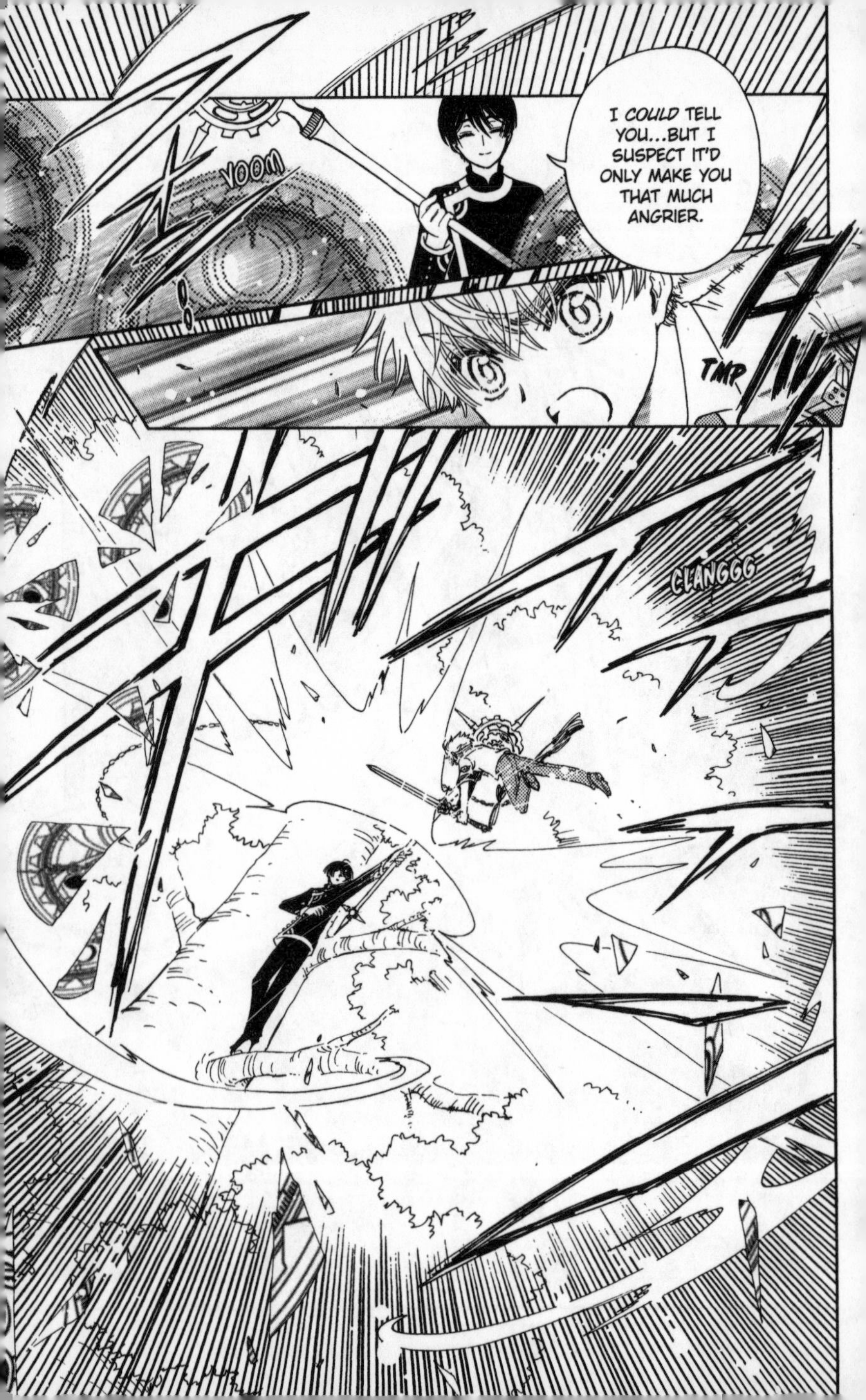
I COULD TELL YOU...BUT I SUSPECT IT'D ONLY MAKE YOU THAT MUCH ANGRIER.
VOOM
TMP
CLANGGG

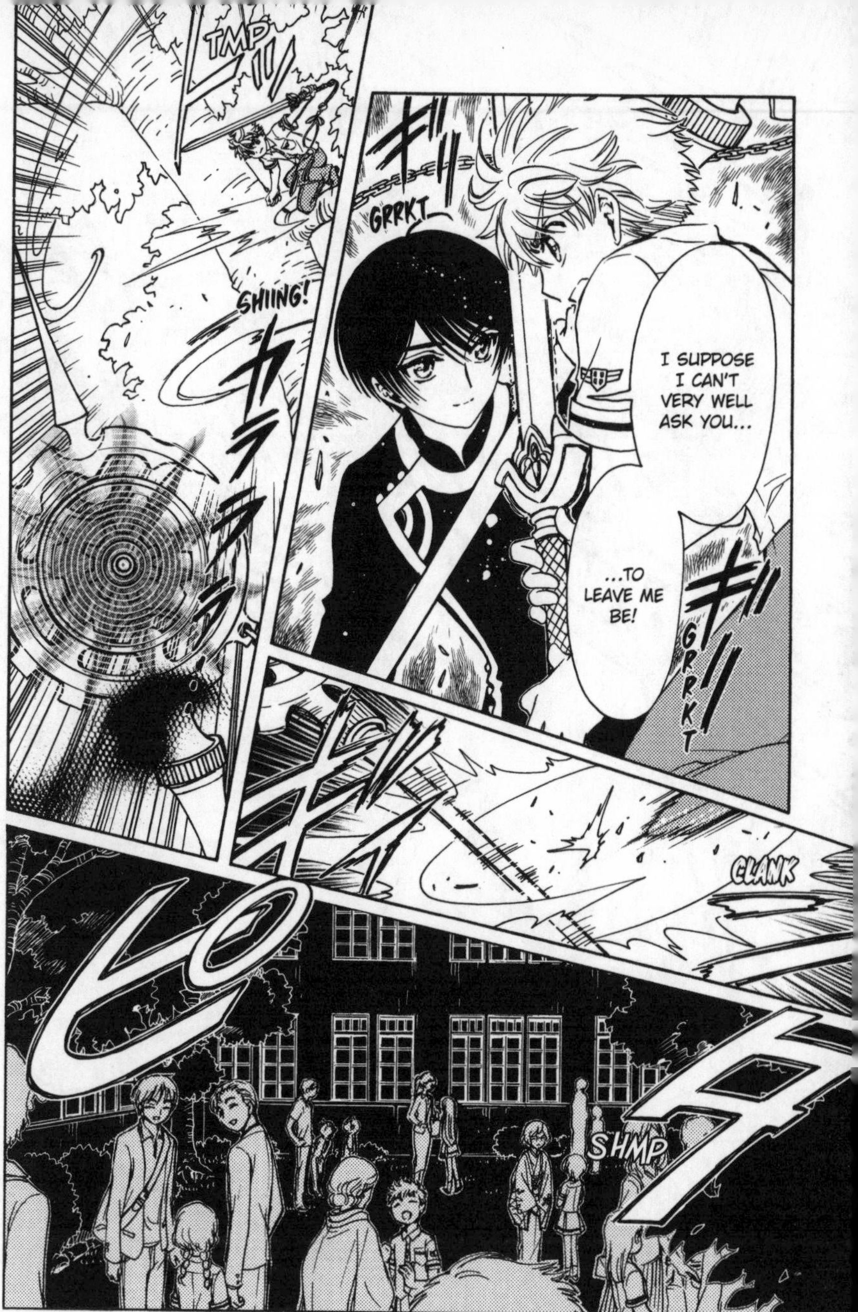
GRRKT
I SUPPOSE I CAN'T VERY WELL ASK YOU...
...TO LEAVE ME BE!
GRRKT
TMP
SHIING!
CLANK
SHMP

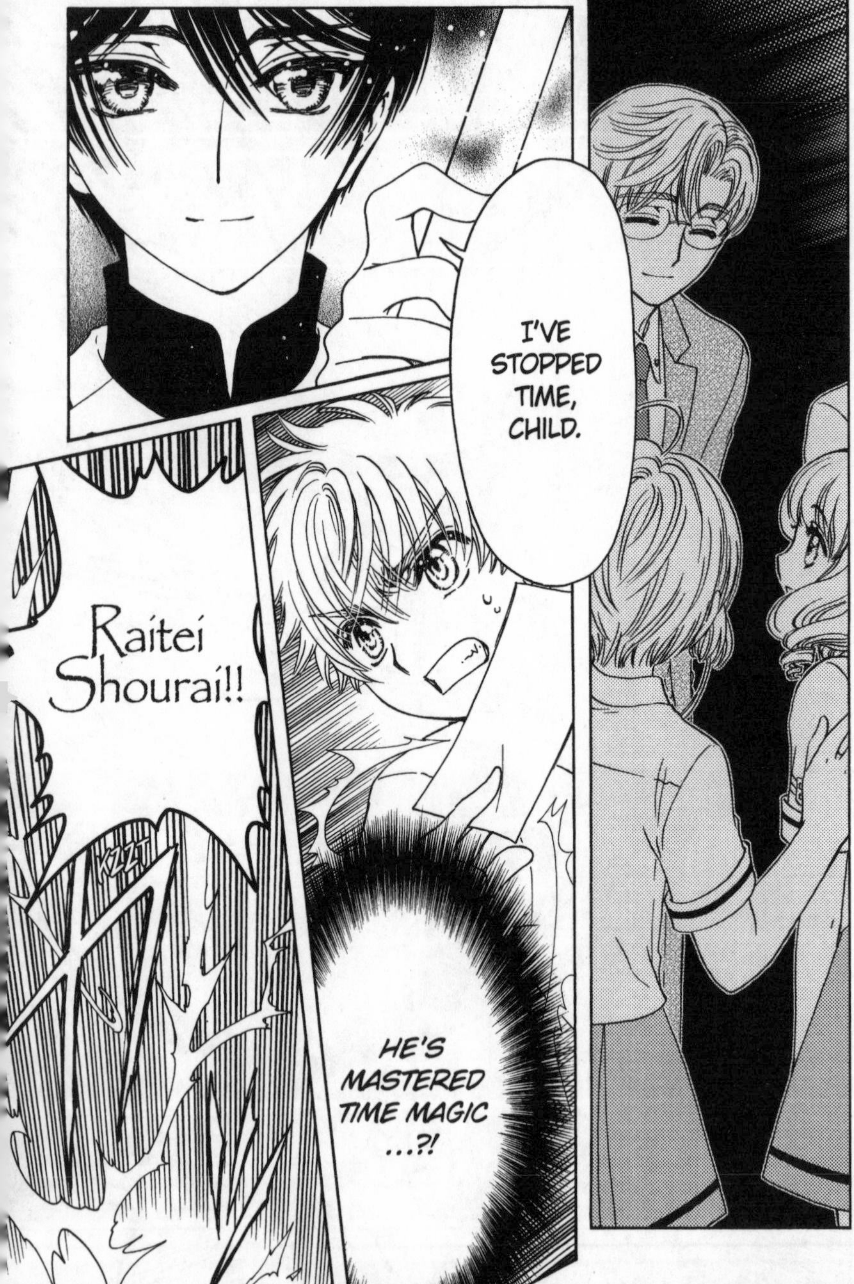
I'VE STOPPED TIME, CHILD.
HE'S MASTERED TIME MAGIC ...?!
Raitei Shourai!!
KZZT

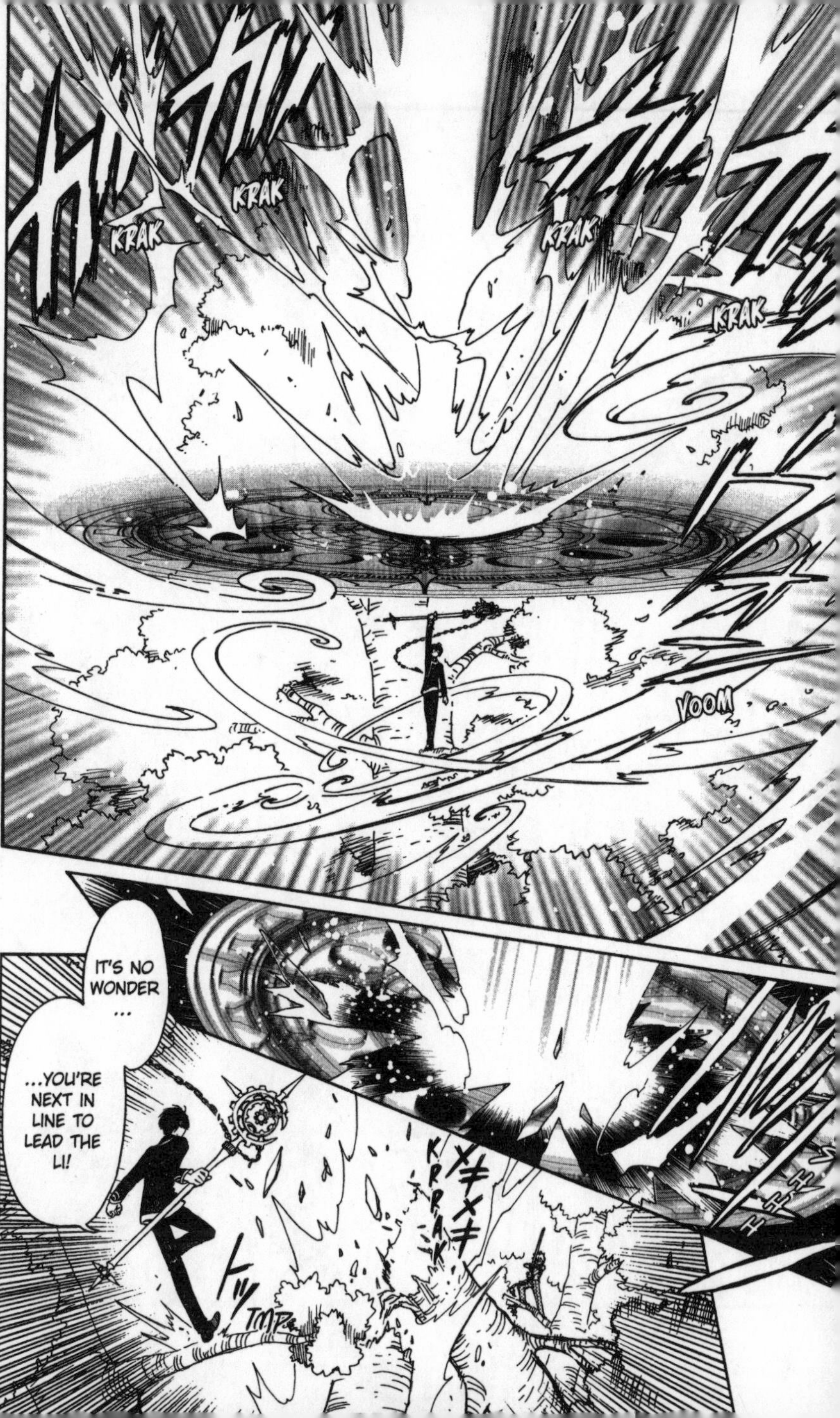
KRAK
KRAK
VOOM
KRAK
KRAK
IT'S NO WONDER ...
...YOU'RE NEXT IN LINE TO LEAD THE LI!
KRRRAK
TMP

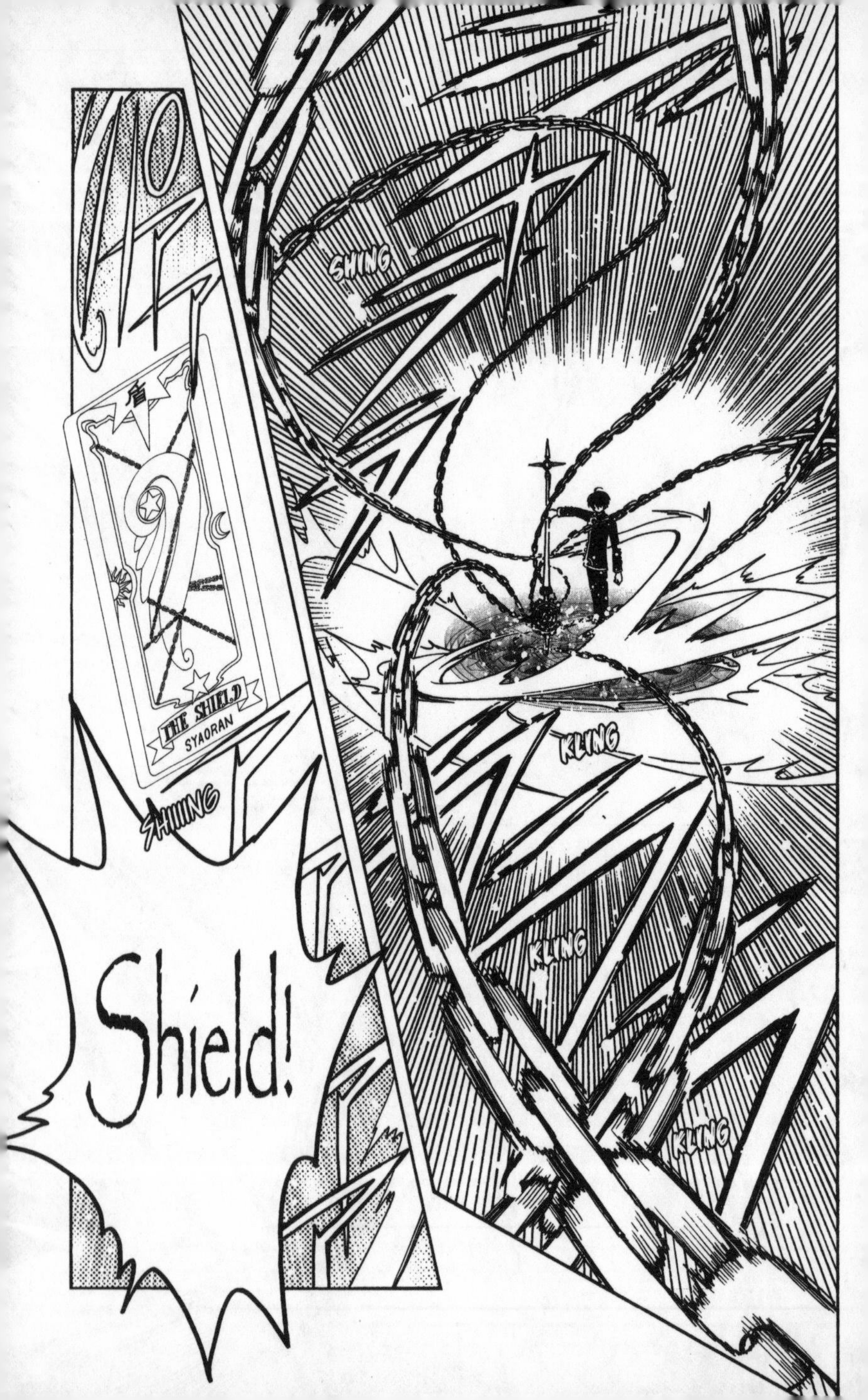
SHING
KLING
KLING
KLING
THE SHIELD
SYAORAN
SHIIIING
Shield!

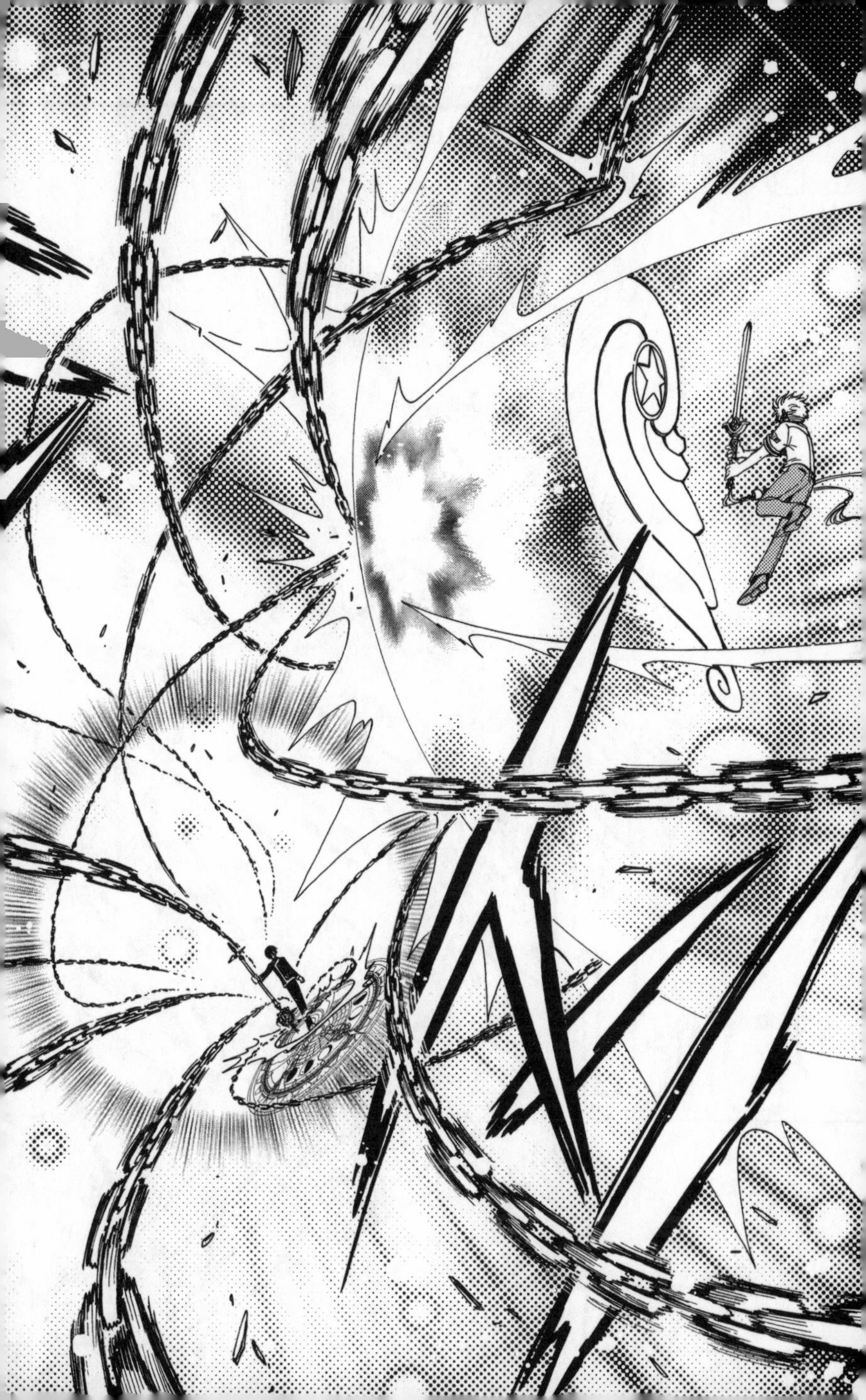

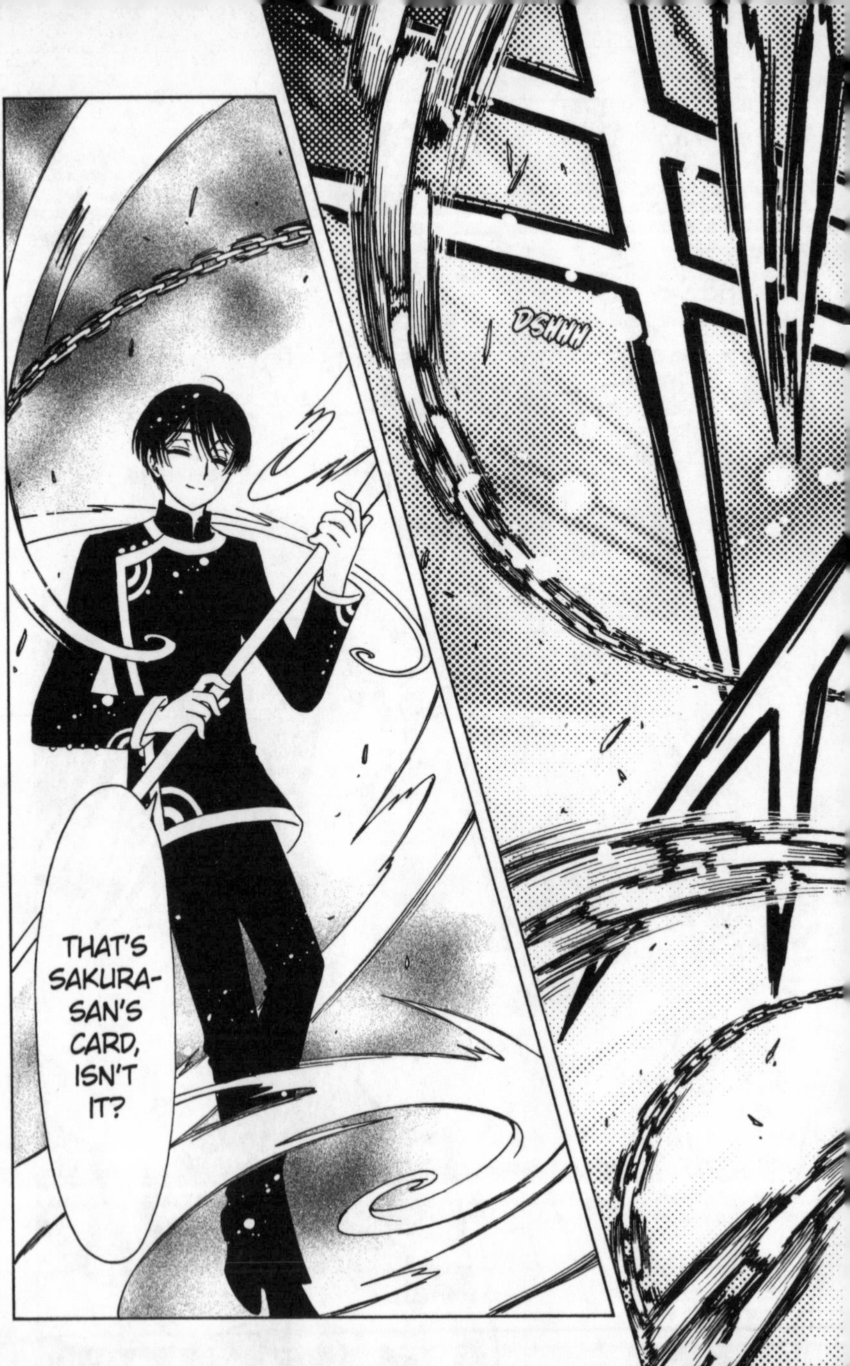
DSHWW
THAT'S SAKURA-SAN'S CARD, ISN'T IT?

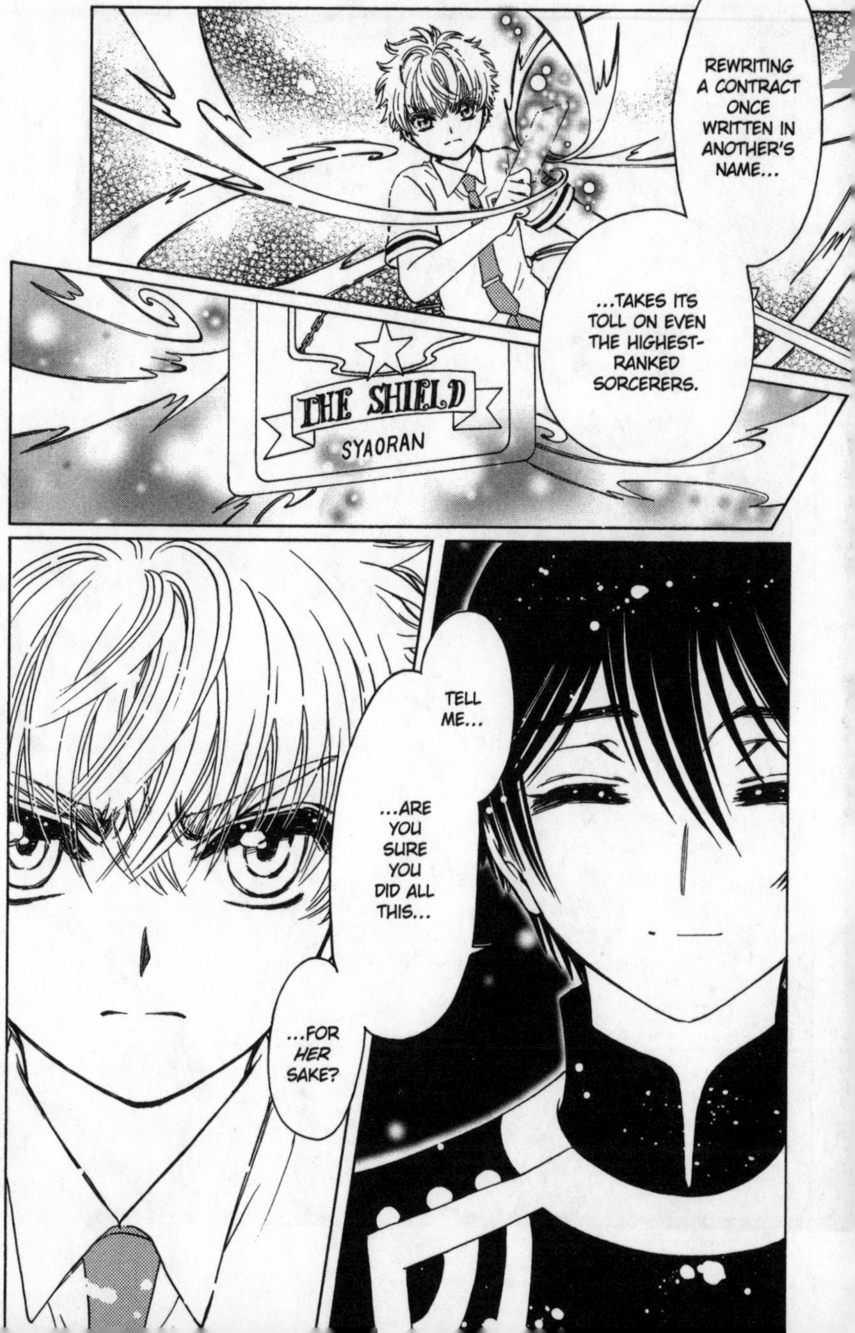
REWRITING A CONTRACT ONCE WRITTEN IN ANOTHER'S NAME...
...TAKES ITS TOLL ON EVEN THE HIGHEST-RANKED SORCERERS.
THE SHIELD
SYAORAN
TELL ME...
...ARE YOU SURE YOU DID ALL THIS...
...FOR HER SAKE?

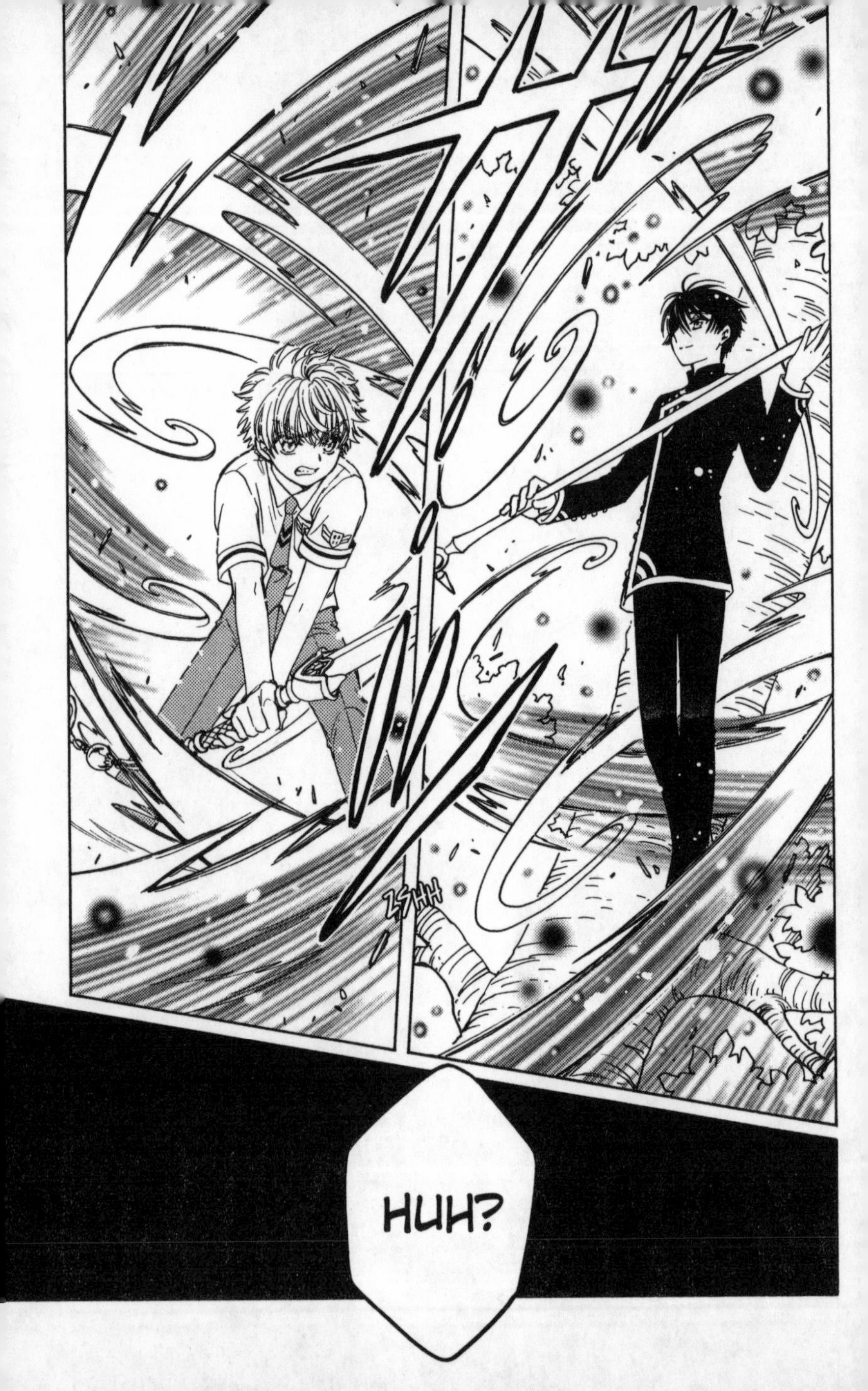
ZSHH
HUH?

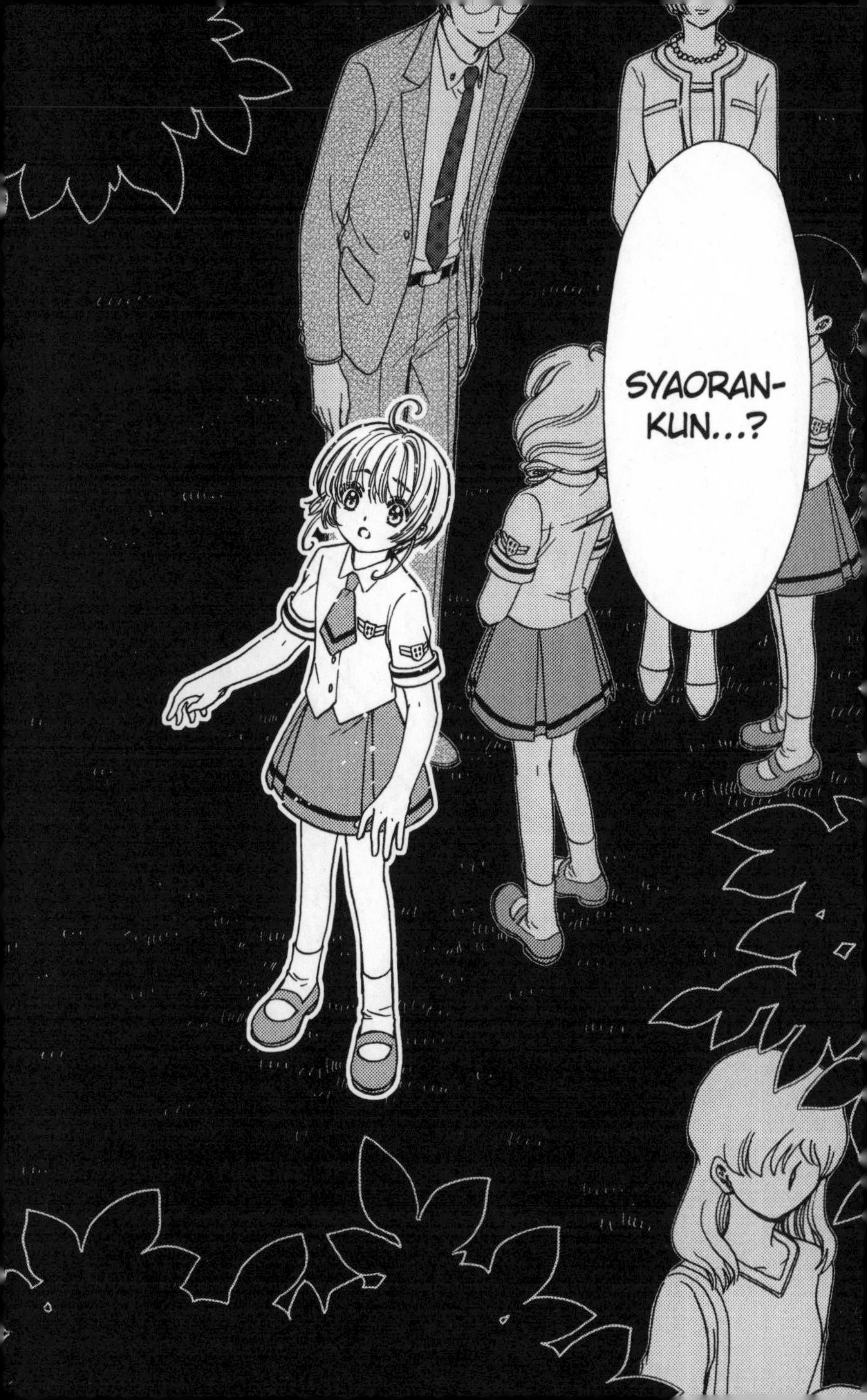
SYAORAN-KUN...?

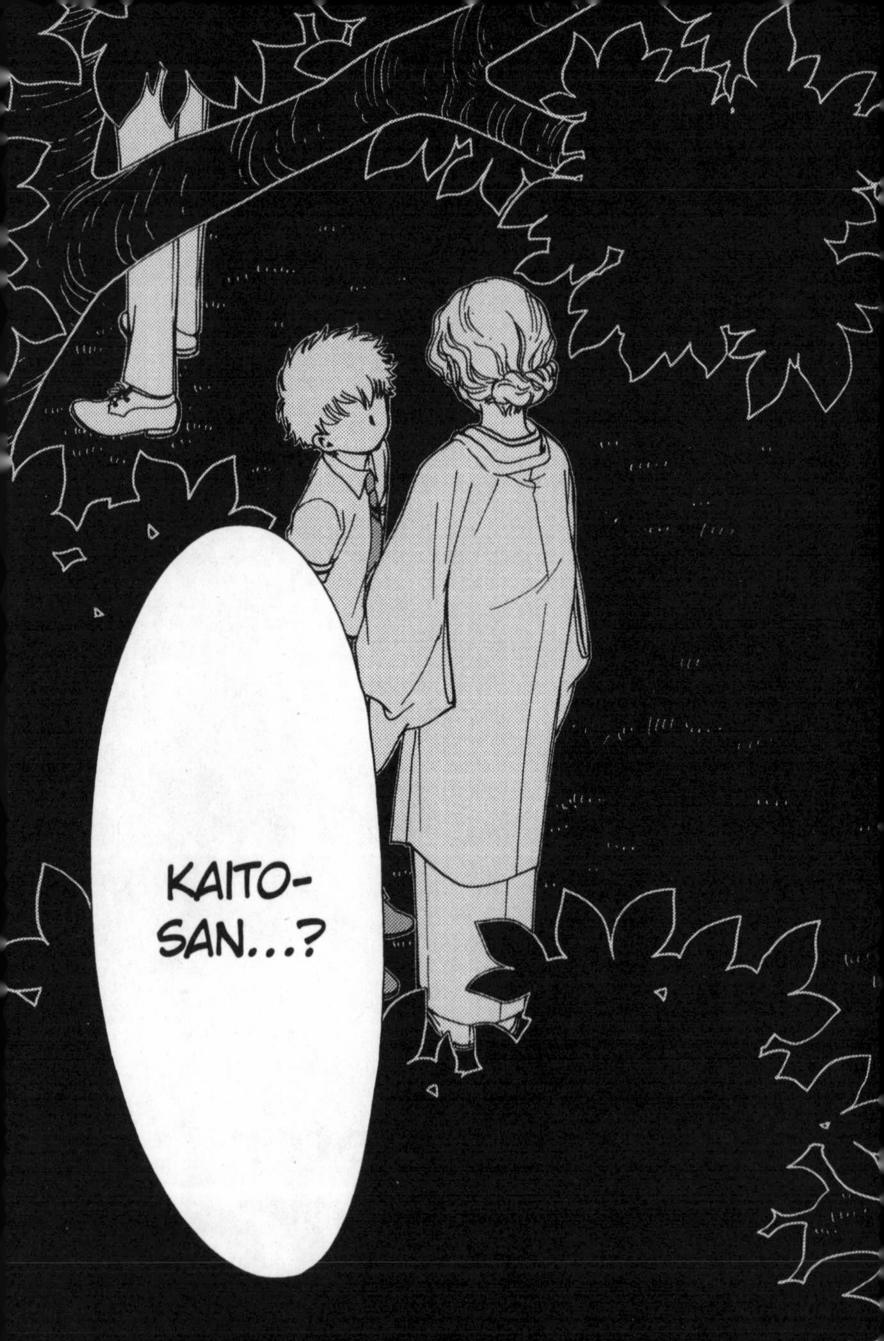
KAITO-SAN...?

✿ To be continued... ✿

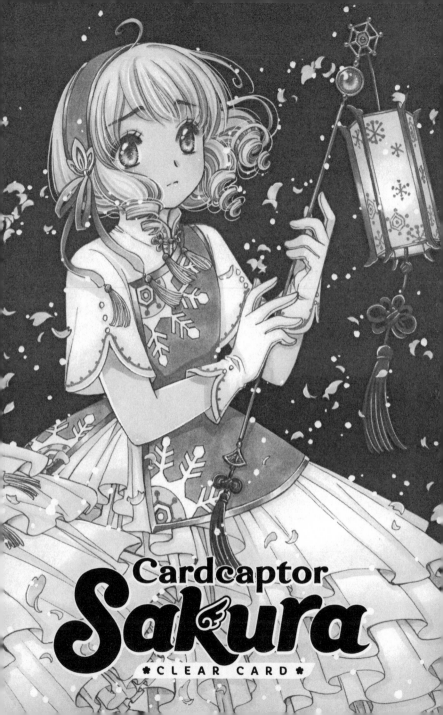

Cardcaptor Sakura

CLEAR CARD

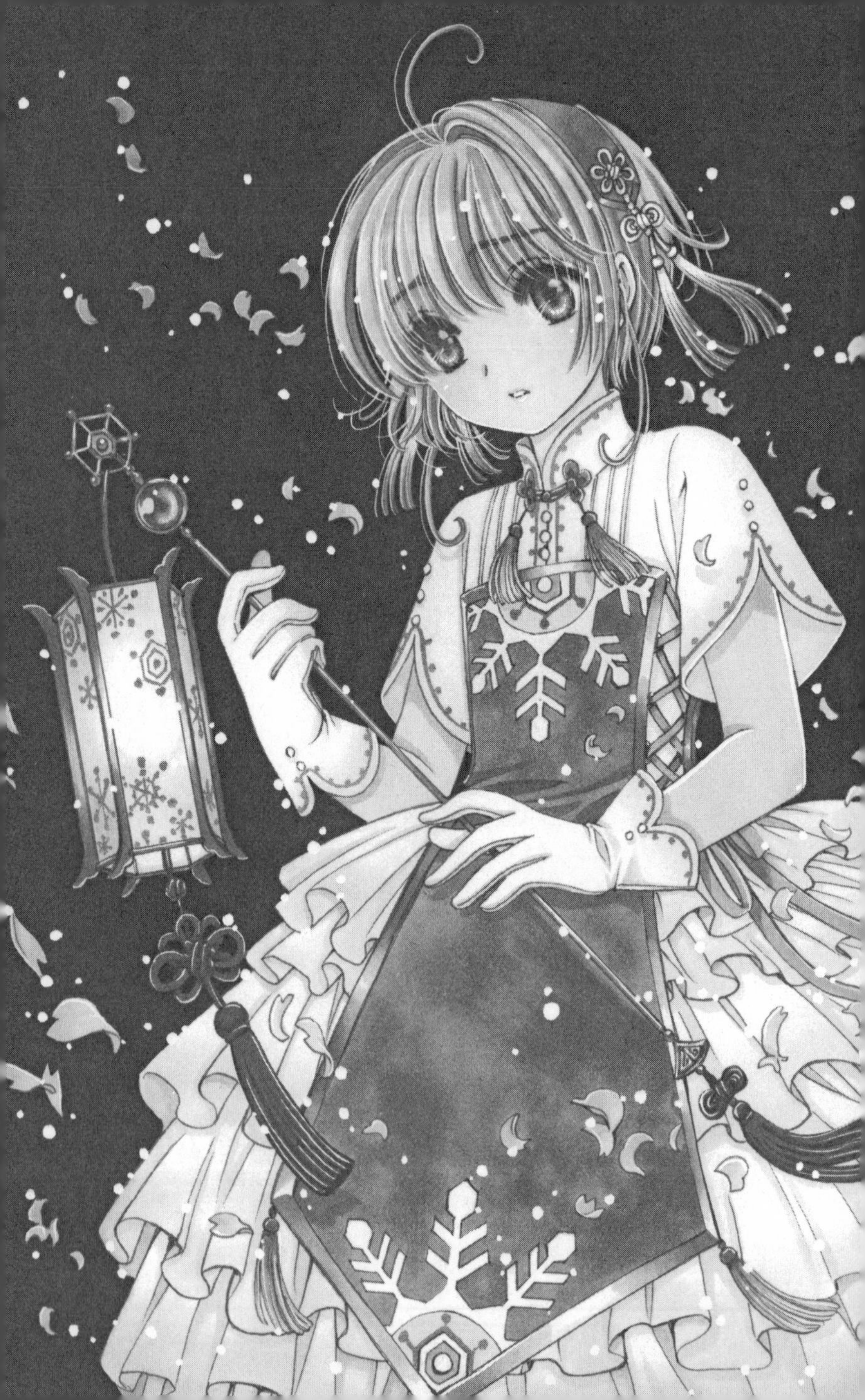

Cardcaptor Sakura
CLEAR CARD

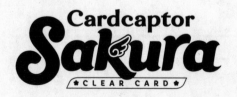

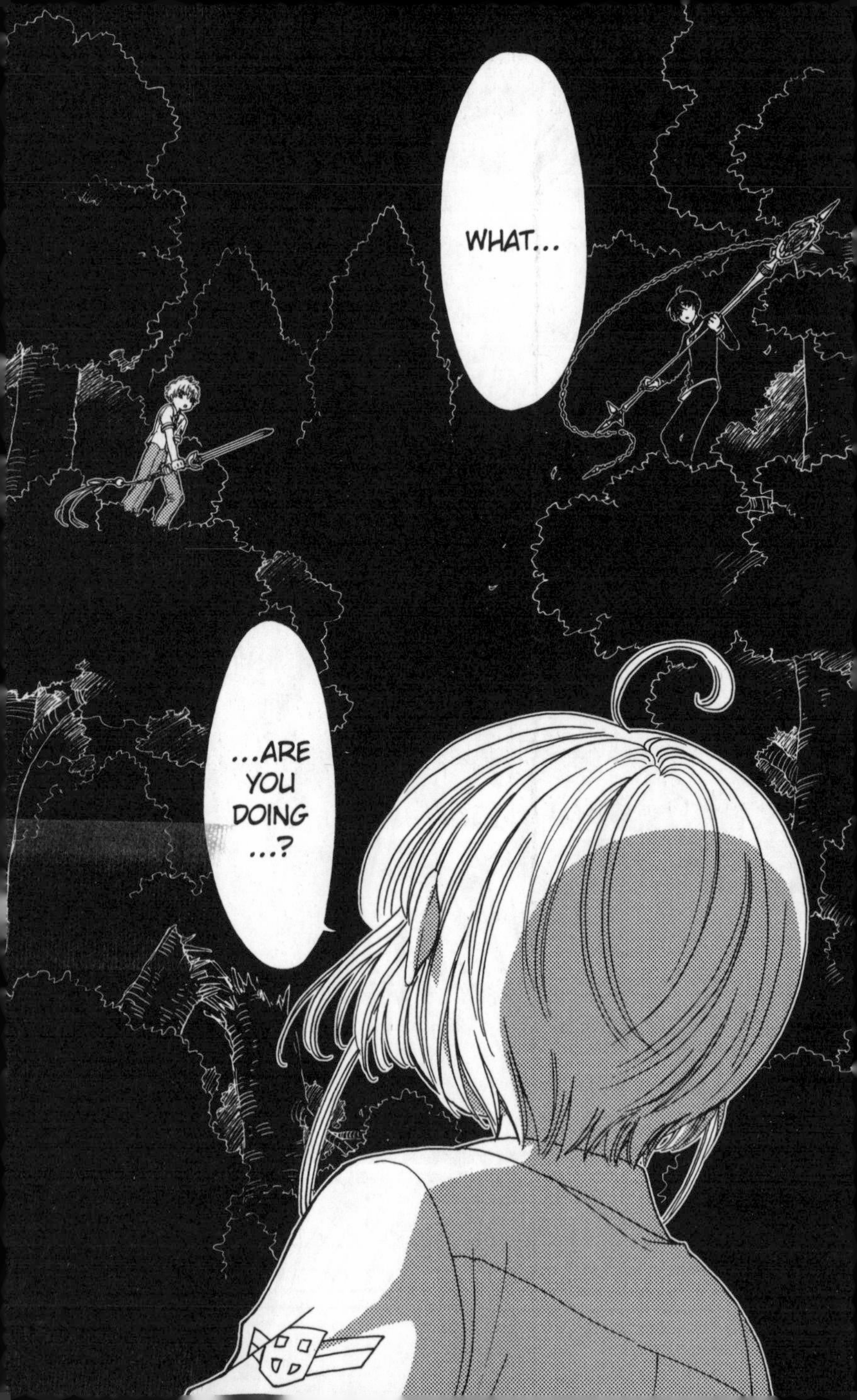
WHAT...
...ARE YOU DOING ...?

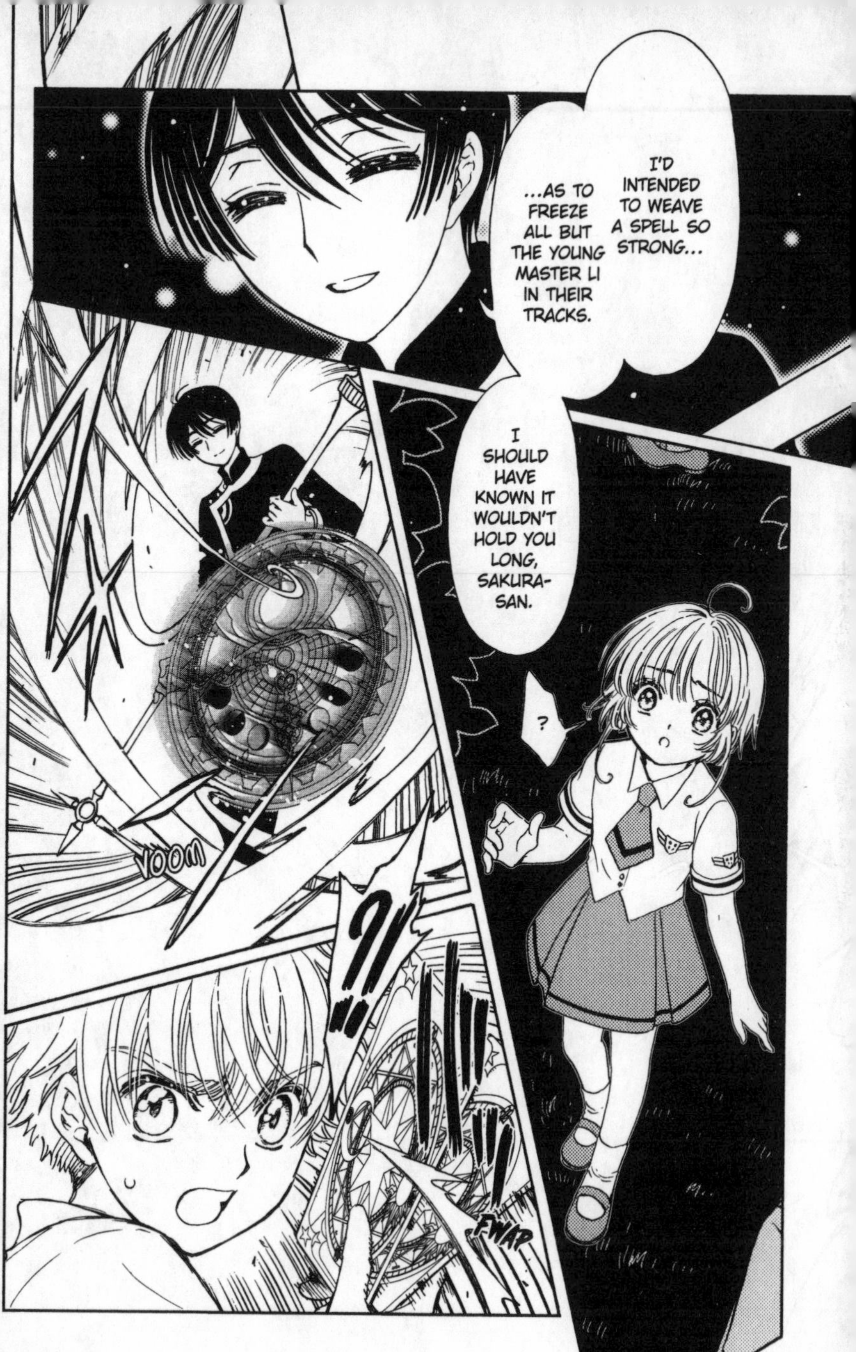
I'D INTENDED TO WEAVE A SPELL SO STRONG...
...AS TO FREEZE ALL BUT THE YOUNG MASTER LI IN THEIR TRACKS.
I SHOULD HAVE KNOWN IT WOULDN'T HOLD YOU LONG, SAKURA-SAN.
?
VOOM
?!
FWAP

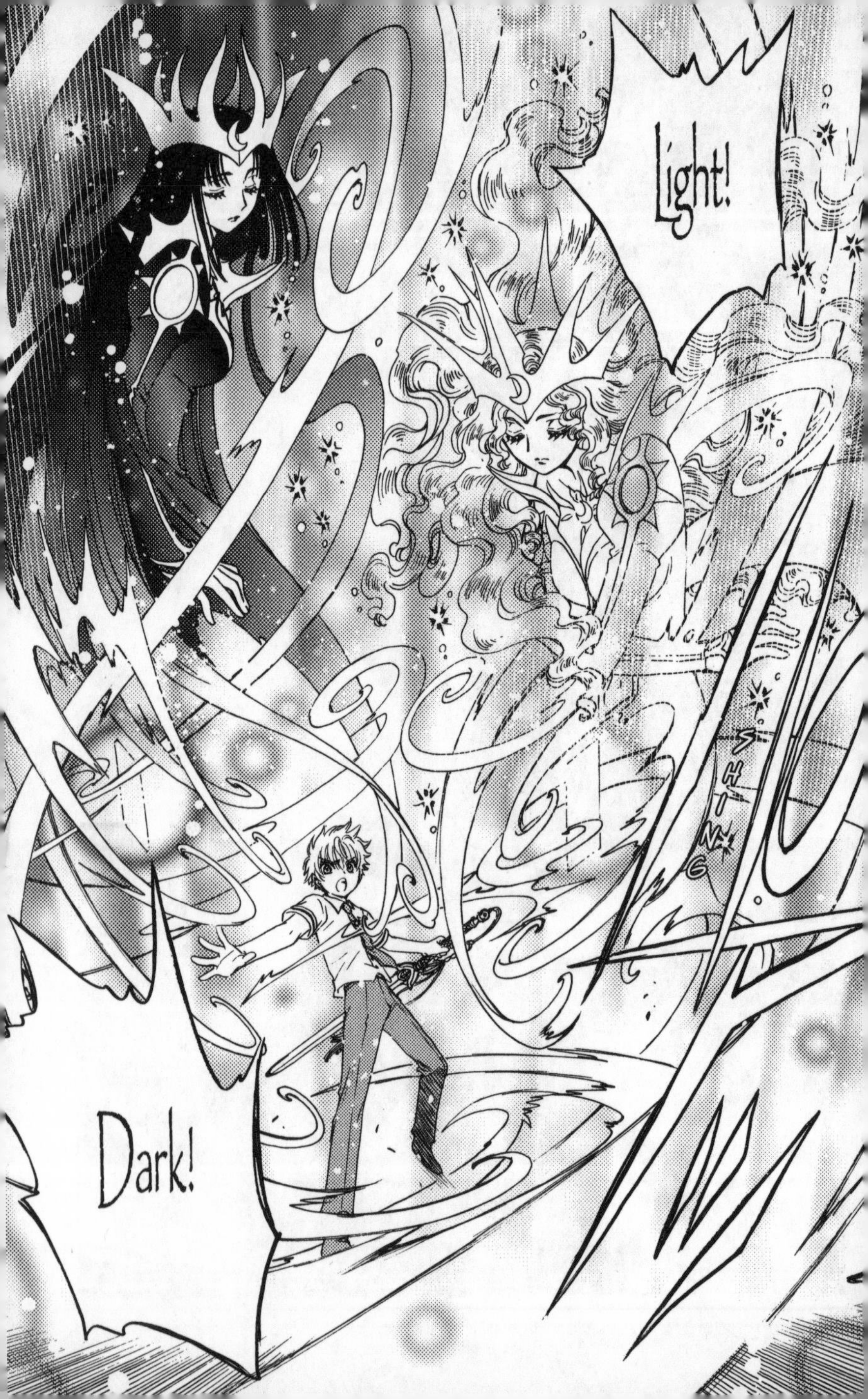
Light!
SHINING
Dark!

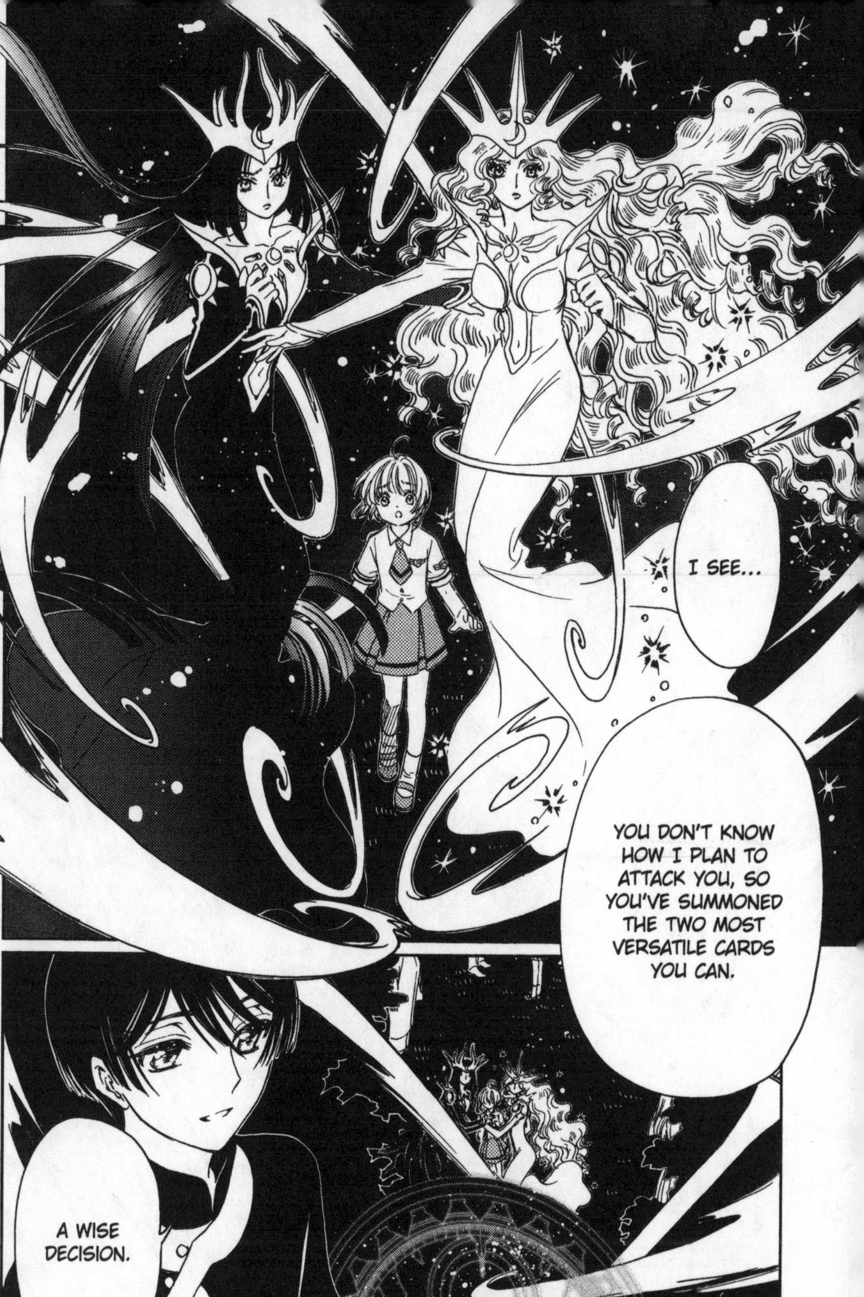
I SEE...
YOU DON'T KNOW HOW I PLAN TO ATTACK YOU, SO YOU'VE SUMMONED THE TWO MOST VERSATILE CARDS YOU CAN.
A WISE DECISION.

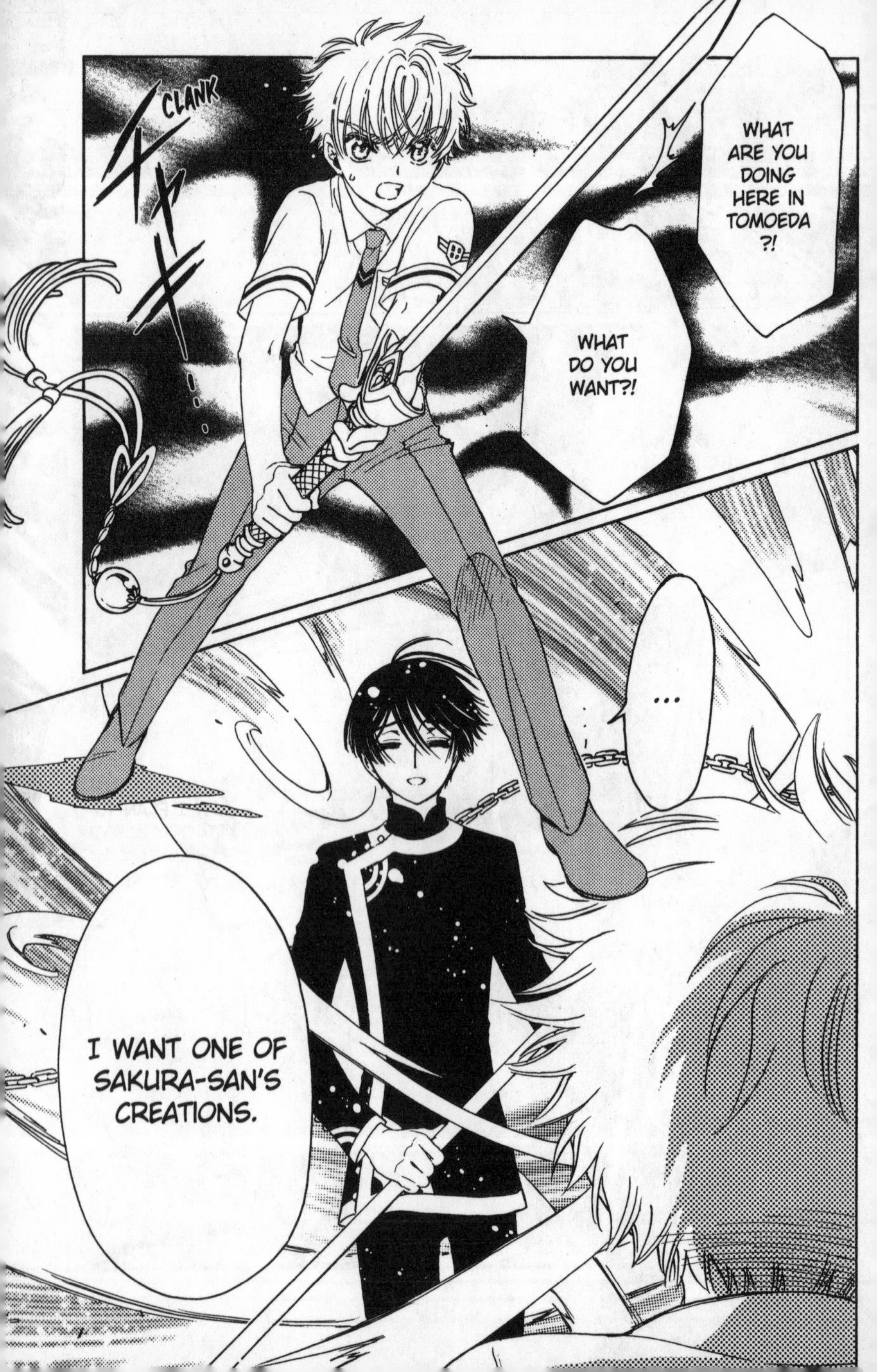
WHAT ARE YOU DOING HERE IN TOMOEDA ?!
WHAT DO YOU WANT?!
CLANK
...
I WANT ONE OF SAKURA-SAN'S CREATIONS.

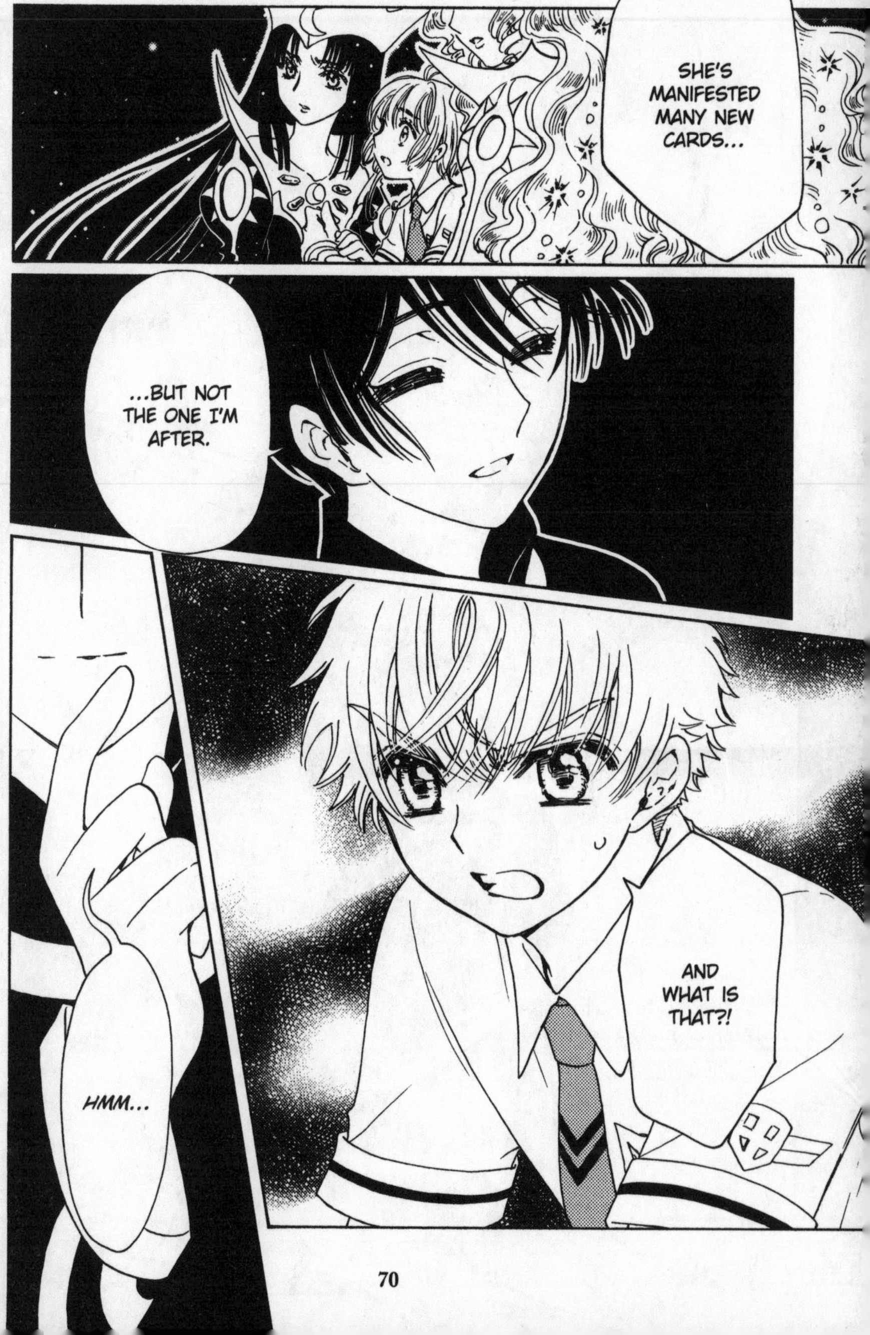
SHE'S MANIFESTED MANY NEW CARDS...
...BUT NOT THE ONE I'M AFTER.
AND WHAT IS THAT?!
HMM...

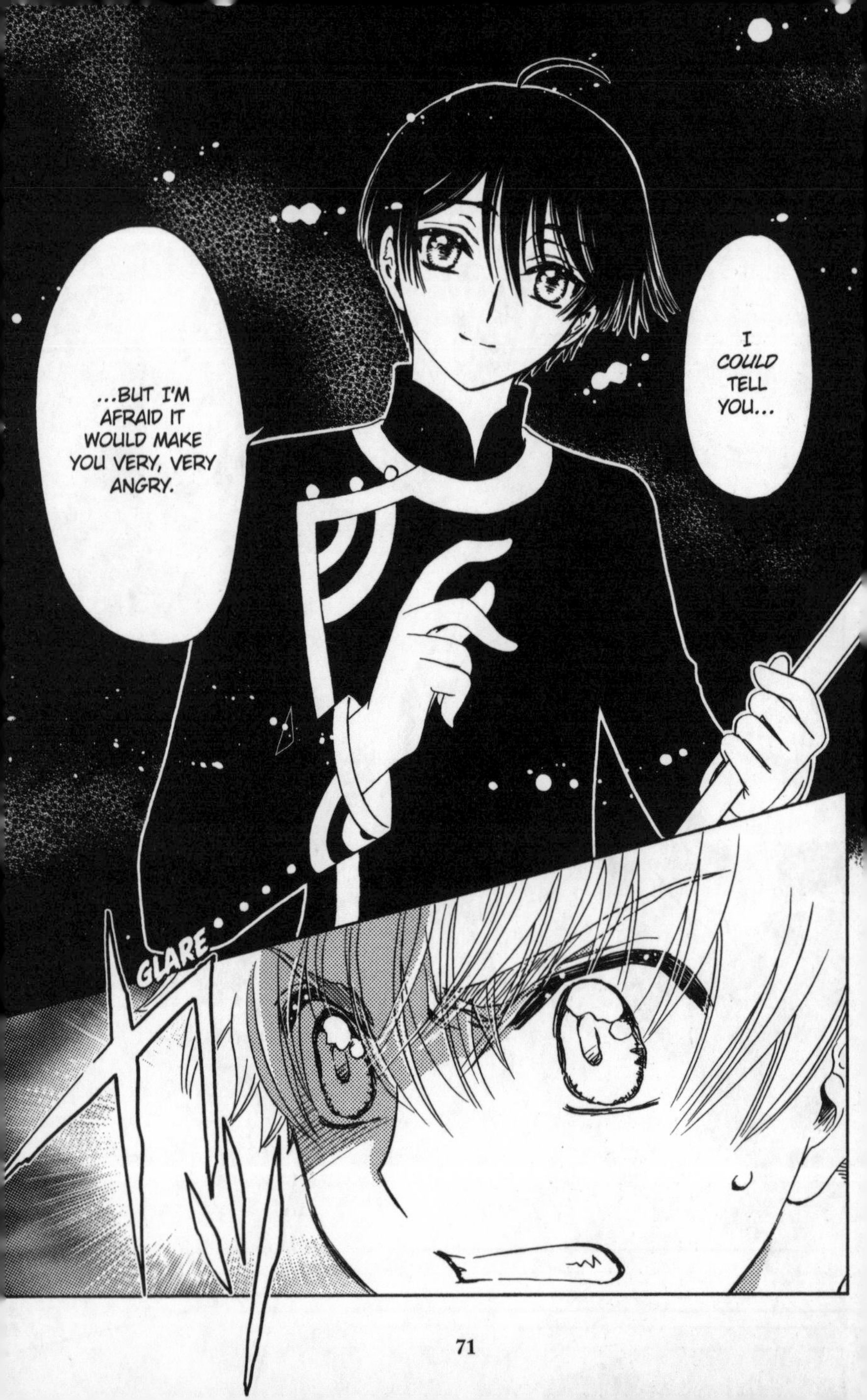
I COULD TELL YOU...
...BUT I'M AFRAID IT WOULD MAKE YOU VERY, VERY ANGRY.
GLARE

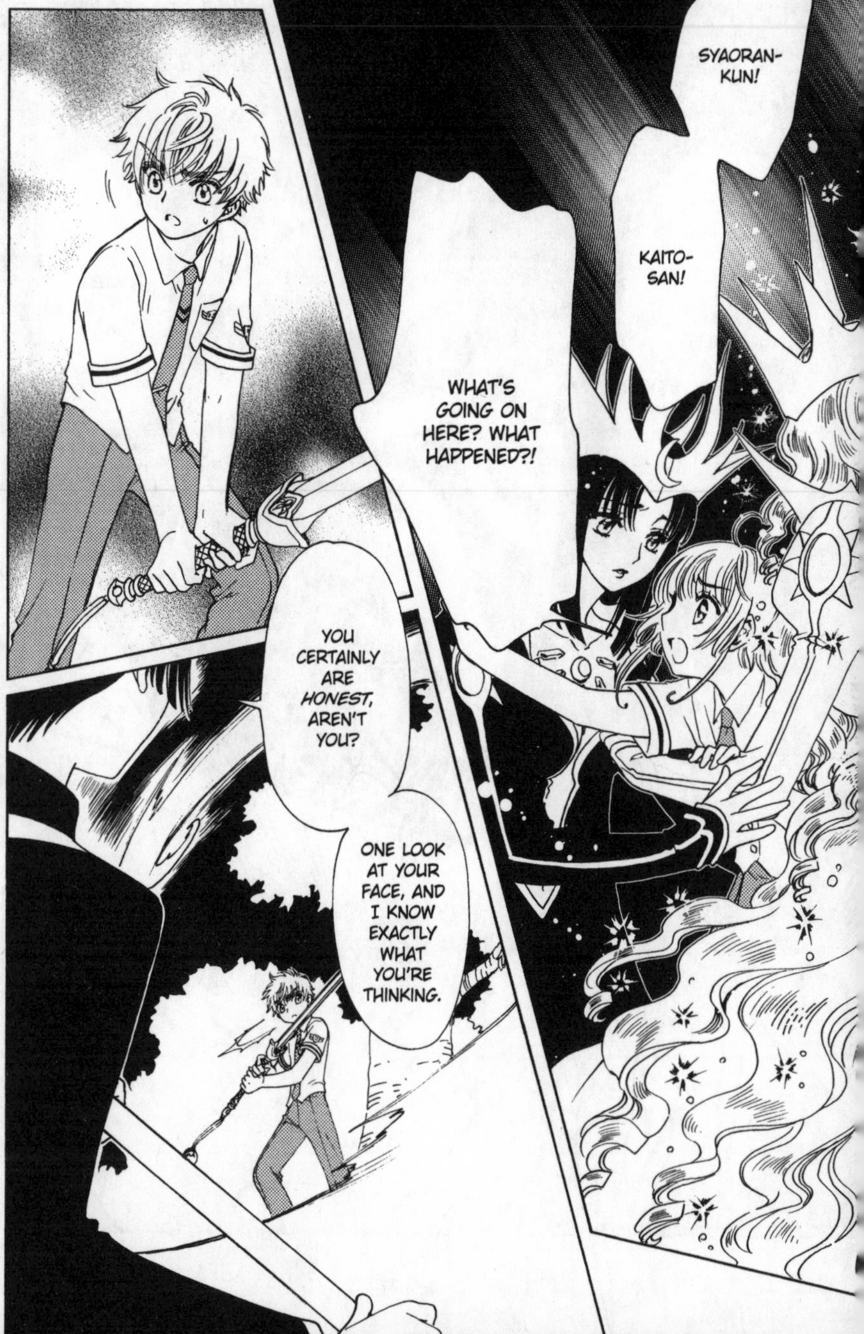
SYAORAN-KUN!
KAITO-SAN!
WHAT'S GOING ON HERE? WHAT HAPPENED?!
YOU CERTAINLY ARE *HONEST*, AREN'T YOU?
ONE LOOK AT YOUR FACE, AND I KNOW EXACTLY WHAT YOU'RE THINKING.

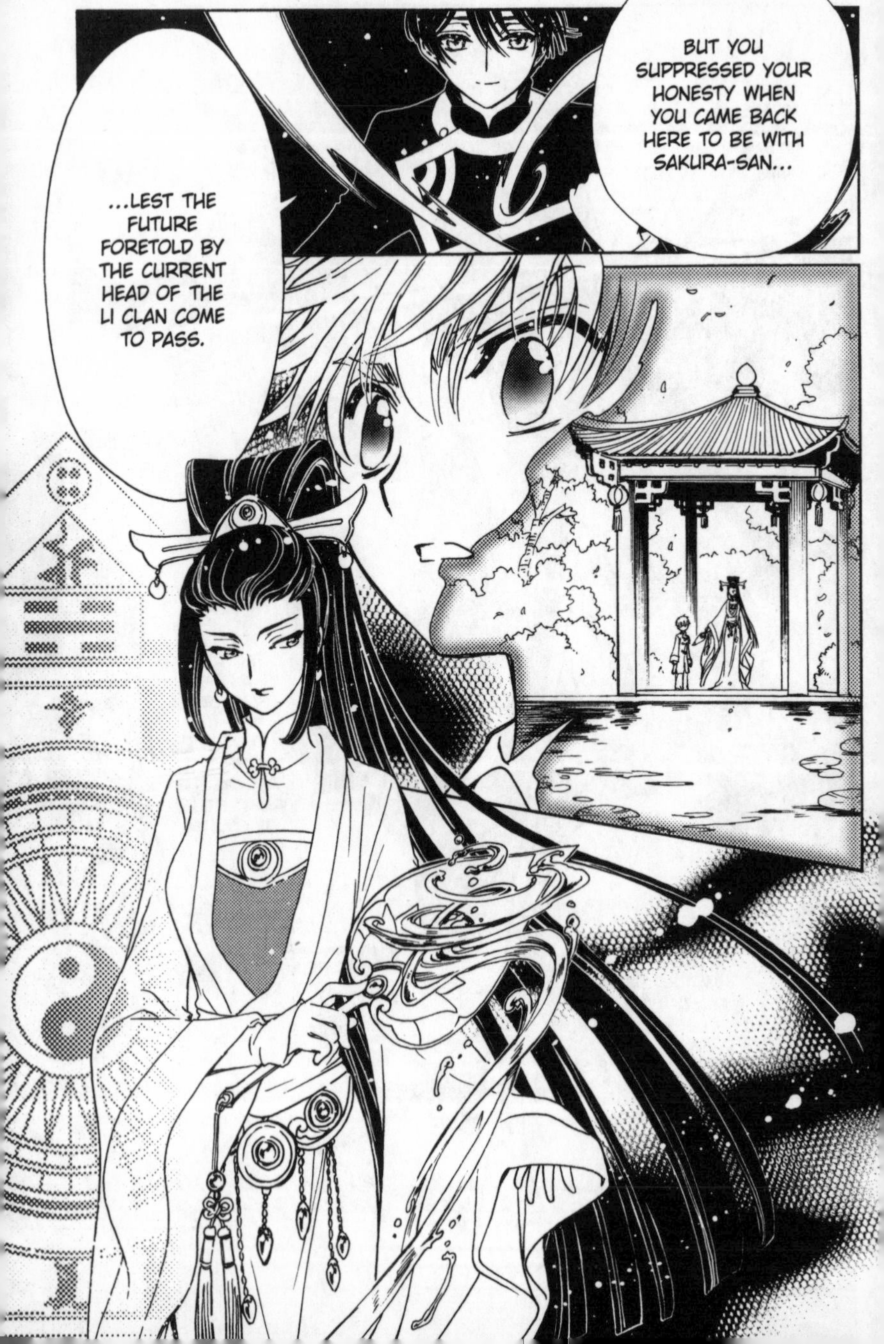
BUT YOU SUPPRESSED YOUR HONESTY WHEN YOU CAME BACK HERE TO BE WITH SAKURA-SAN...
...LEST THE FUTURE FORETOLD BY THE CURRENT HEAD OF THE LI CLAN COME TO PASS.

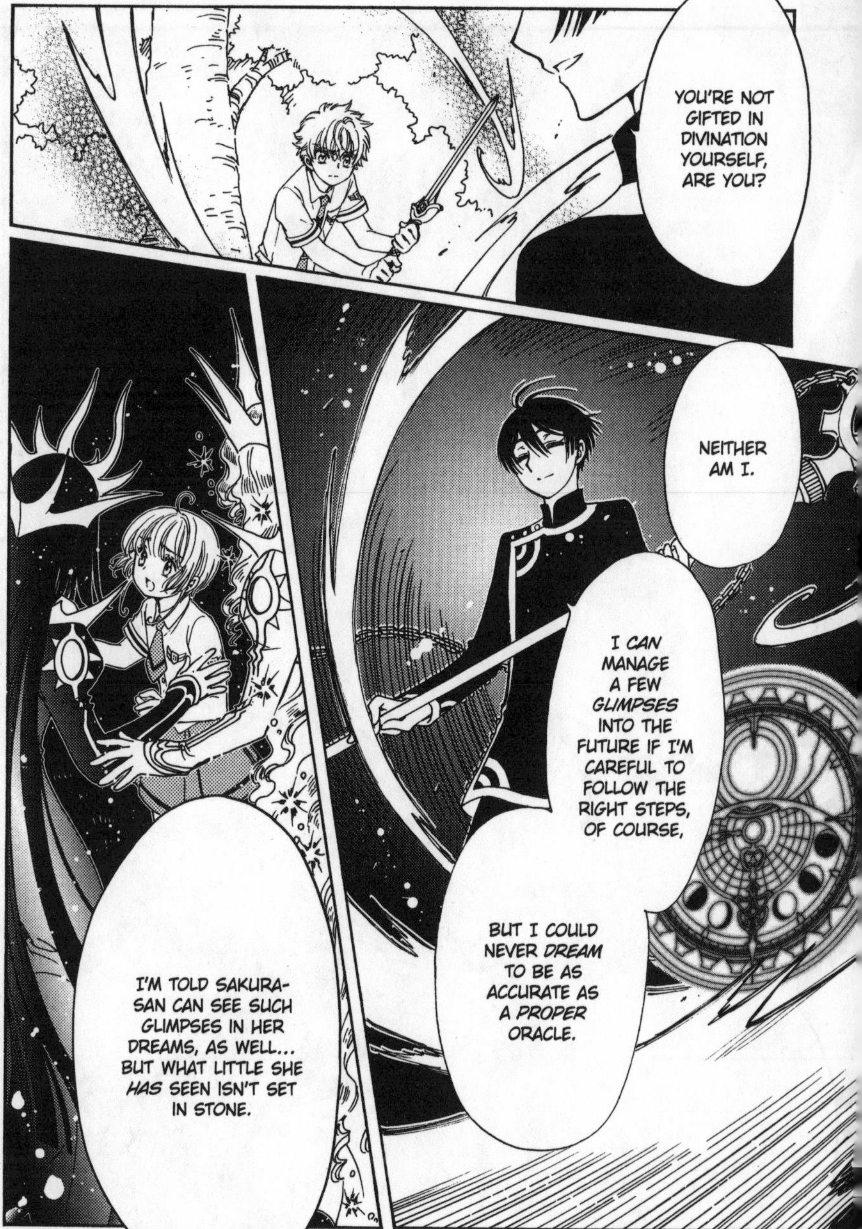
YOU'RE NOT GIFTED IN DIVINATION YOURSELF, ARE YOU?
NEITHER AM I.
I *CAN* MANAGE A FEW *GLIMPSES* INTO THE FUTURE IF I'M CAREFUL TO FOLLOW THE RIGHT STEPS, OF COURSE,
BUT I COULD NEVER *DREAM* TO BE AS ACCURATE AS A *PROPER* ORACLE.
I'M TOLD SAKURA-SAN CAN SEE SUCH GLIMPSES IN HER DREAMS, AS WELL... BUT WHAT LITTLE SHE *HAS* SEEN ISN'T SET IN STONE.

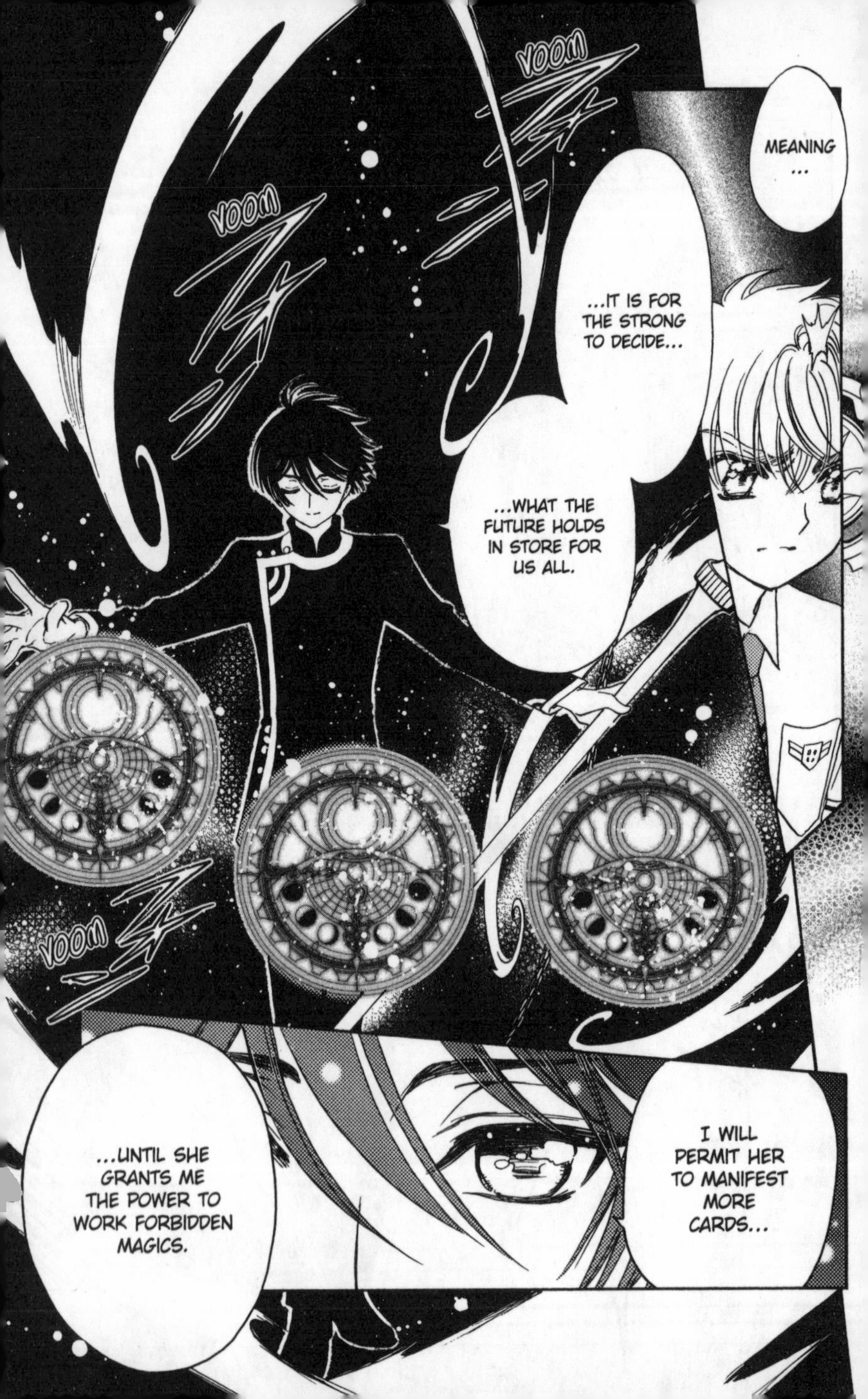
VOOM
MEANING ...
...IT IS FOR THE STRONG TO DECIDE...
VOOM
...WHAT THE FUTURE HOLDS IN STORE FOR US ALL.
VOOM
I WILL PERMIT HER TO MANIFEST MORE CARDS...
...UNTIL SHE GRANTS ME THE POWER TO WORK FORBIDDEN MAGICS.

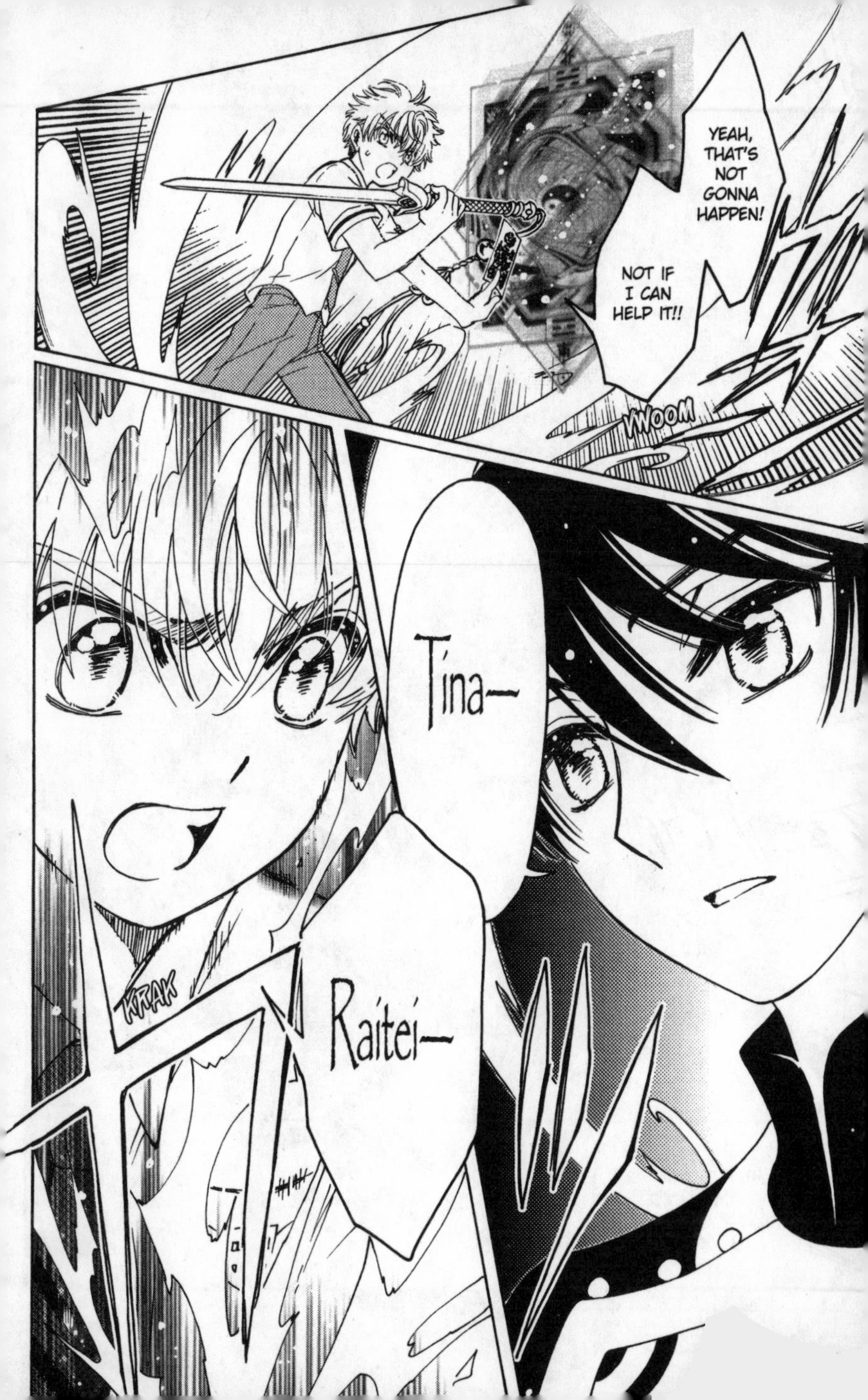
YEAH, THAT'S NOT GONNA HAPPEN!
NOT IF I CAN HELP IT!!
VWOOM
Tina—
Raitei—
KRAK

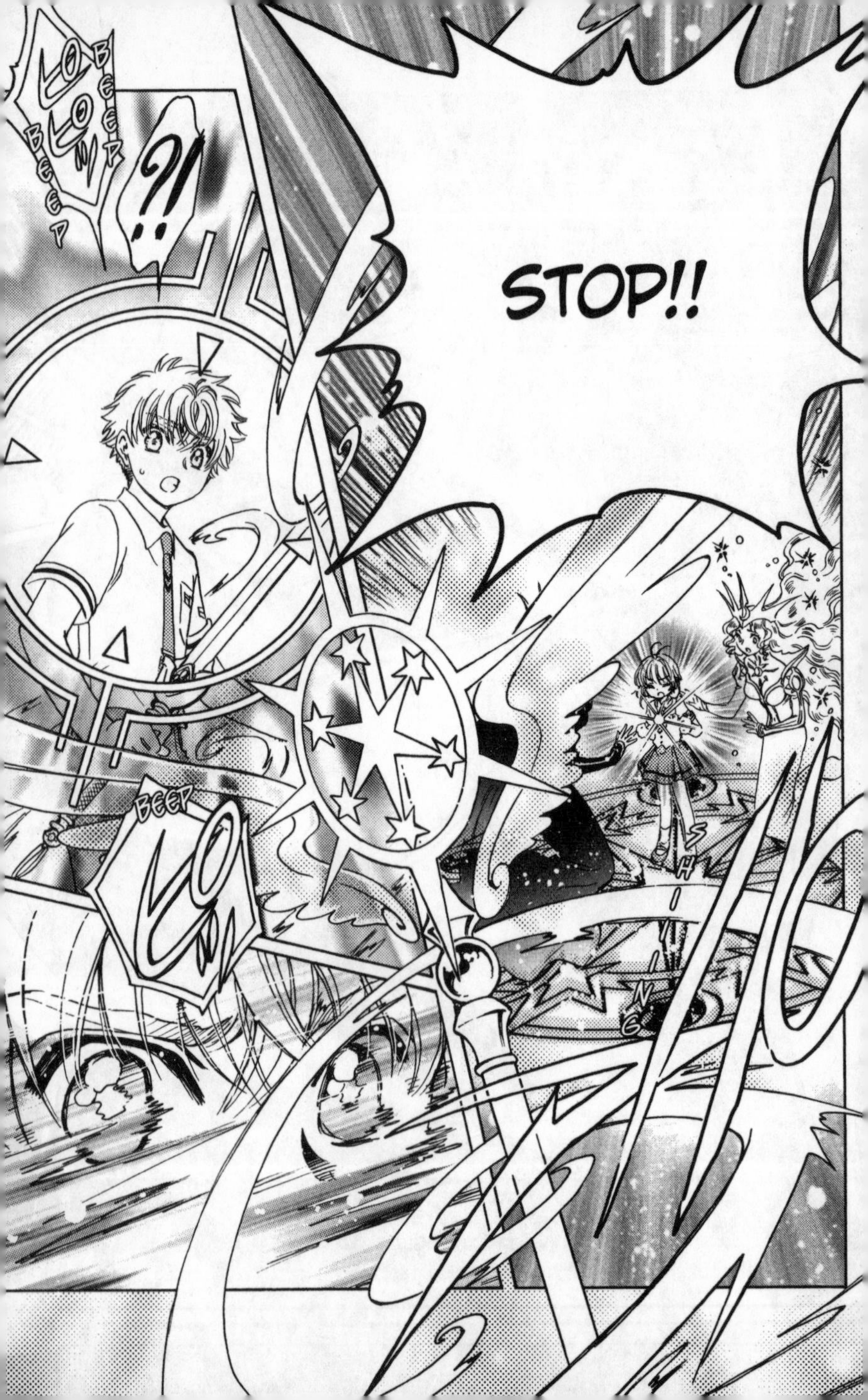
STOP!!
SHIING
BEEP BEEP
?!
!
BEEP

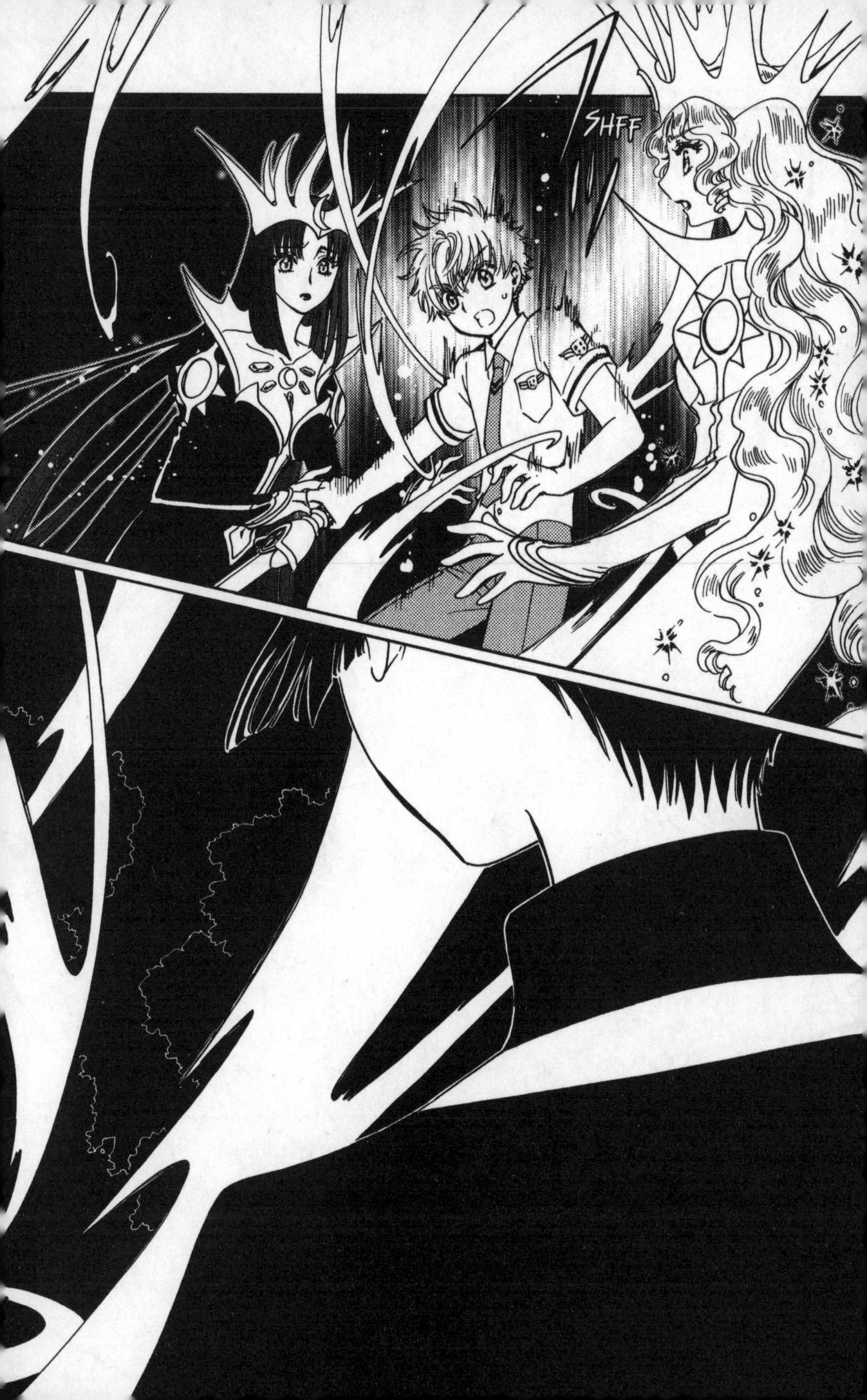
SHFF

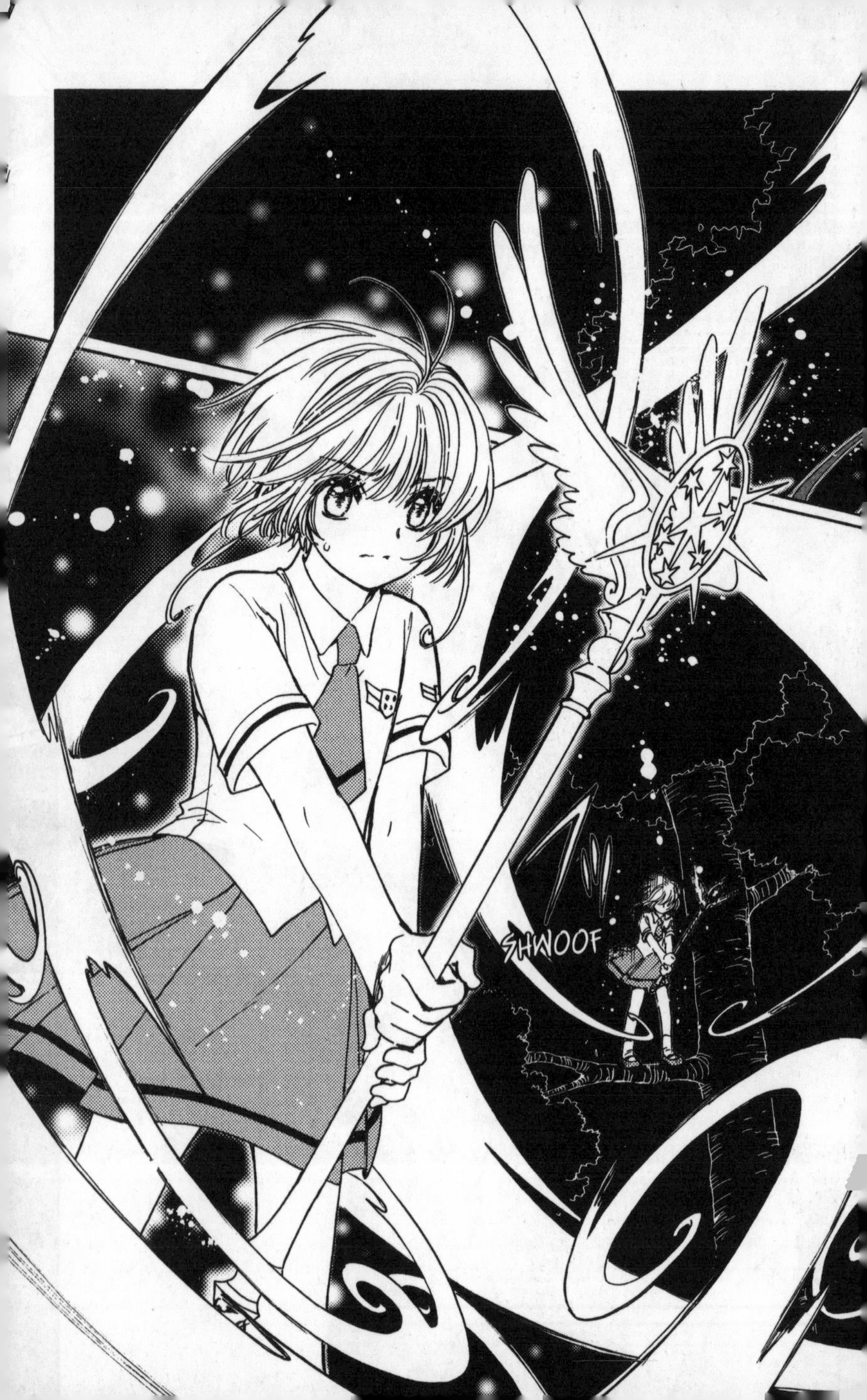
SHWOOF

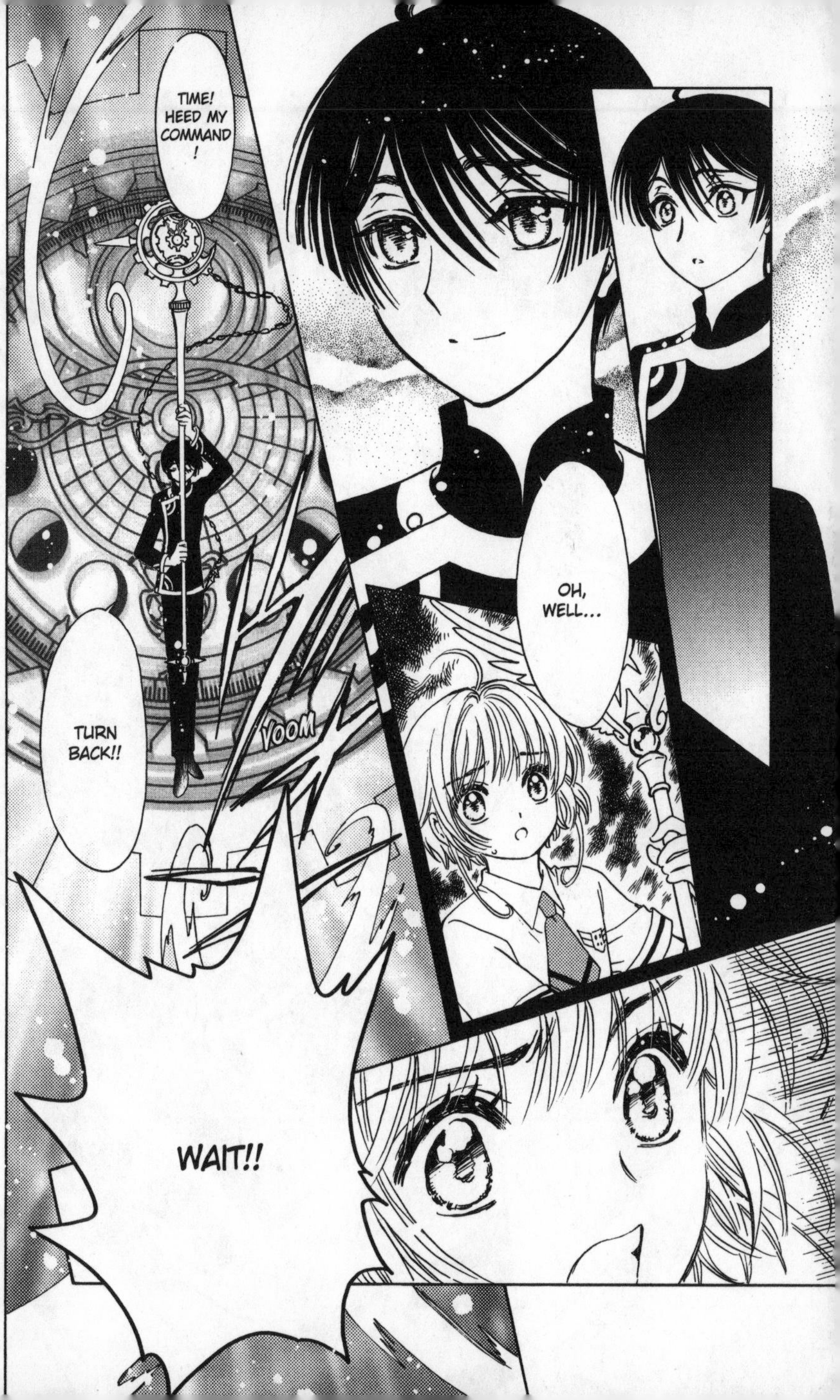
OH, WELL...
TIME! HEED MY COMMAND !
TURN BACK!!
VOOM
WAIT!!

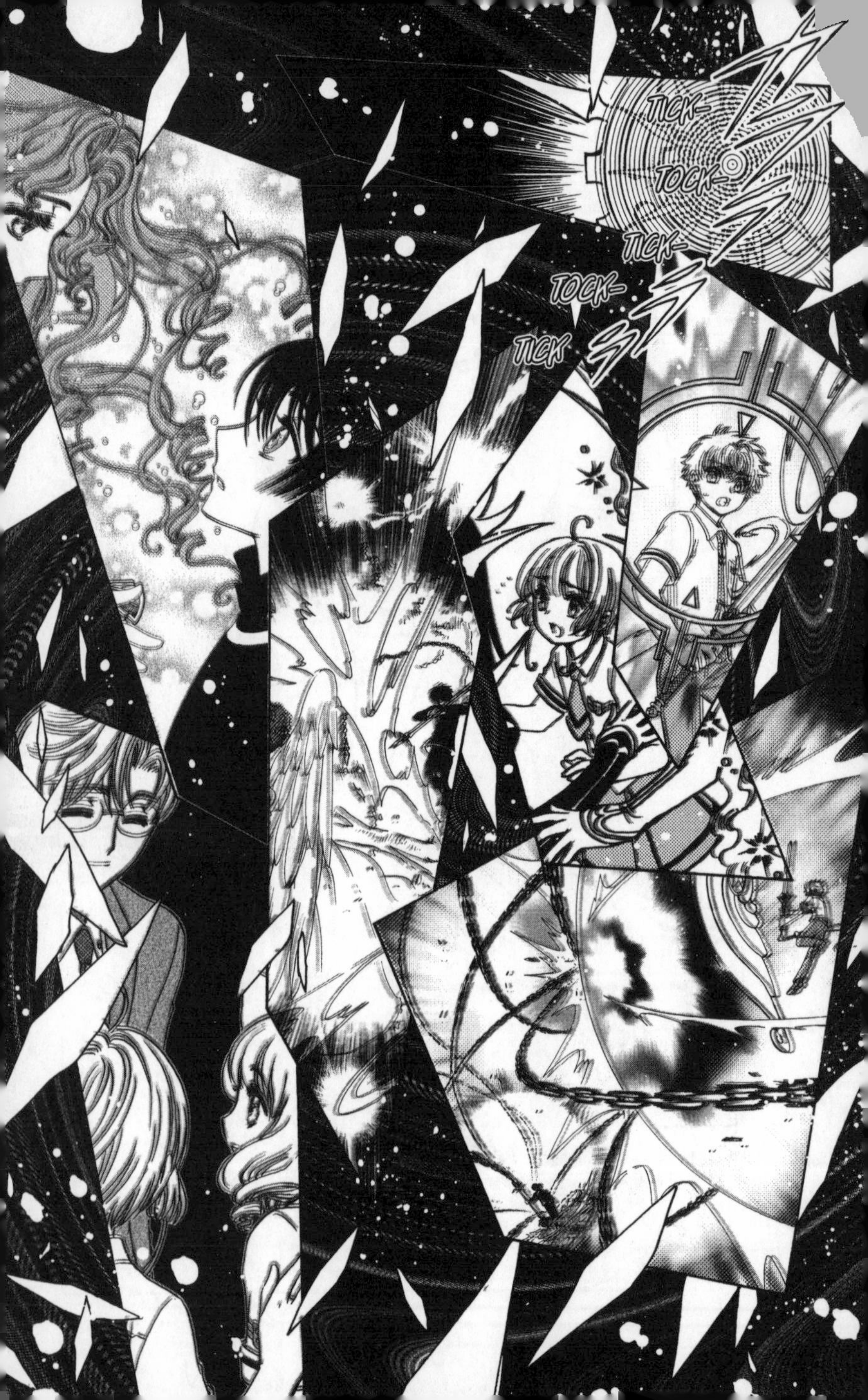

TICK-
TOCK-
TICK-
TOCK-
TICK

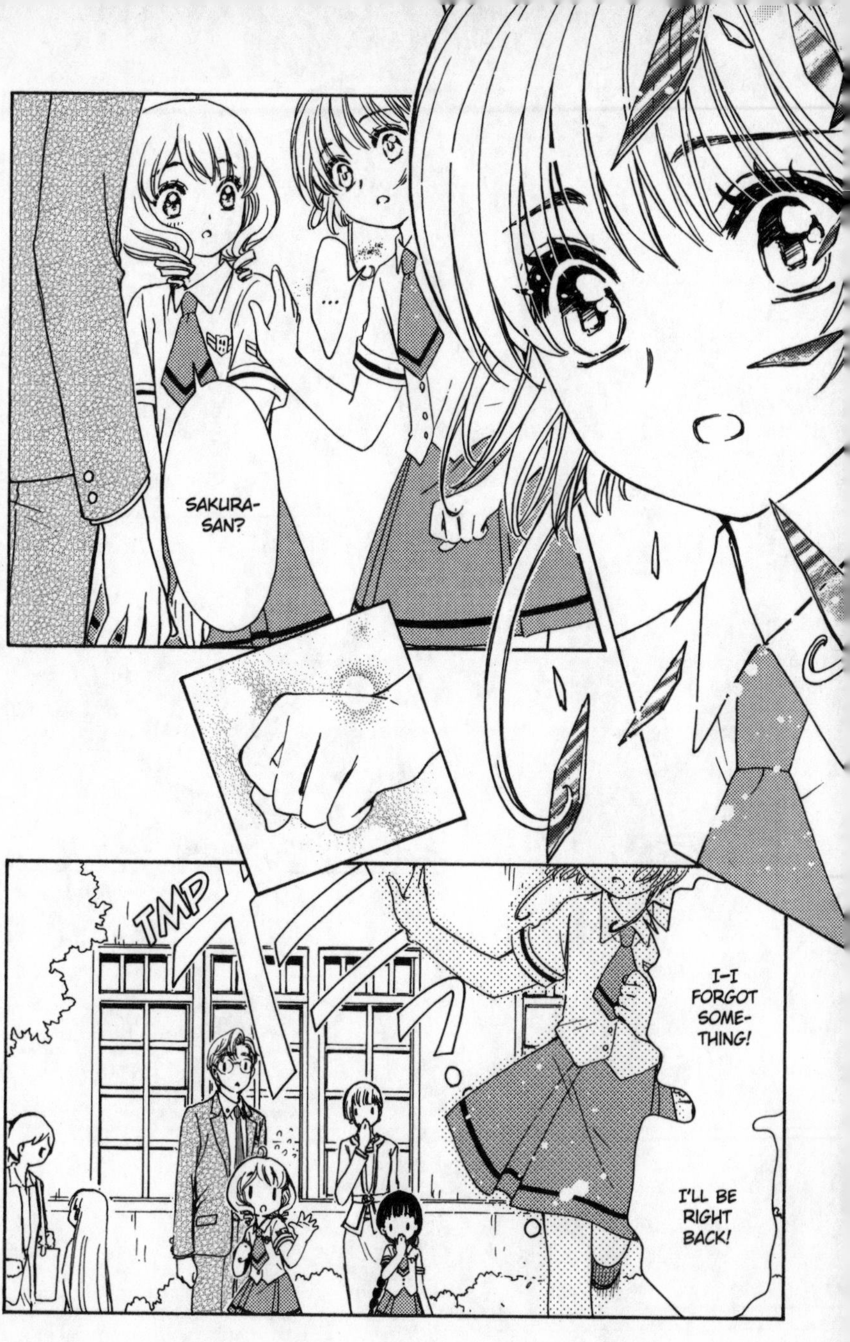
...
SAKURA-
SAN?
TMP
I-I
FORGOT
SOME-
THING!
I'LL BE
RIGHT
BACK!

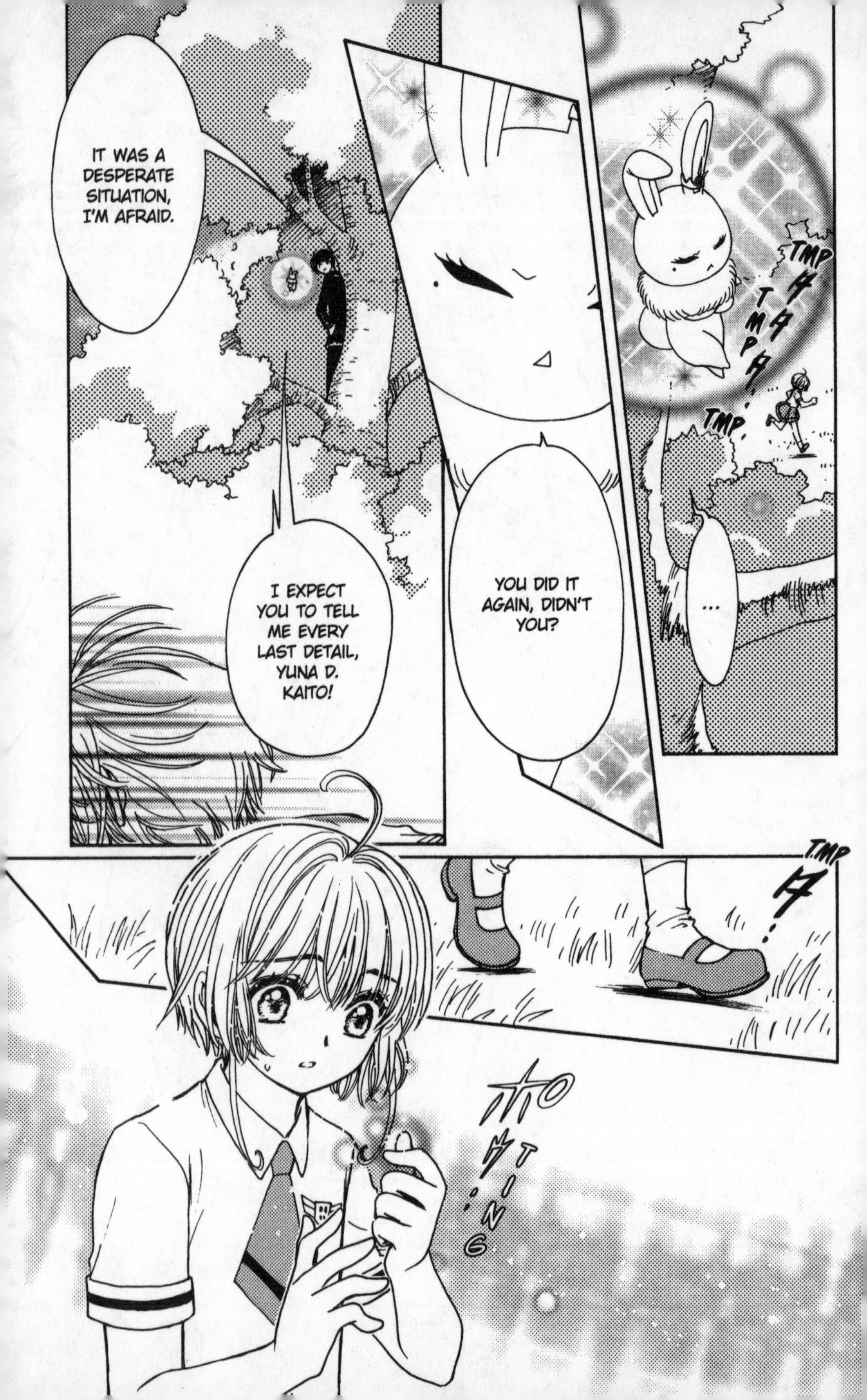
TMP
TMP
TMP
...
YOU DID IT AGAIN, DIDN'T YOU?
IT WAS A DESPERATE SITUATION, I'M AFRAID.
I EXPECT YOU TO TELL ME EVERY LAST DETAIL, YUNA D. KAITO!
TMP
TING

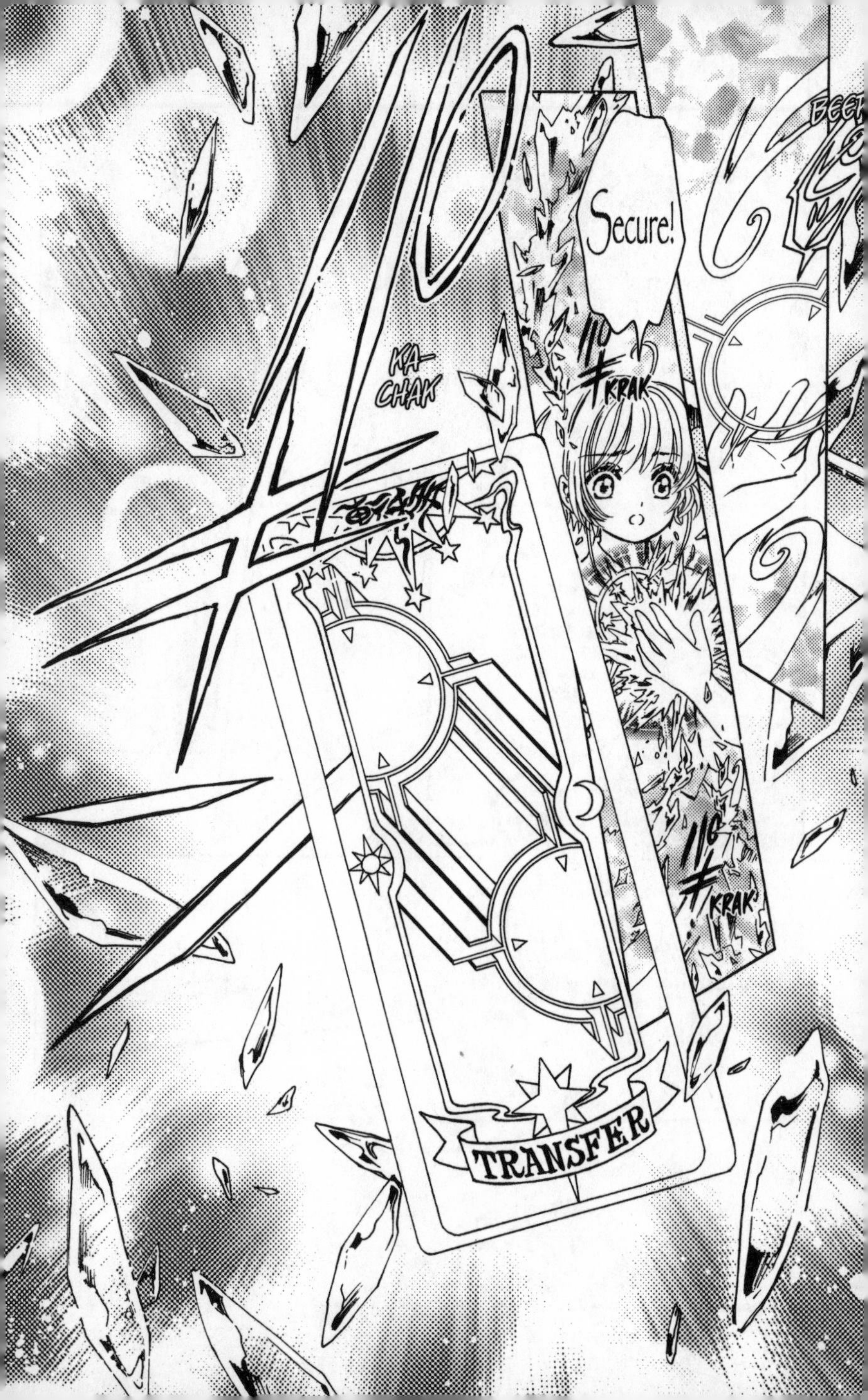
Secure!
KRAK
KA-CHAK
KRAK
TRANSFER

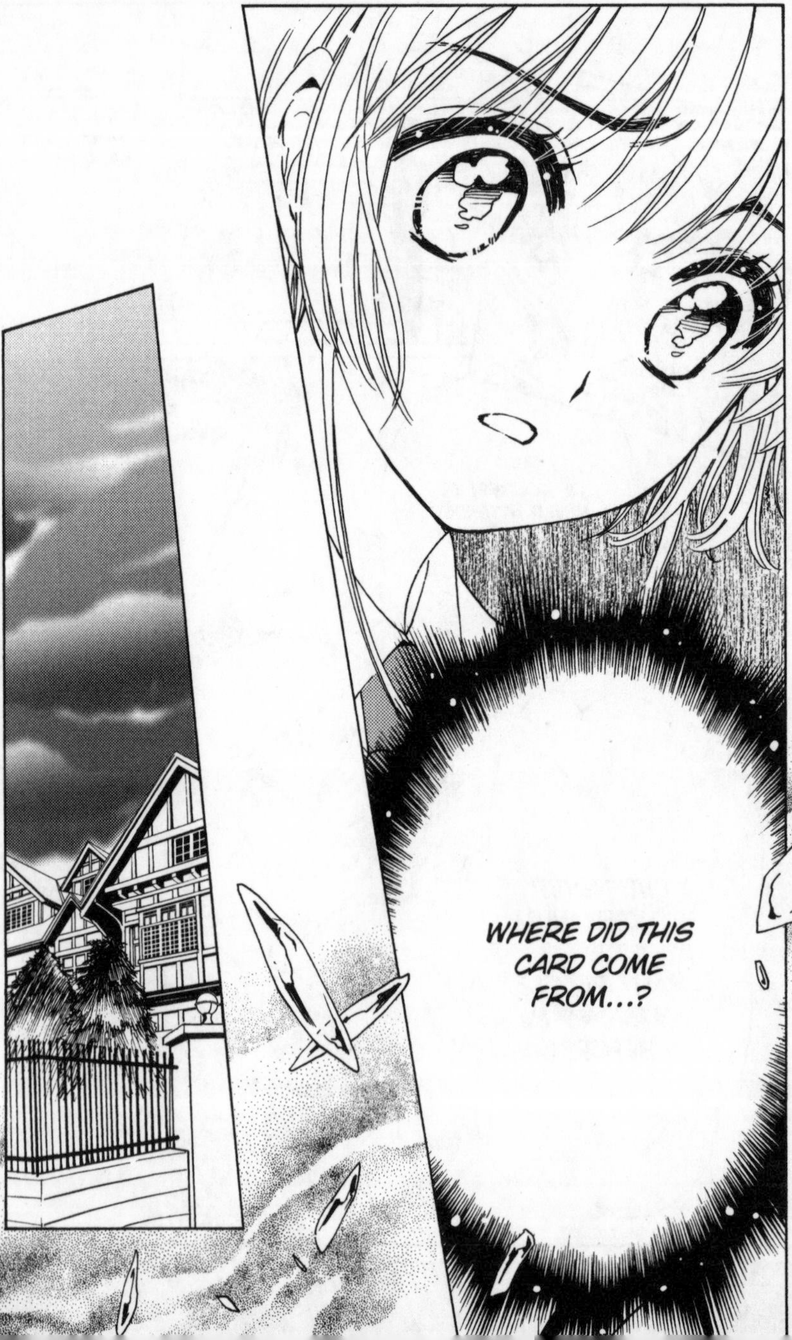
WHERE DID THIS CARD COME FROM...?

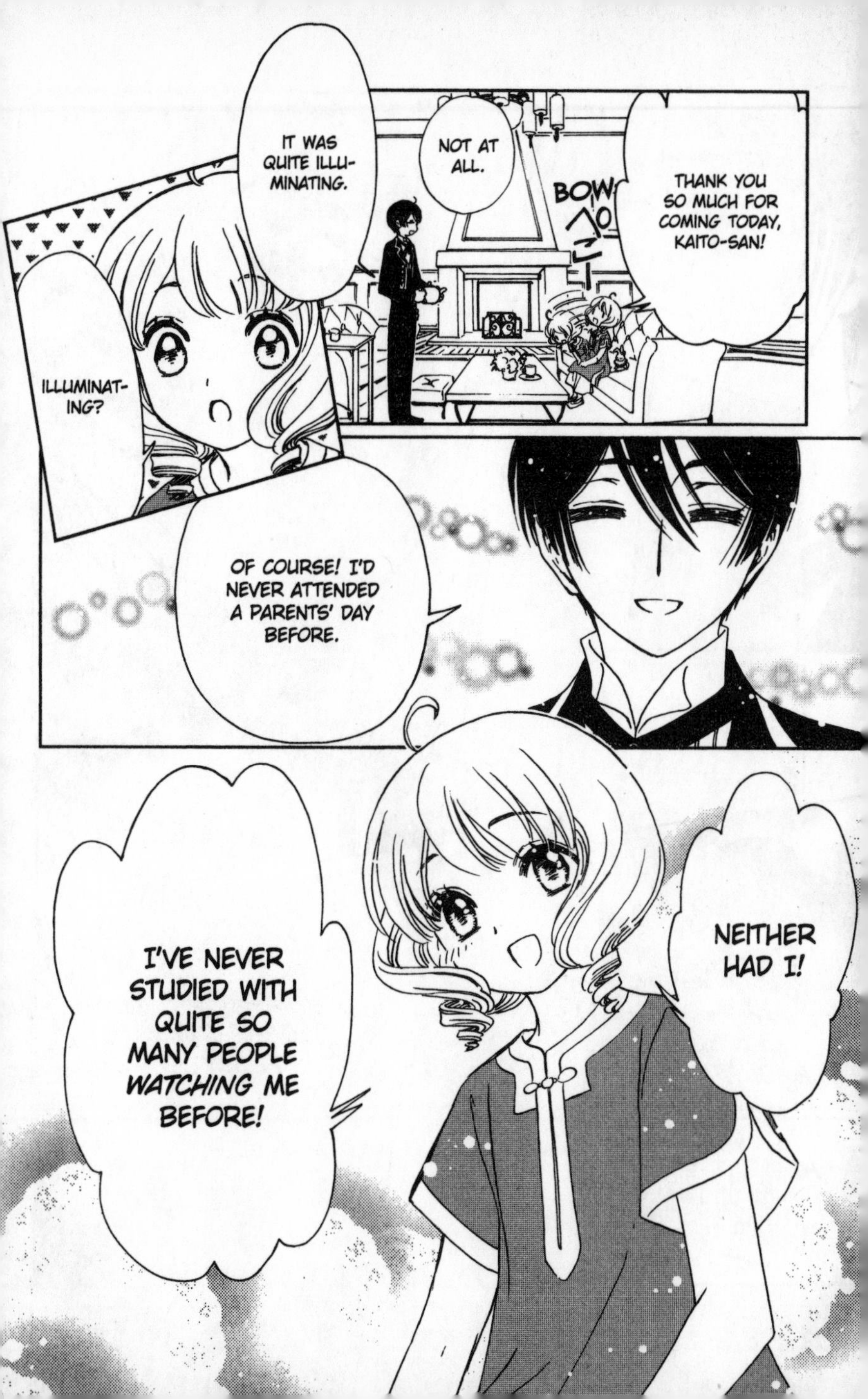
THANK YOU SO MUCH FOR COMING TODAY, KAITO-SAN!
BOW
NOT AT ALL.
IT WAS QUITE ILLUMINATING.
ILLUMINATING?
OF COURSE! I'D NEVER ATTENDED A PARENTS' DAY BEFORE.
NEITHER HAD I!
I'VE NEVER STUDIED WITH QUITE SO MANY PEOPLE WATCHING ME BEFORE!

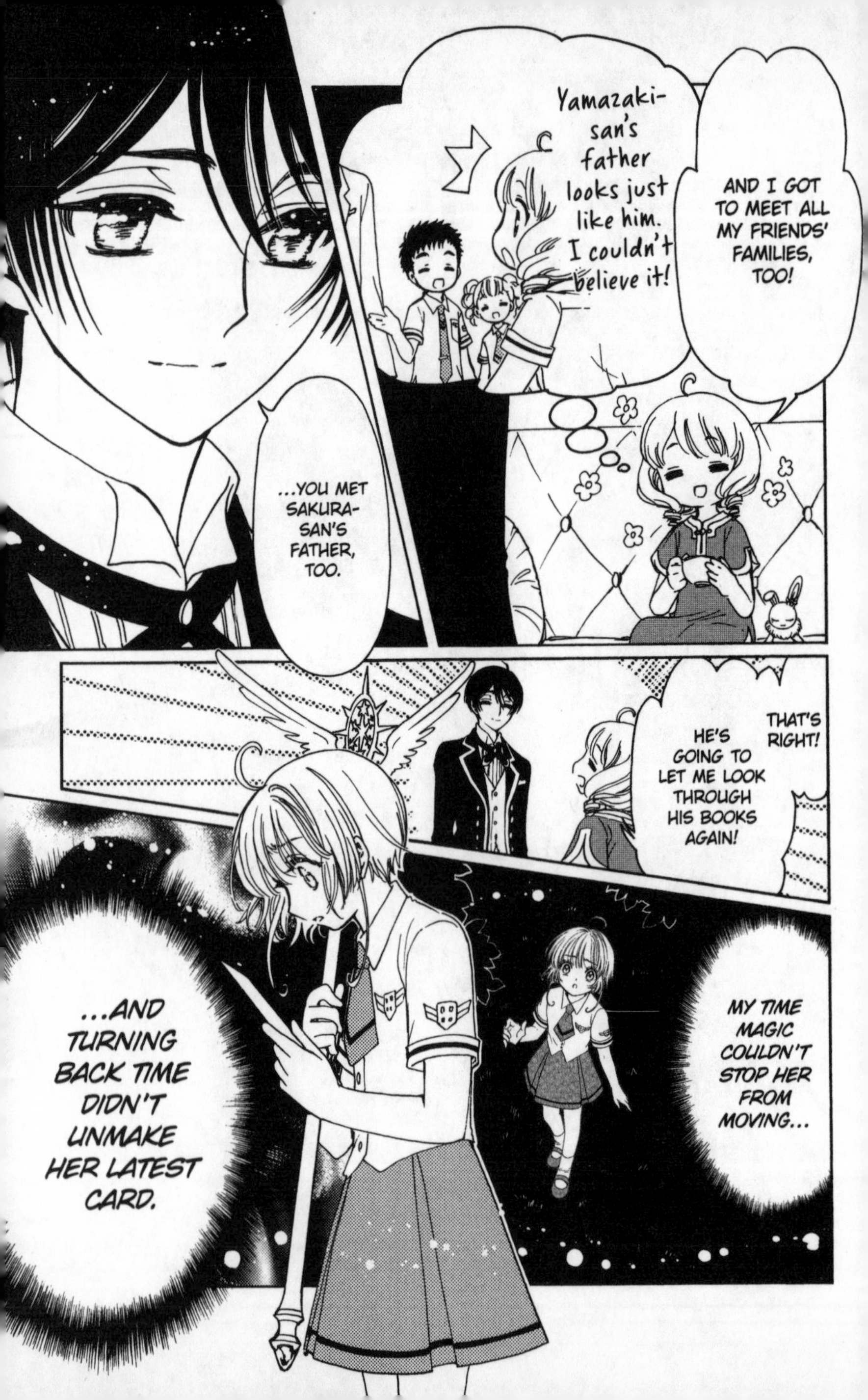
Yamazaki-san's father looks just like him. I couldn't believe it!
AND I GOT TO MEET ALL MY FRIENDS' FAMILIES, TOO!
...YOU MET SAKURA-SAN'S FATHER, TOO.
THAT'S RIGHT! HE'S GOING TO LET ME LOOK THROUGH HIS BOOKS AGAIN!
MY TIME MAGIC COULDN'T STOP HER FROM MOVING...
...AND TURNING BACK TIME DIDN'T UNMAKE HER LATEST CARD.

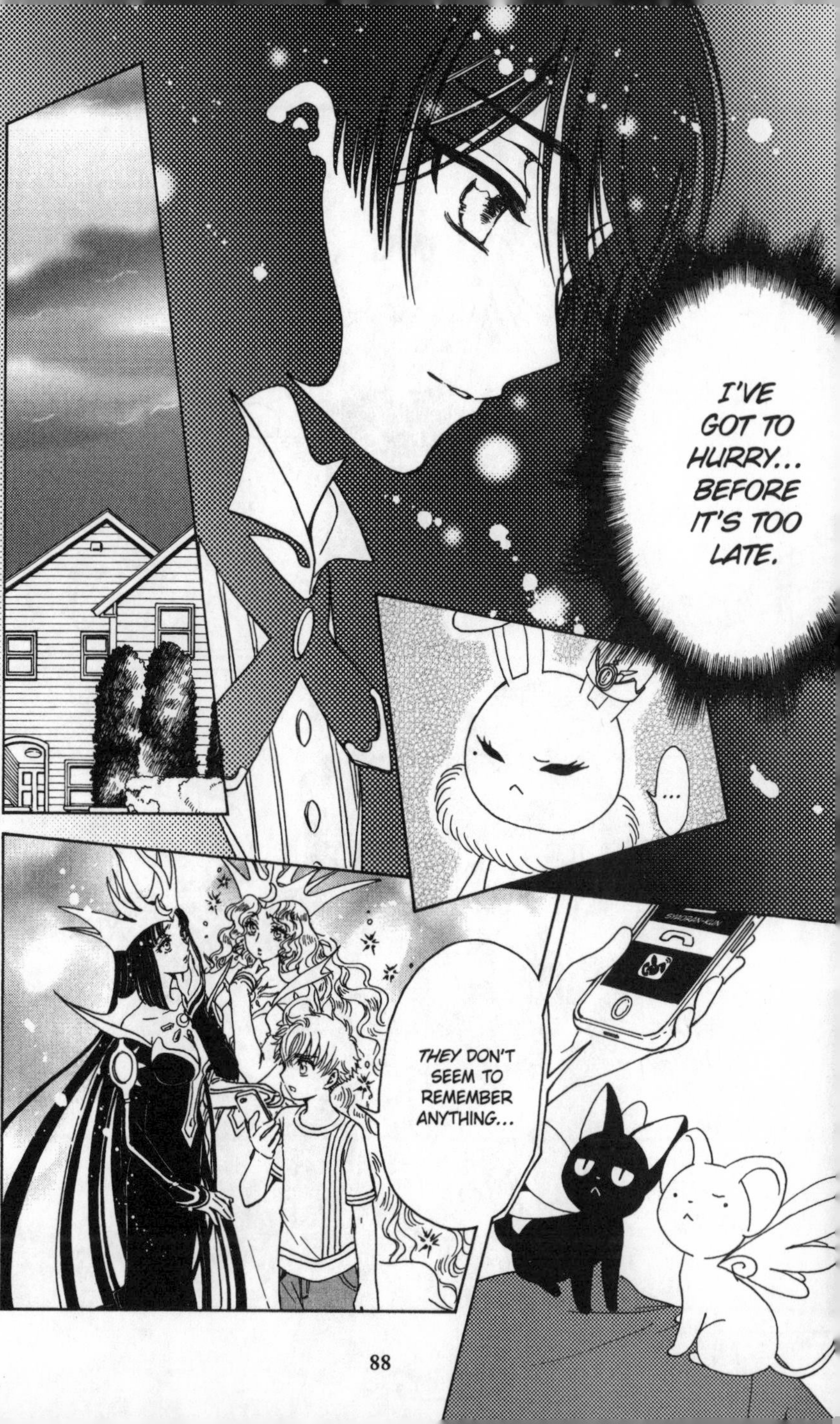
I'VE GOT TO HURRY... BEFORE IT'S TOO LATE.
...
THEY DON'T SEEM TO REMEMBER ANYTHING...

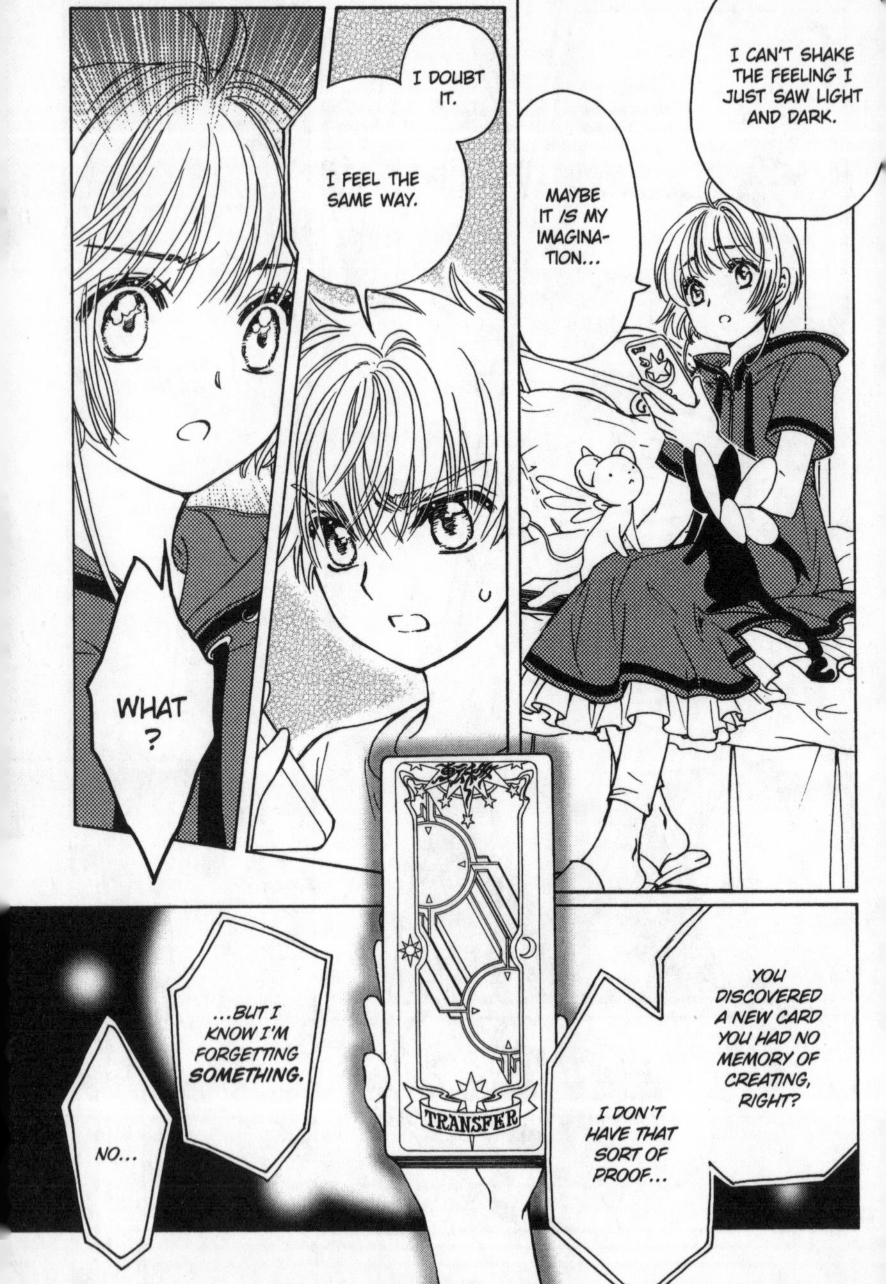
I CAN'T SHAKE THE FEELING I JUST SAW LIGHT AND DARK.
MAYBE IT IS MY IMAGINATION...
I DOUBT IT.
I FEEL THE SAME WAY.
WHAT?
YOU DISCOVERED A NEW CARD YOU HAD NO MEMORY OF CREATING, RIGHT?
I DON'T HAVE THAT SORT OF PROOF...
TRANSFER
...BUT I KNOW I'M FORGETTING SOMETHING.
NO...

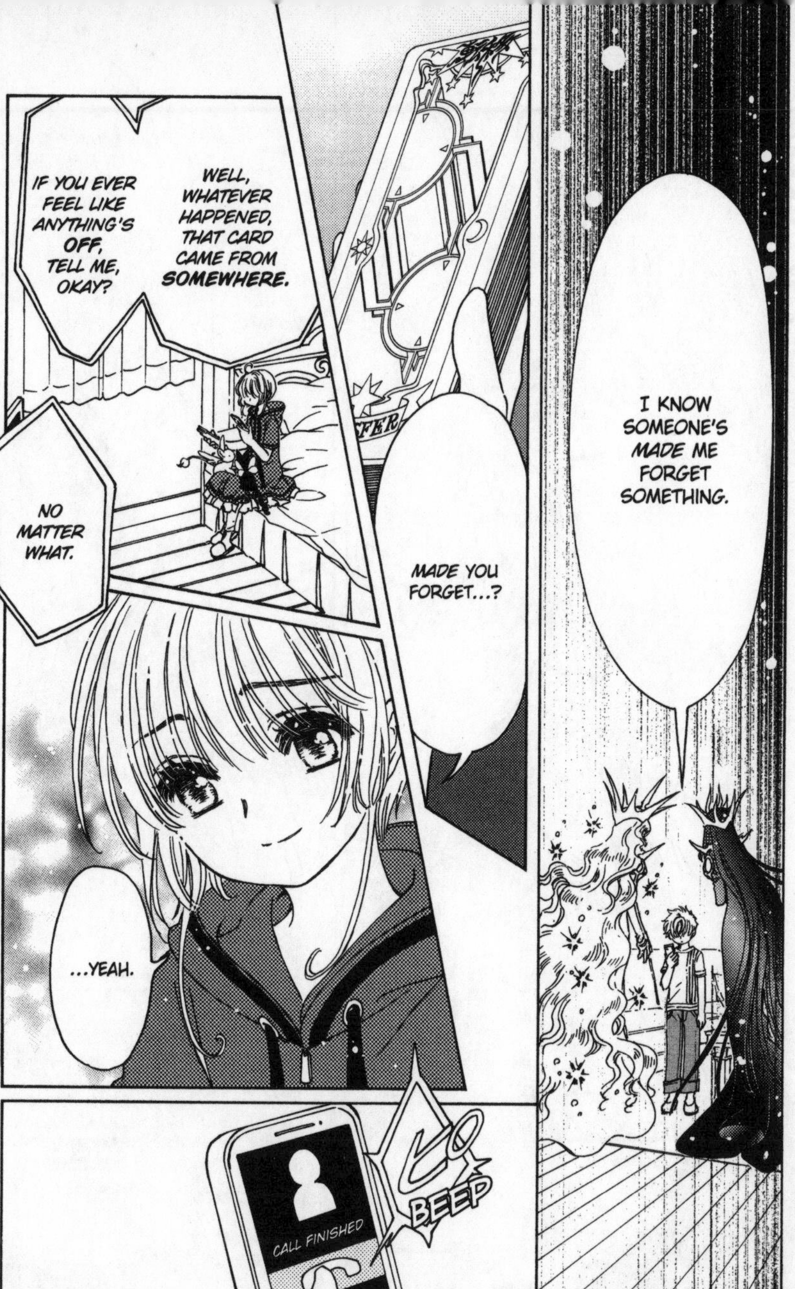
I KNOW SOMEONE'S MADE ME FORGET SOMETHING.
MADE YOU FORGET...?
WELL, WHATEVER HAPPENED, THAT CARD CAME FROM SOMEWHERE.
IF YOU EVER FEEL LIKE ANYTHING'S OFF, TELL ME, OKAY?
NO MATTER WHAT.
...YEAH.
BEEP
CALL FINISHED

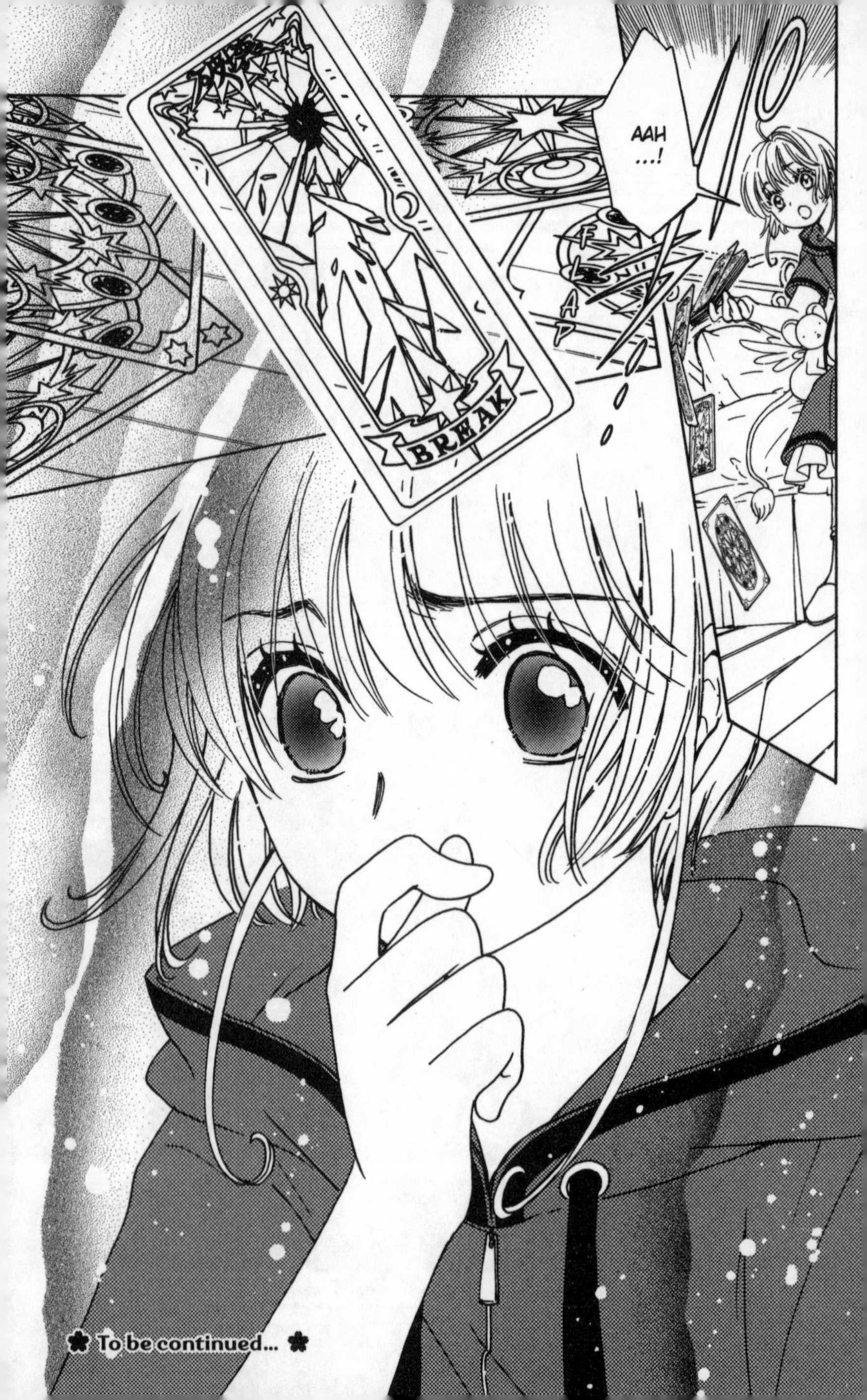
AAH ...!
FLAP
BREAK
To be continued...

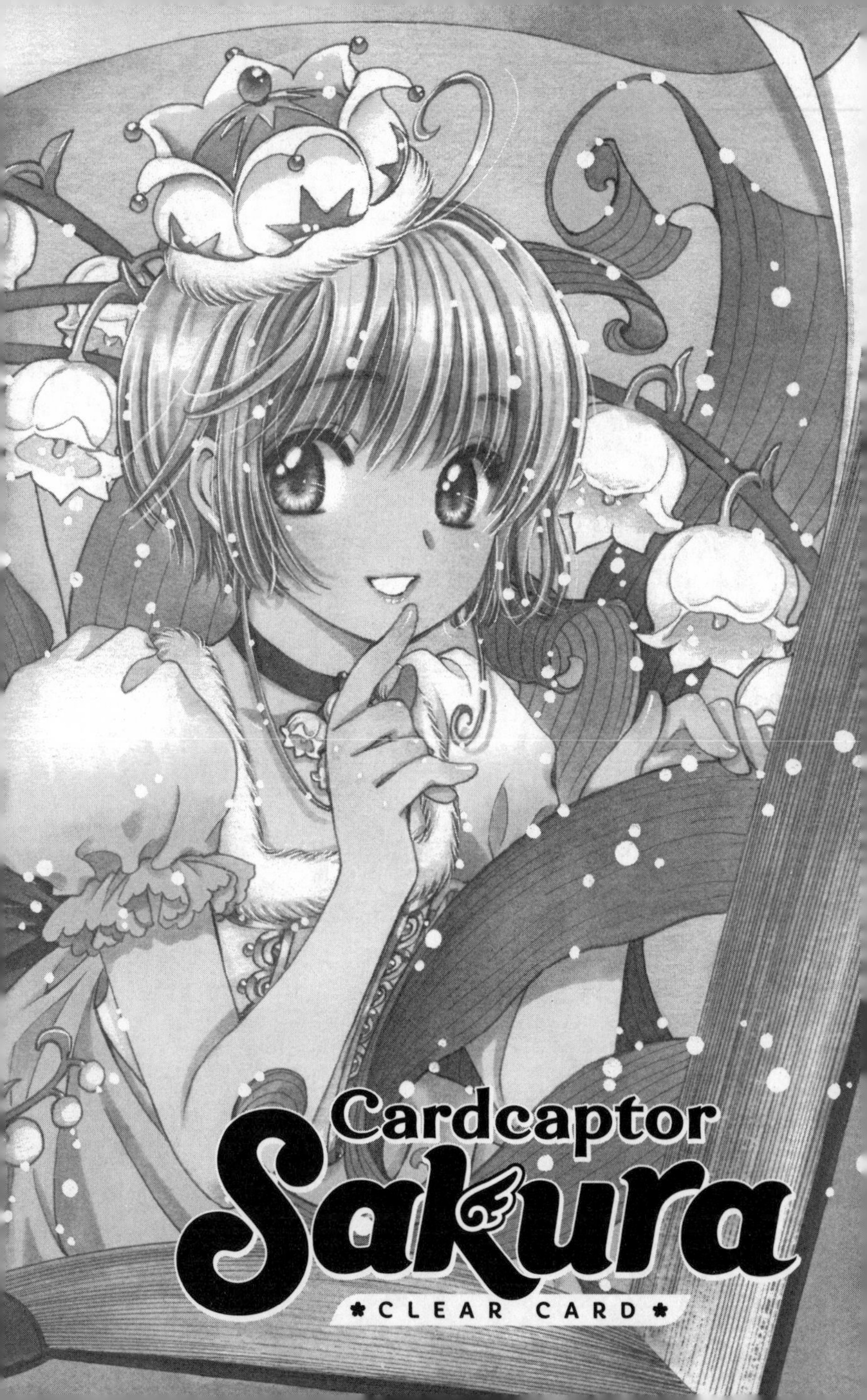
Cardcaptor
Sakura
CLEAR CARD

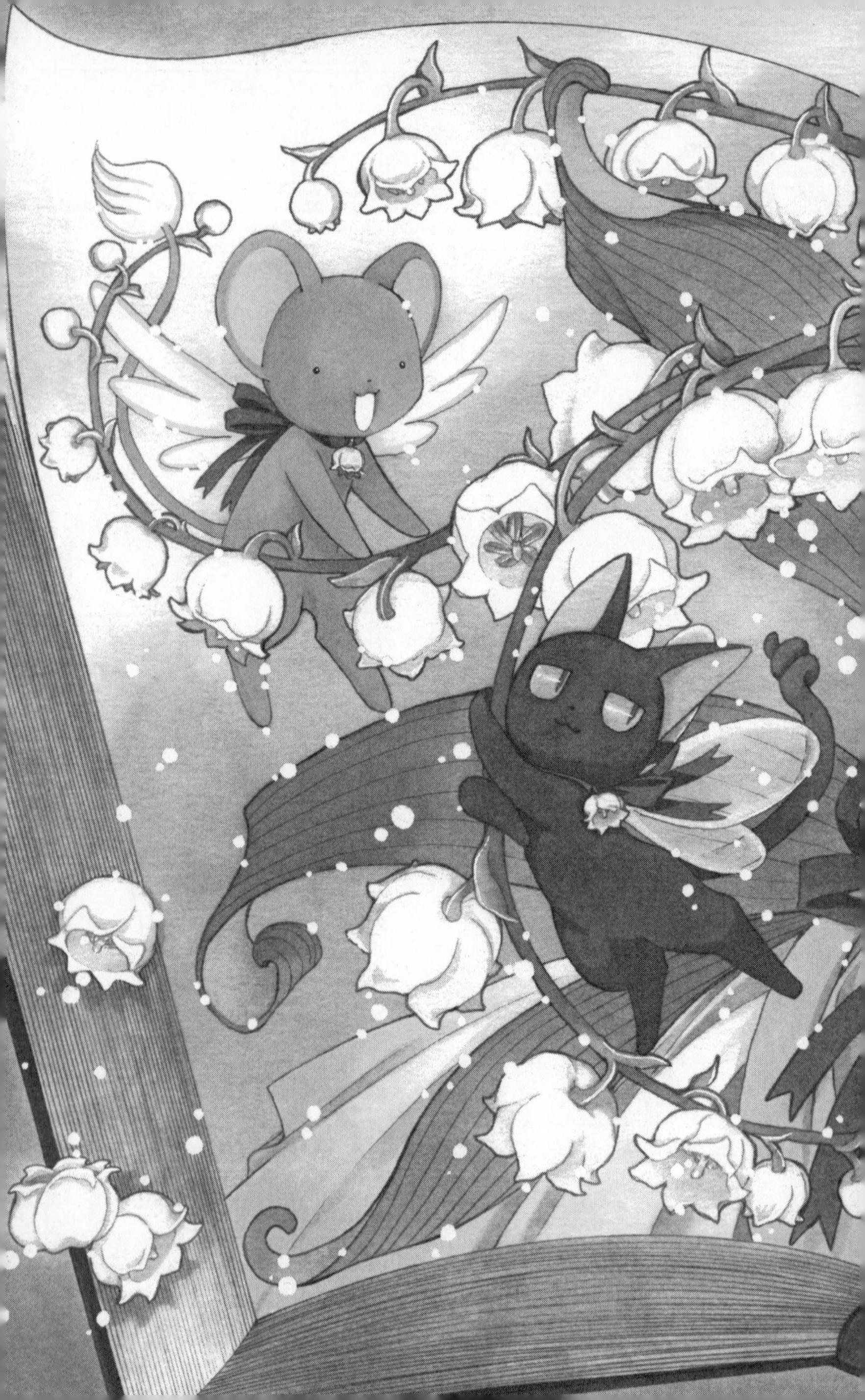

Cardcaptor Sakura

CLEAR CARD

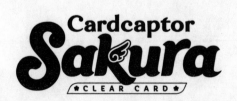

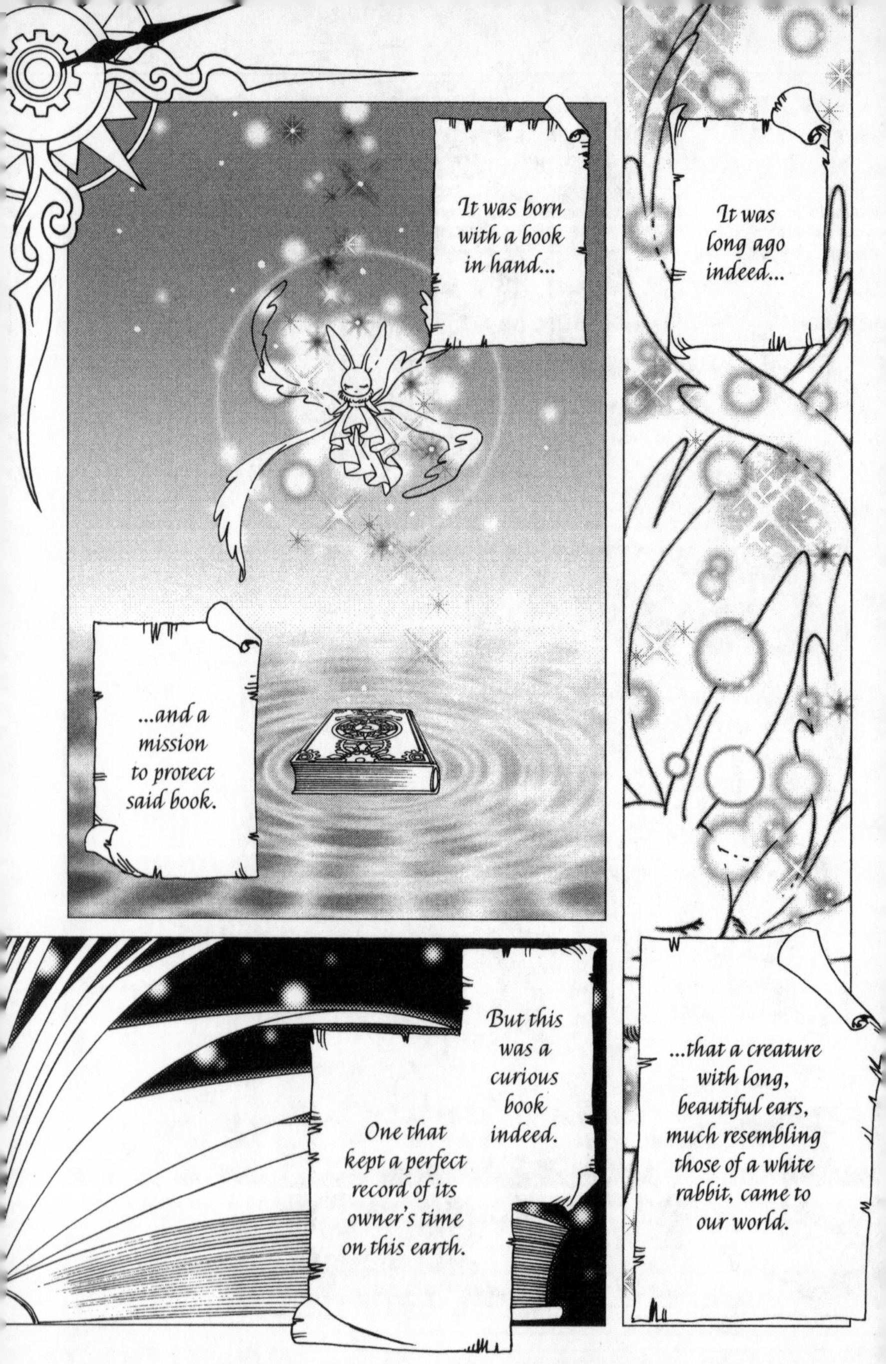
It was long ago indeed...
...that a creature with long, beautiful ears, much resembling those of a white rabbit, came to our world.
It was born with a book in hand...
...and a mission to protect said book.
But this was a curious book indeed.
One that kept a perfect record of its owner's time on this earth.

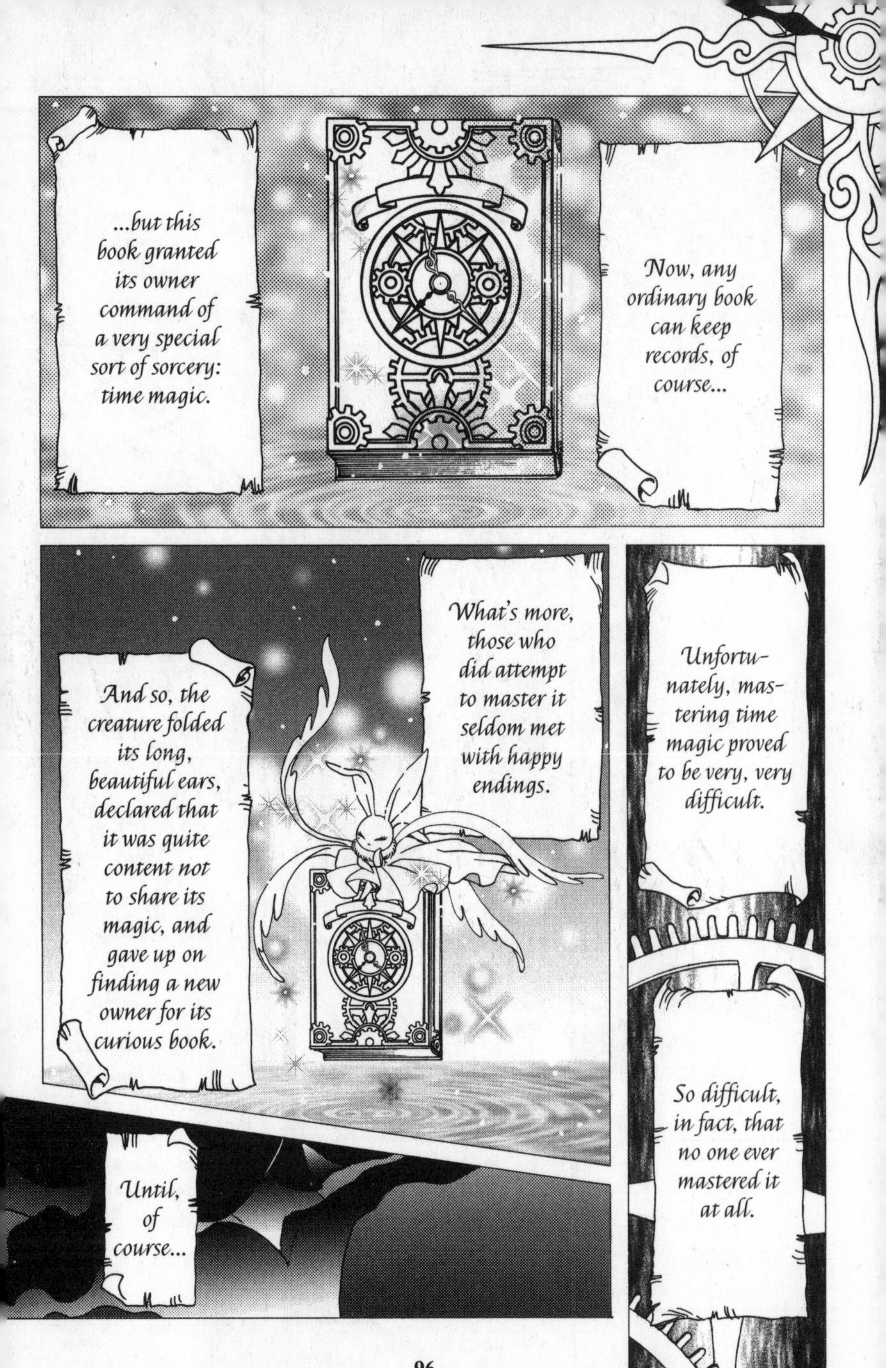
Now, any ordinary book can keep records, of course...
...but this book granted its owner command of a very special sort of sorcery: time magic.
Unfortunately, mastering time magic proved to be very, very difficult.
So difficult, in fact, that no one ever mastered it at all.
What's more, those who did attempt to master it seldom met with happy endings.
And so, the creature folded its long, beautiful ears, declared that it was quite content not to share its magic, and gave up on finding a new owner for its curious book.
Until, of course...

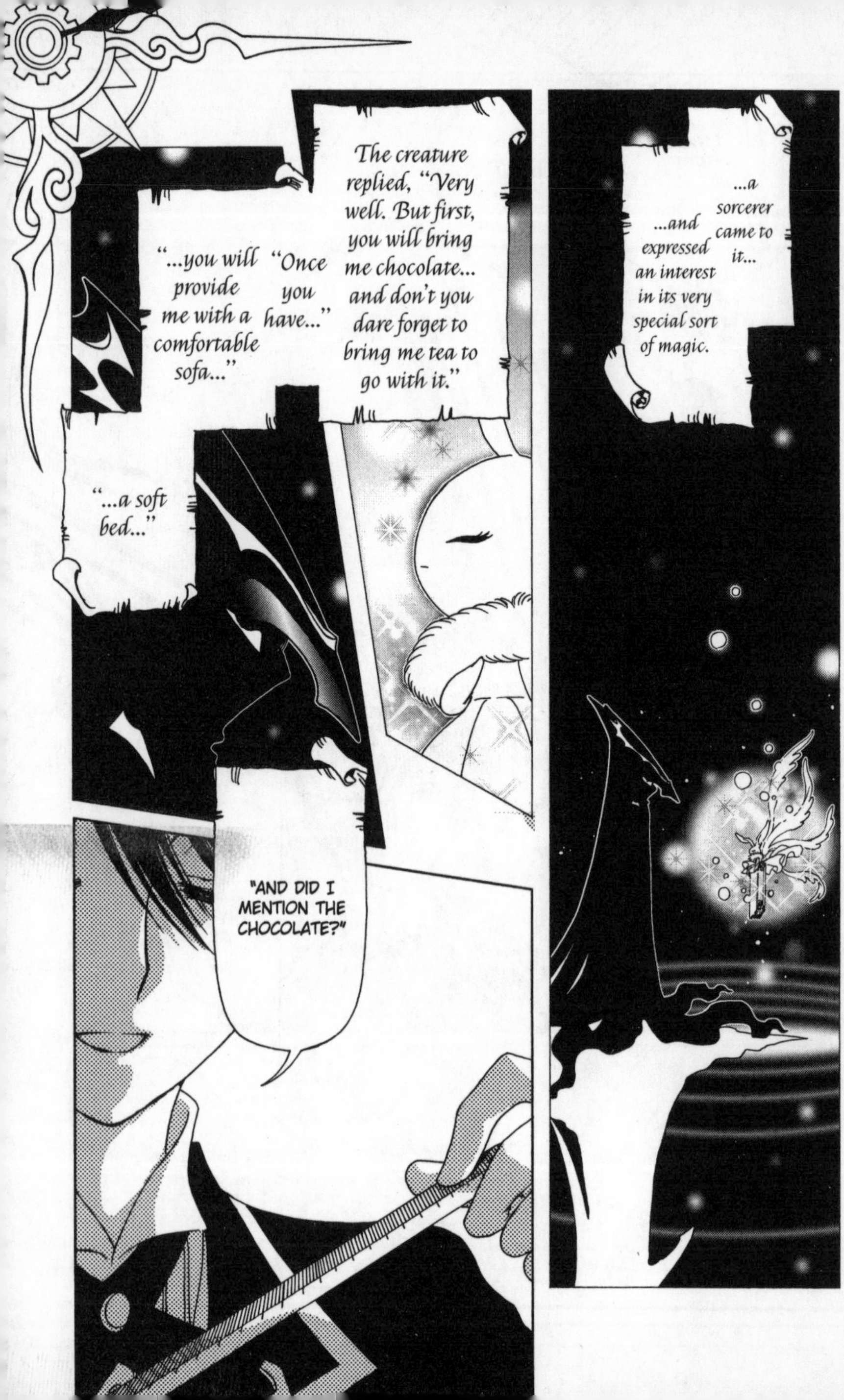
...a sorcerer came to it...
...and expressed an interest in its very special sort of magic.
The creature replied, "Very well. But first, you will bring me chocolate... and don't you dare forget to bring me tea to go with it."
"Once you have..."
"...you will provide me with a comfortable sofa..."
"...a soft bed..."
"AND DID I MENTION THE CHOCOLATE?"

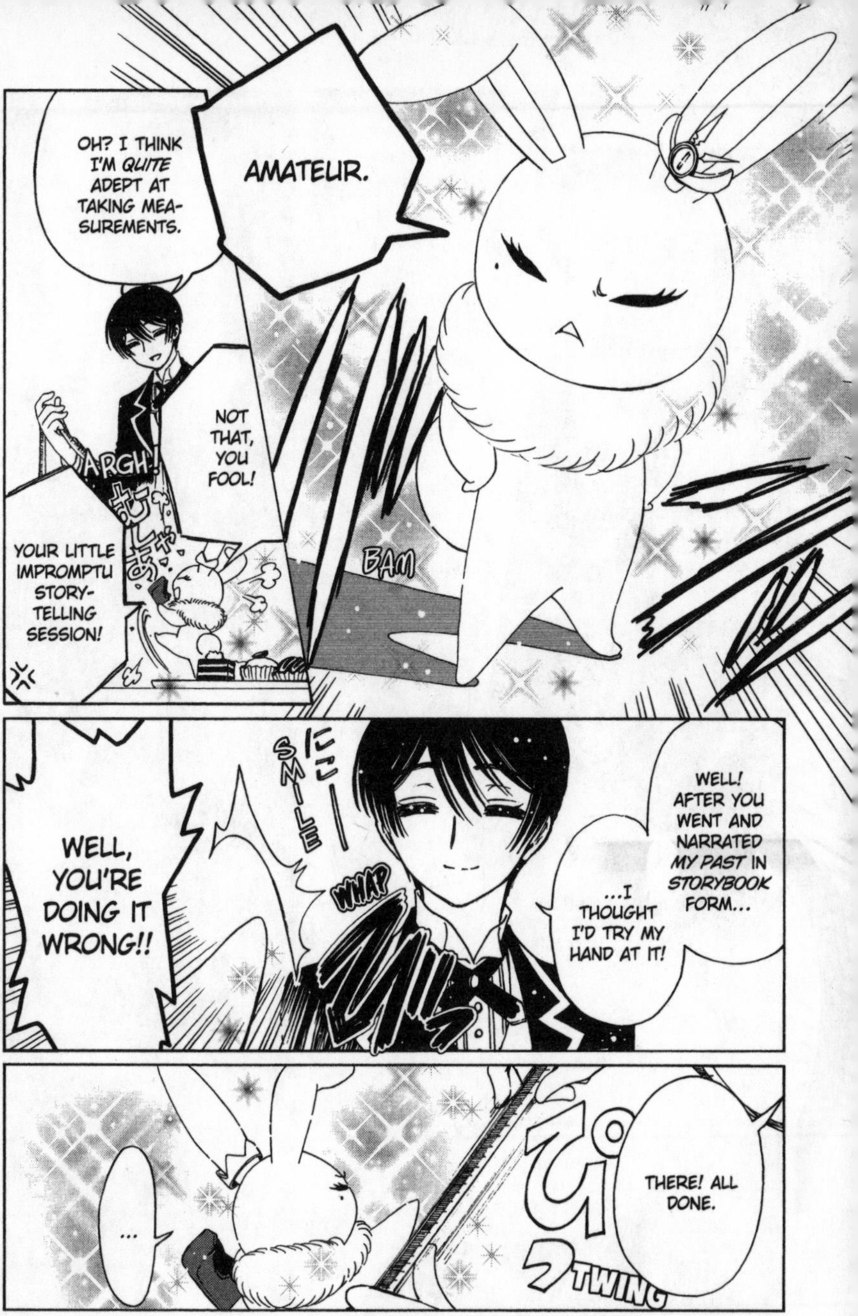
AMATEUR.
OH? I THINK I'M *QUITE* ADEPT AT TAKING MEA-SUREMENTS.
NOT THAT, YOU FOOL!
ARGH!
YOUR LITTLE IMPROMPTU STORY-TELLING SESSION!
BAM
WELL! AFTER YOU WENT AND NARRATED *MY PAST* IN *STORYBOOK* FORM...
...I THOUGHT I'D TRY MY HAND AT IT!
SMILE
WHAP
WELL, YOU'RE DOING IT WRONG!!
THERE! ALL DONE.
TWING
...

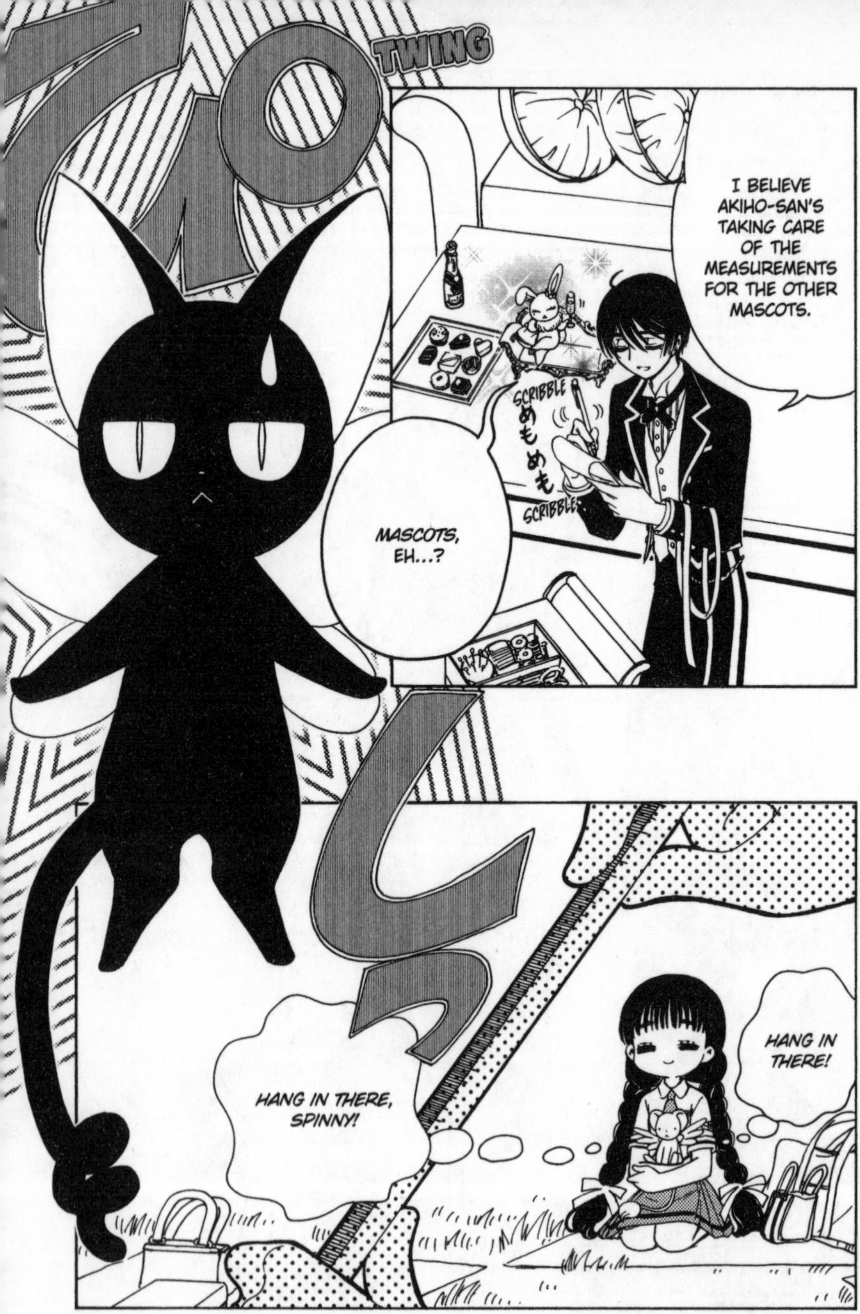
I BELIEVE AKIHO-SAN'S TAKING CARE OF THE MEASUREMENTS FOR THE OTHER MASCOTS.
SCRIBBLE
めもめも
SCRIBBLE
TWING
MASCOTS, EH...?
HANG IN THERE!
HANG IN THERE, SPINNY!

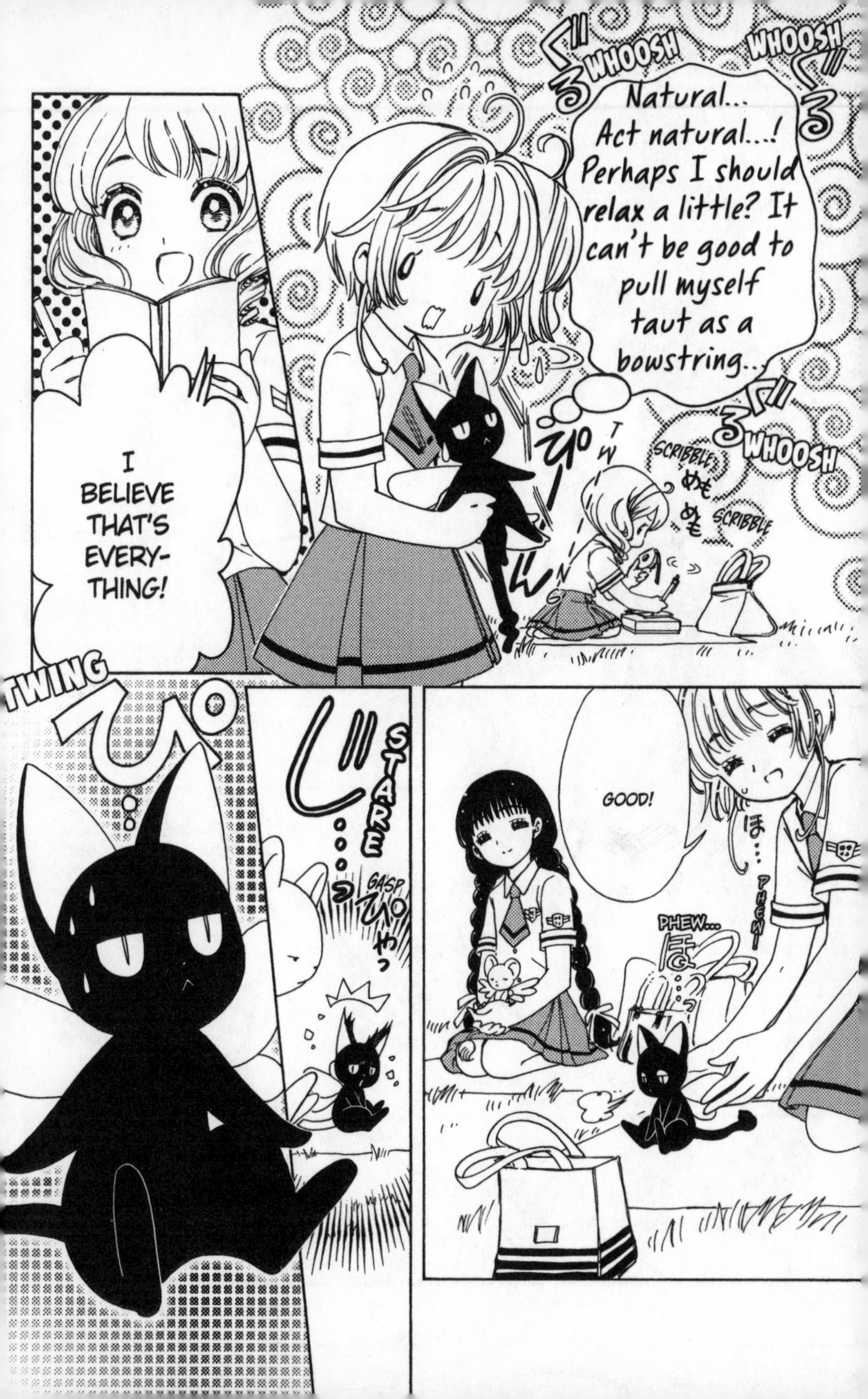
ぐる WHOOSH
WHOOSH ぐる
Natural... Act natural...! Perhaps I should relax a little? It can't be good to pull myself taut as a bowstring...
ぐる WHOOSH
ぴーん TWING
SCRIBBLE めも
めも SCRIBBLE
I BELIEVE THAT'S EVERYTHING!
GOOD!
ほ… PHEW!
PHEW... ほっ
じーっ STARE
GASP ぴゃっ
TWING ぴ

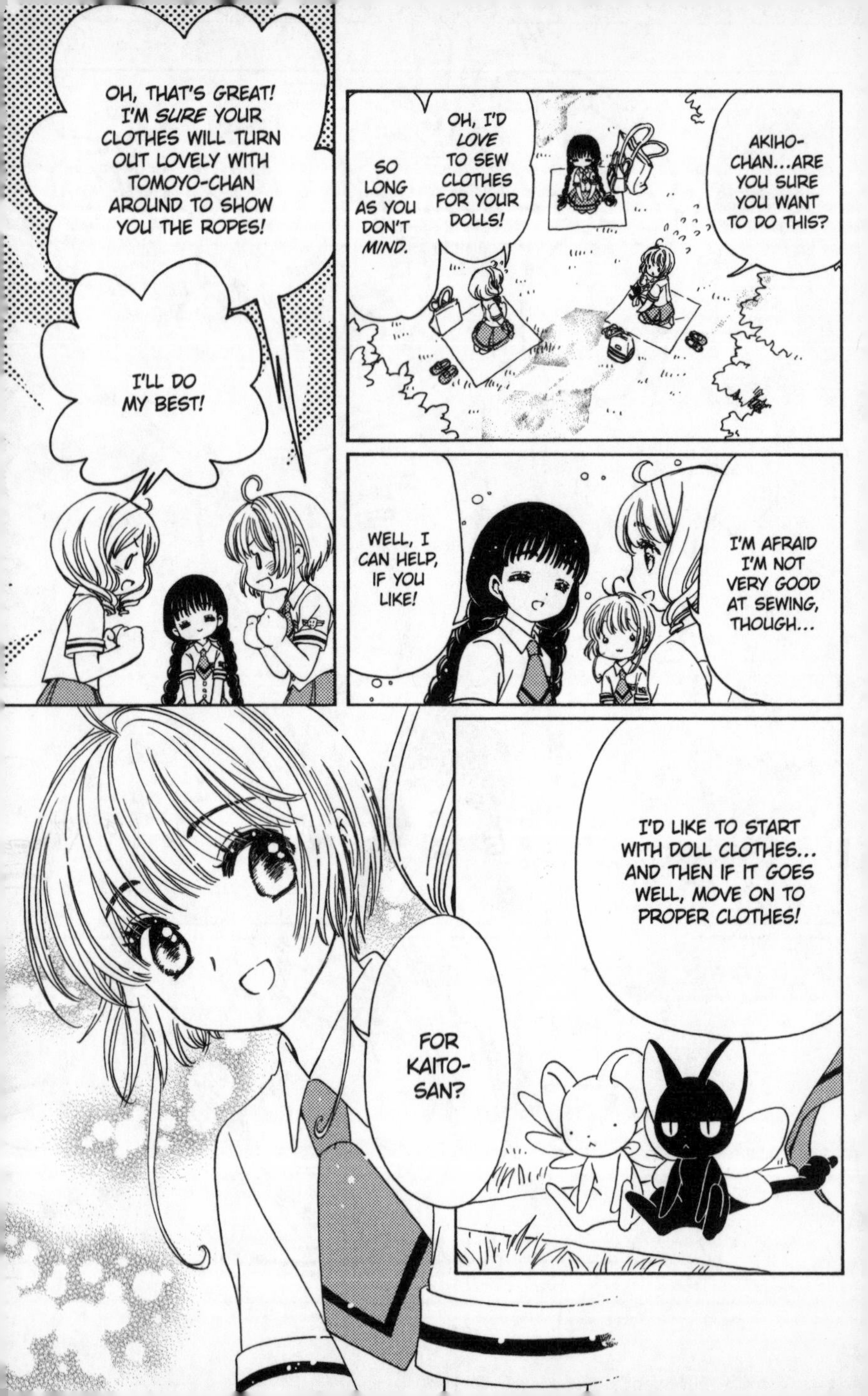
AKIHO-CHAN...ARE YOU SURE YOU WANT TO DO THIS?
OH, I'D *LOVE* TO SEW CLOTHES FOR YOUR DOLLS!
SO LONG AS YOU DON'T *MIND*.
I'M AFRAID I'M NOT VERY GOOD AT SEWING, THOUGH...
WELL, I CAN HELP, IF YOU LIKE!
OH, THAT'S GREAT! I'M *SURE* YOUR CLOTHES WILL TURN OUT LOVELY WITH TOMOYO-CHAN AROUND TO SHOW YOU THE ROPES!
I'LL DO MY BEST!
I'D LIKE TO START WITH DOLL CLOTHES... AND THEN IF IT GOES WELL, MOVE ON TO PROPER CLOTHES!
FOR KAITO-SAN?

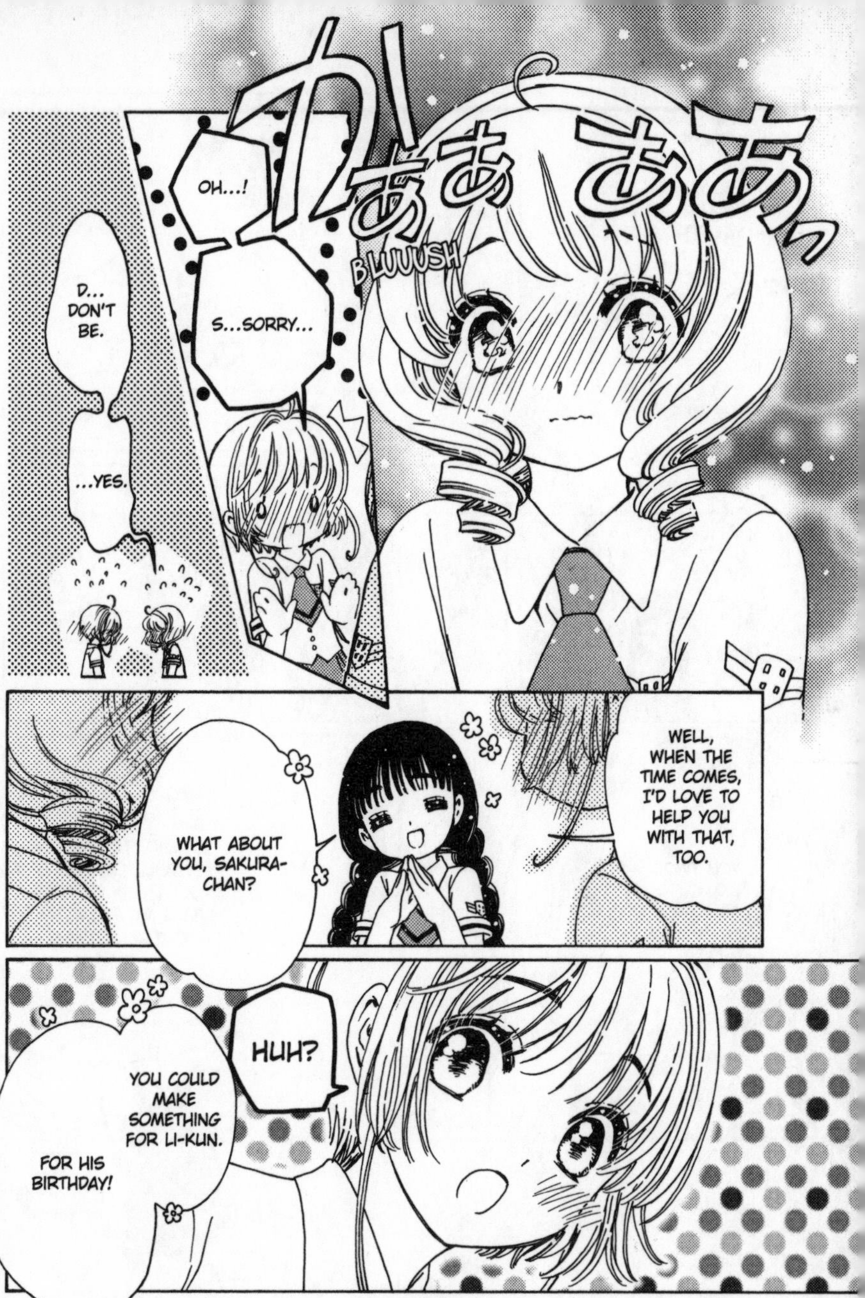

かああ あああっ
BLUUUSH
OH...!
S...SORRY...
D... DON'T BE.
...YES.
WELL, WHEN THE TIME COMES, I'D LOVE TO HELP YOU WITH THAT, TOO.
WHAT ABOUT YOU, SAKURA-CHAN?
HUH?
YOU COULD MAKE SOMETHING FOR LI-KUN.
FOR HIS BIRTHDAY!

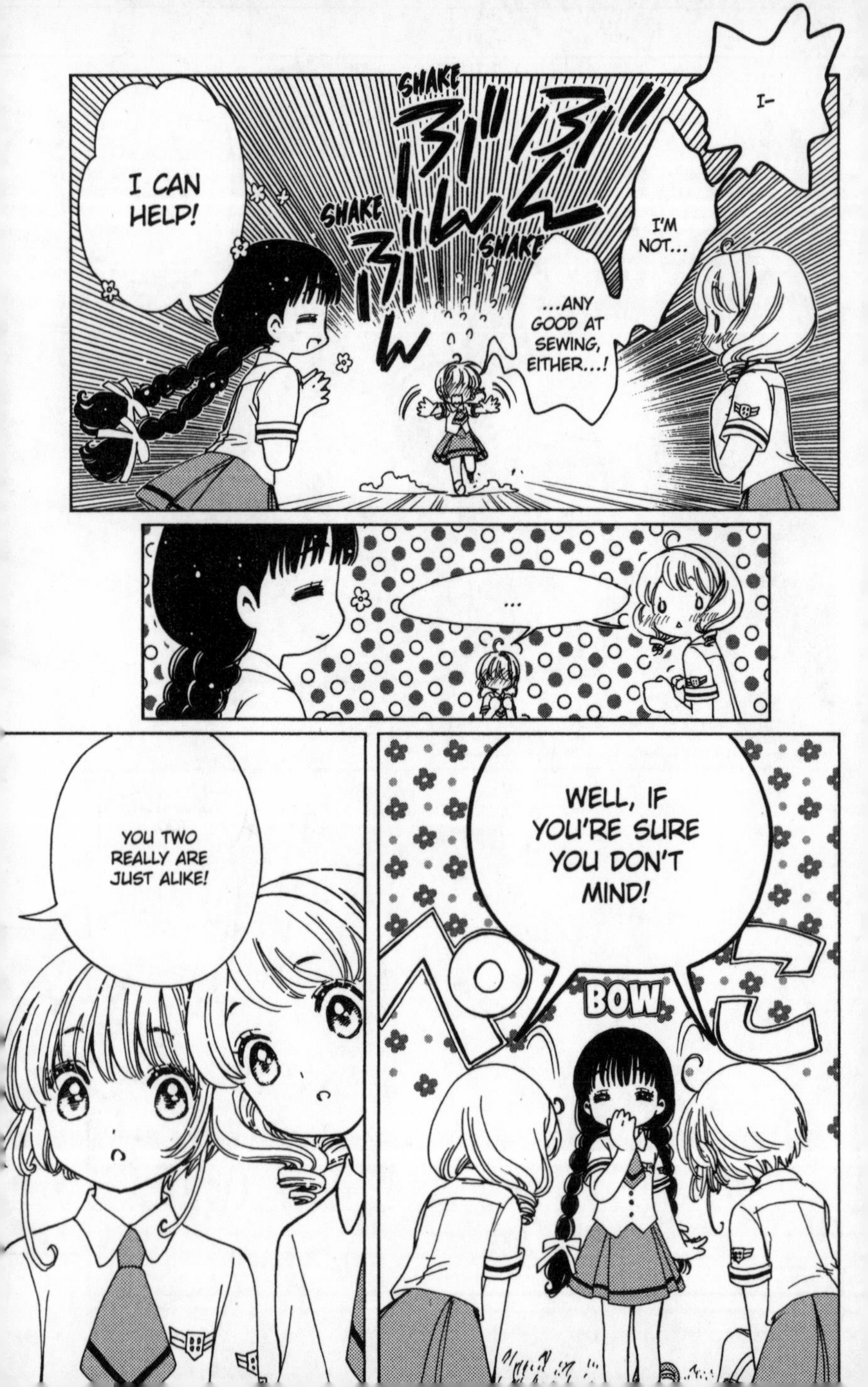
I–
I'M NOT...
...ANY GOOD AT SEWING, EITHER...!
SHAKE
SHAKE
SHAKE
I CAN HELP!
...
WELL, IF YOU'RE SURE YOU DON'T MIND!
BOW
YOU TWO REALLY ARE JUST ALIKE!

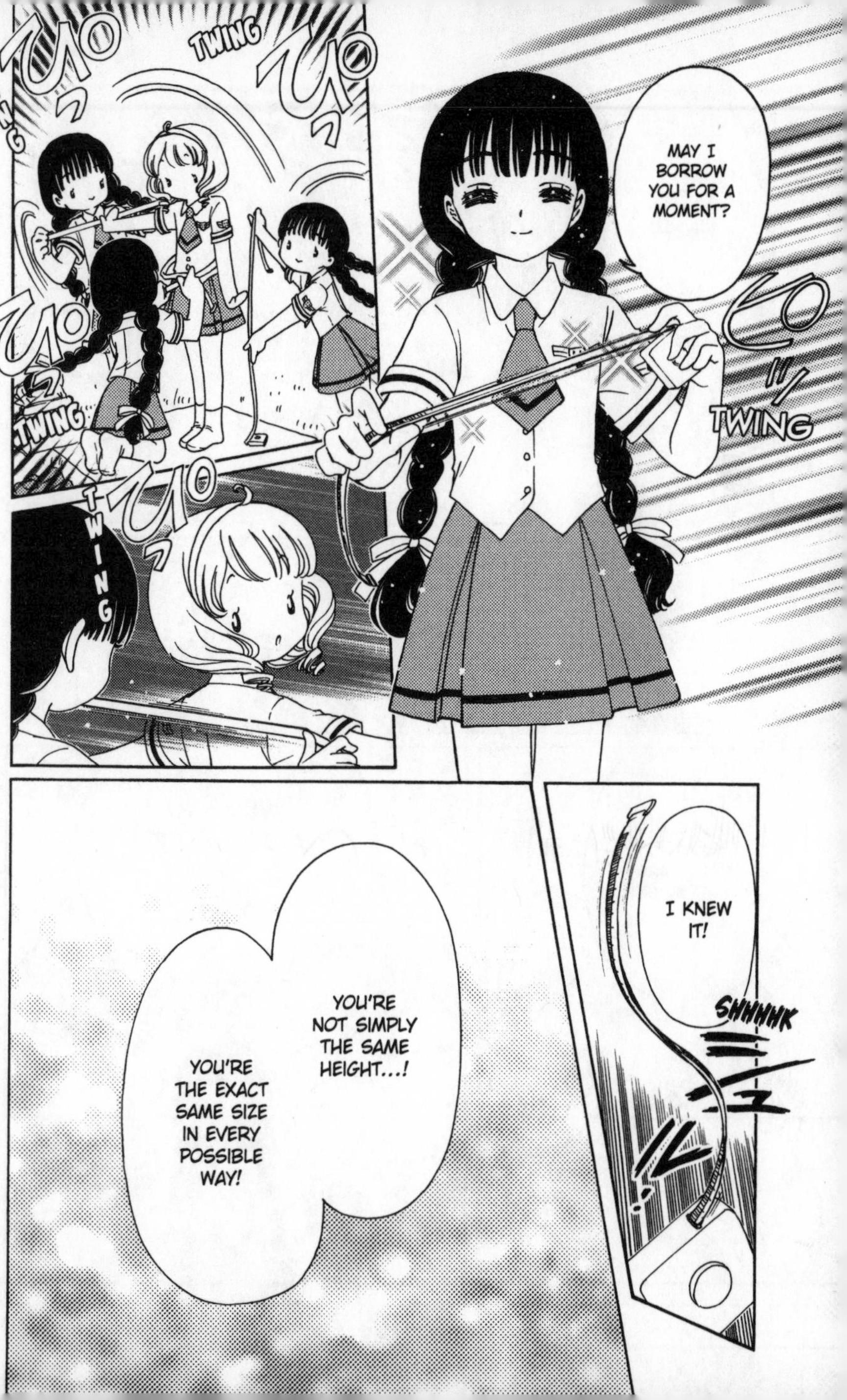
MAY I BORROW YOU FOR A MOMENT?
TWING
TWING
TWING
TWING
I KNEW IT!
SHHHHK
YOU'RE NOT SIMPLY THE SAME HEIGHT...!
YOU'RE THE EXACT SAME SIZE IN EVERY POSSIBLE WAY!

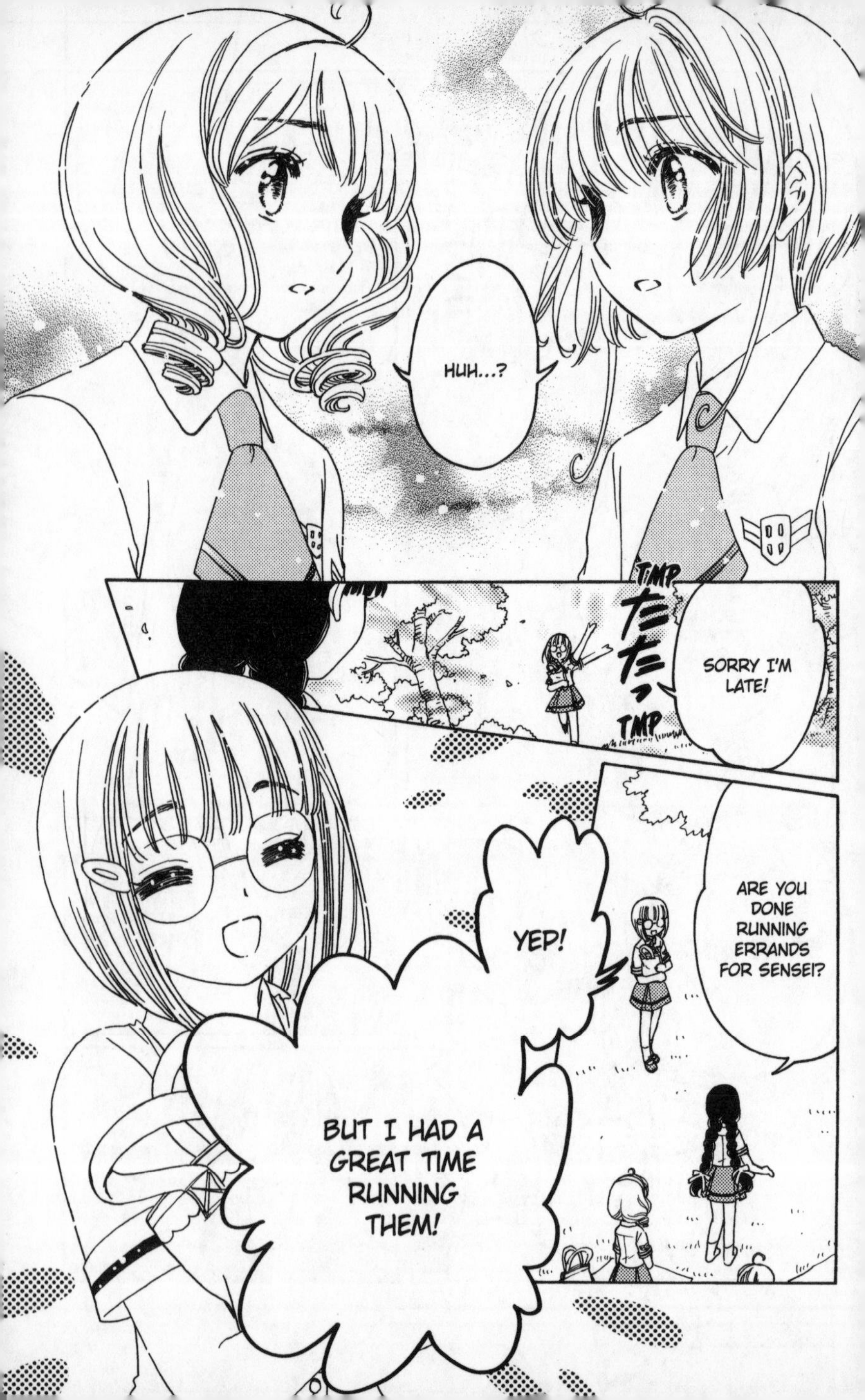
HUH...?
TMP
TMP
SORRY I'M LATE!
ARE YOU DONE RUNNING ERRANDS FOR SENSEI?
YEP!
BUT I HAD A GREAT TIME RUNNING THEM!

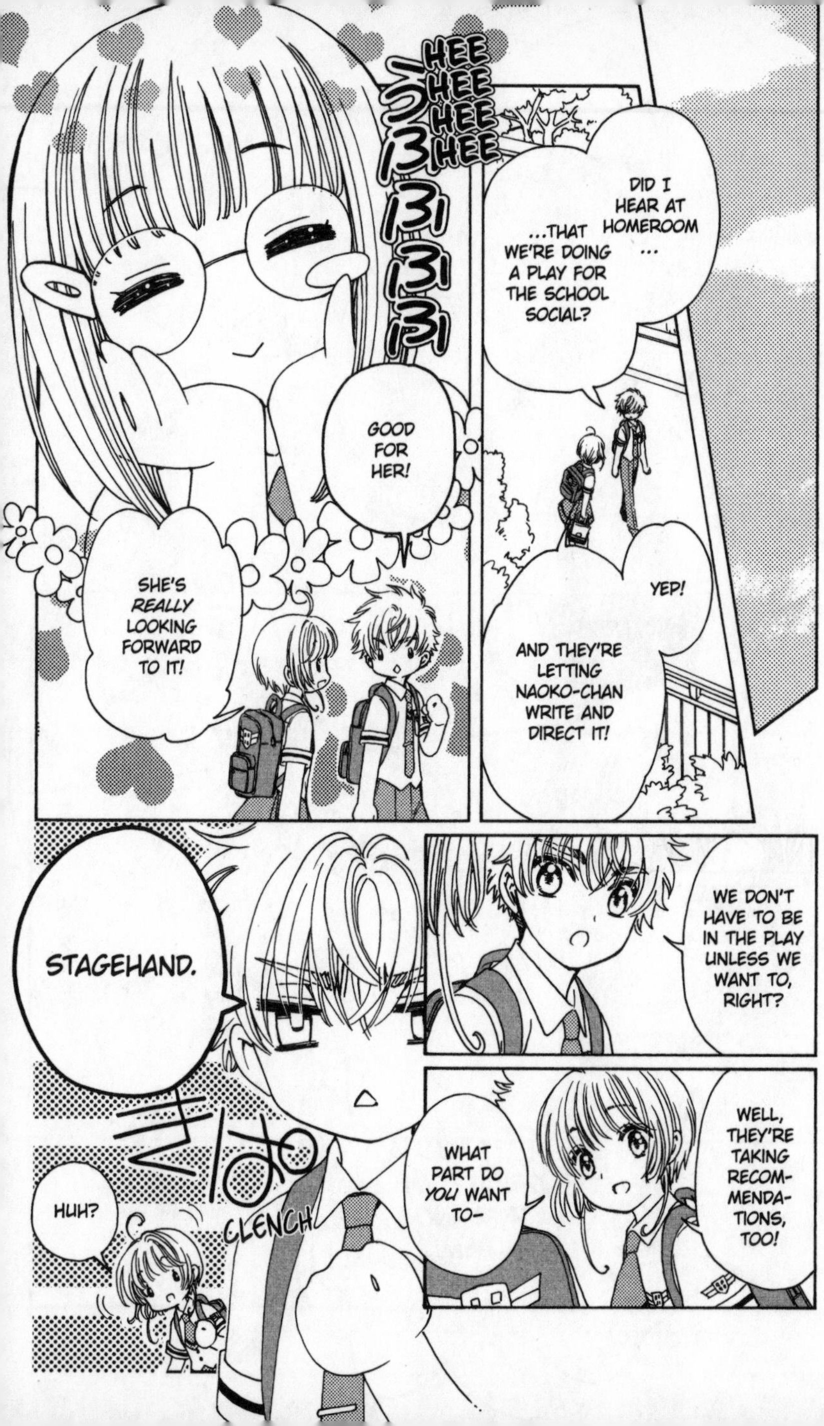
DID I HEAR AT HOMEROOM ...
...THAT WE'RE DOING A PLAY FOR THE SCHOOL SOCIAL?
YEP!
AND THEY'RE LETTING NAOKO-CHAN WRITE AND DIRECT IT!
HEE HEE HEE HEE
GOOD FOR HER!
SHE'S *REALLY* LOOKING FORWARD TO IT!
WE DON'T HAVE TO BE IN THE PLAY UNLESS WE WANT TO, RIGHT?
WELL, THEY'RE TAKING RECOMMENDATIONS, TOO!
WHAT PART DO *YOU* WANT TO-
STAGEHAND.
CLENCH
HUH?

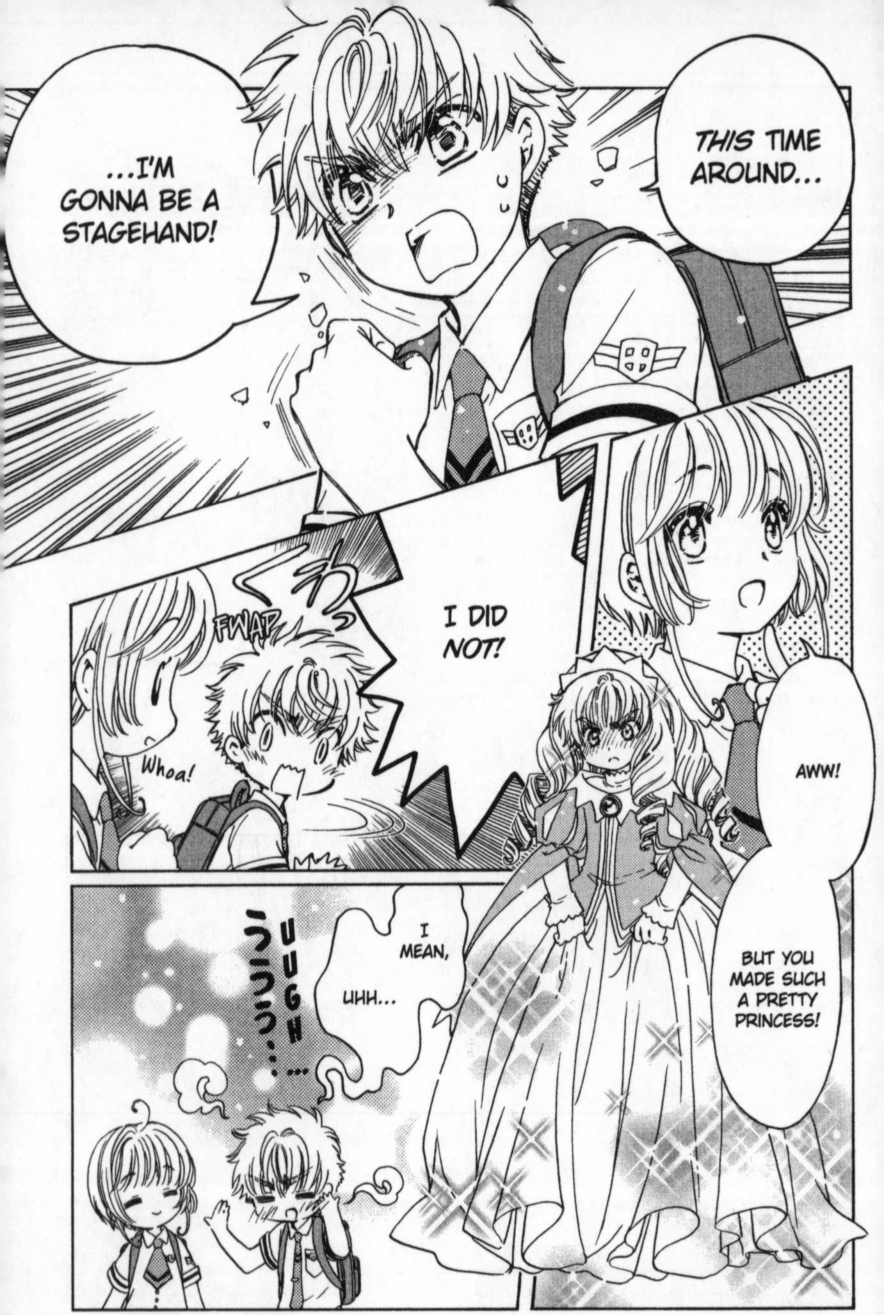
THIS TIME AROUND...
...I'M GONNA BE A STAGEHAND!
AWW!
BUT YOU MADE SUCH A PRETTY PRINCESS!
くわっ
FWAP
I DID NOT!
Whoa!
I MEAN,
UHH...
ううう…
UUGH...

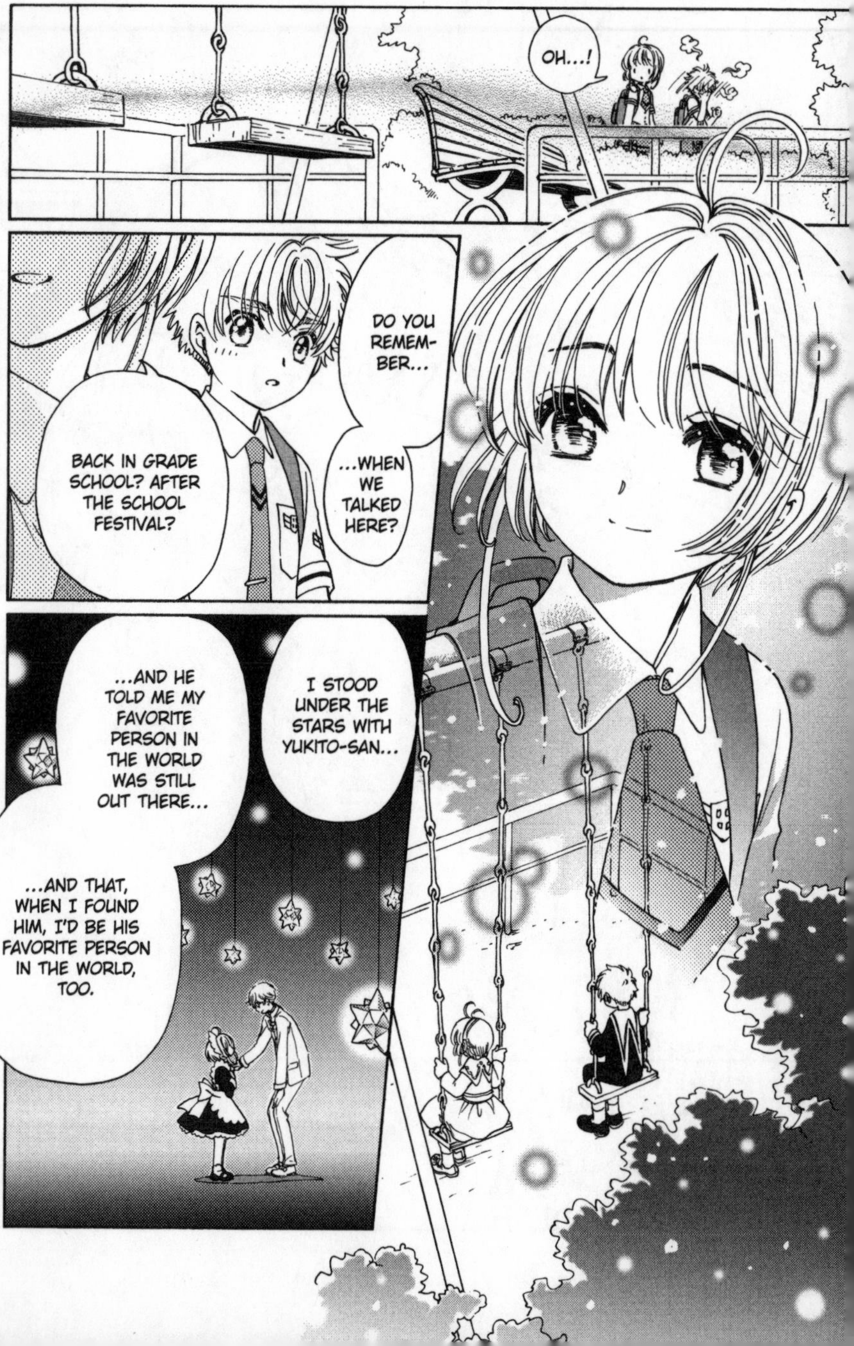

OH...!
DO YOU REMEMBER...
...WHEN WE TALKED HERE?
BACK IN GRADE SCHOOL? AFTER THE SCHOOL FESTIVAL?
I STOOD UNDER THE STARS WITH YUKITO-SAN...
...AND HE TOLD ME MY FAVORITE PERSON IN THE WORLD WAS STILL OUT THERE...
...AND THAT, WHEN I FOUND HIM, I'D BE HIS FAVORITE PERSON IN THE WORLD, TOO.

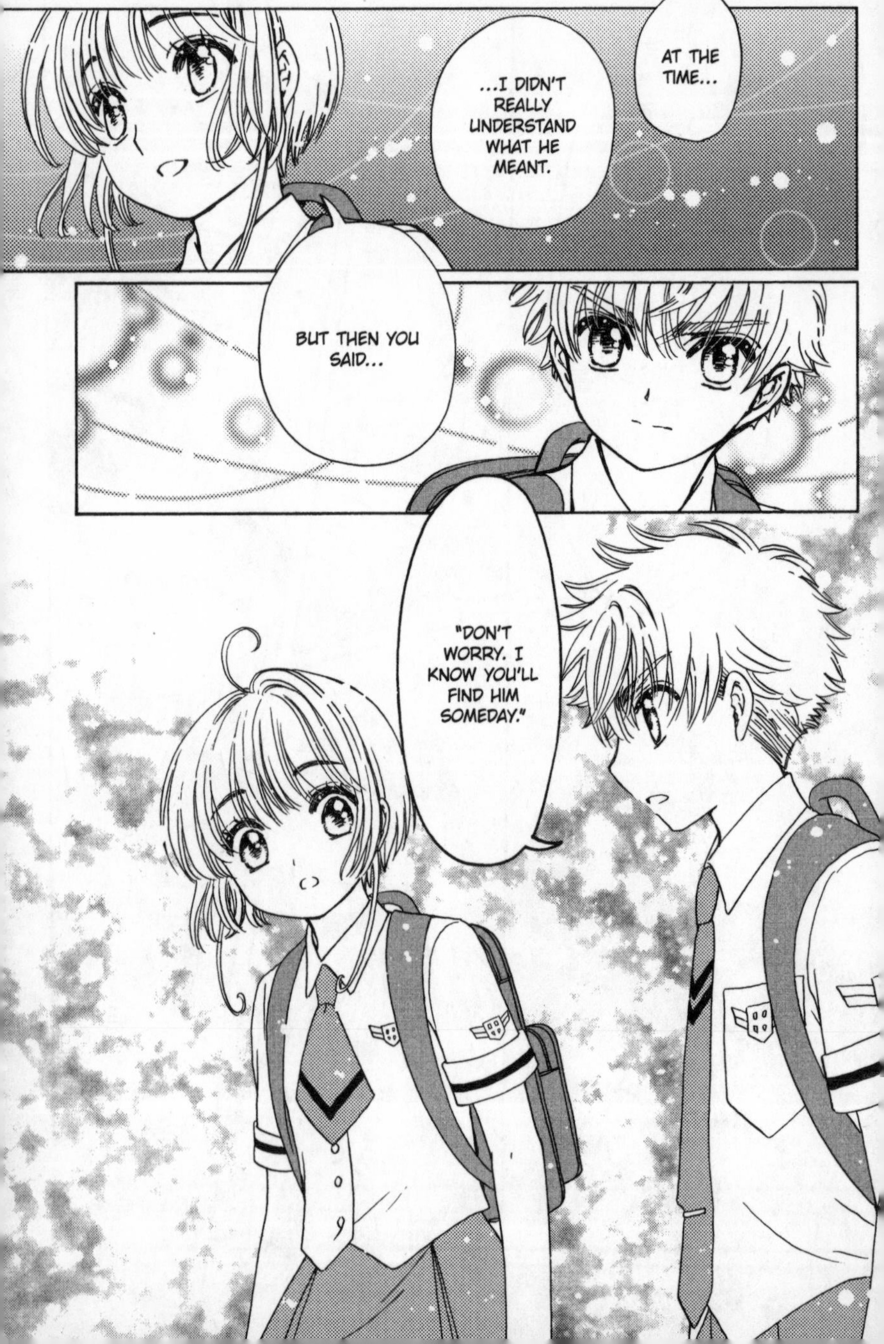
AT THE TIME...
...I DIDN'T REALLY UNDERSTAND WHAT HE MEANT.
BUT THEN YOU SAID...
"DON'T WORRY. I KNOW YOU'LL FIND HIM SOMEDAY."

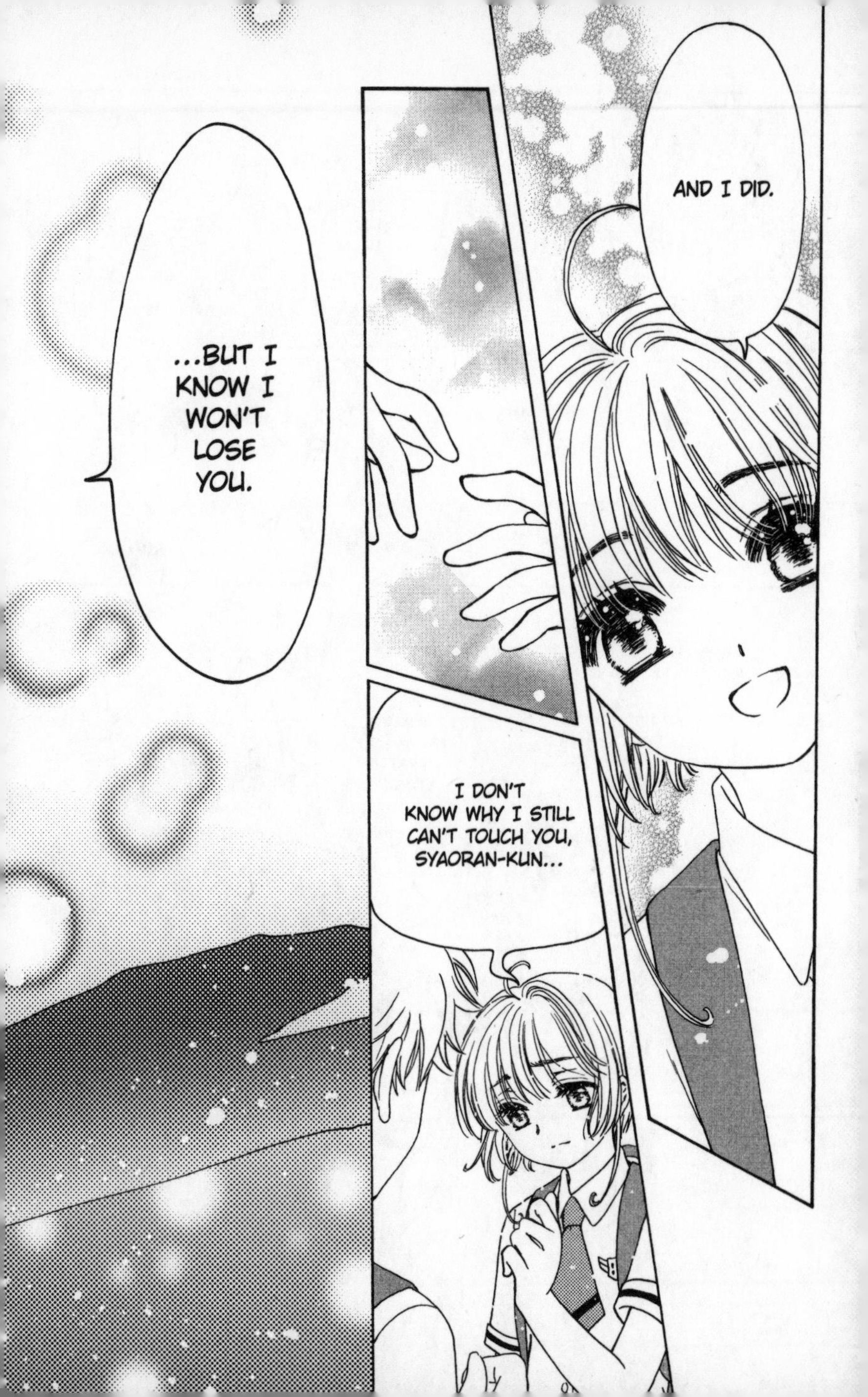
AND I DID.
I DON'T KNOW WHY I STILL CAN'T TOUCH YOU, SYAORAN-KUN...
...BUT I KNOW I WON'T LOSE YOU.

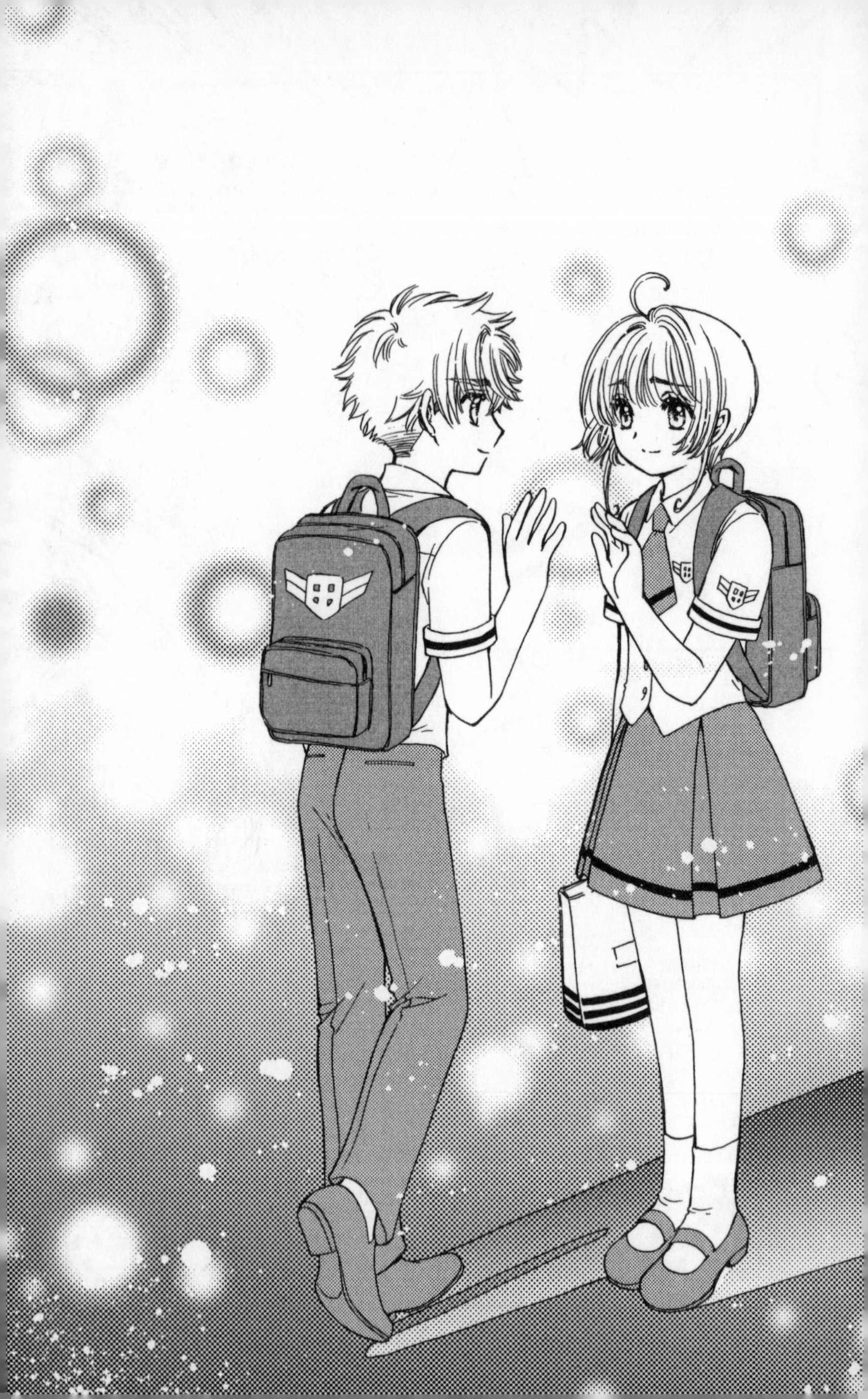

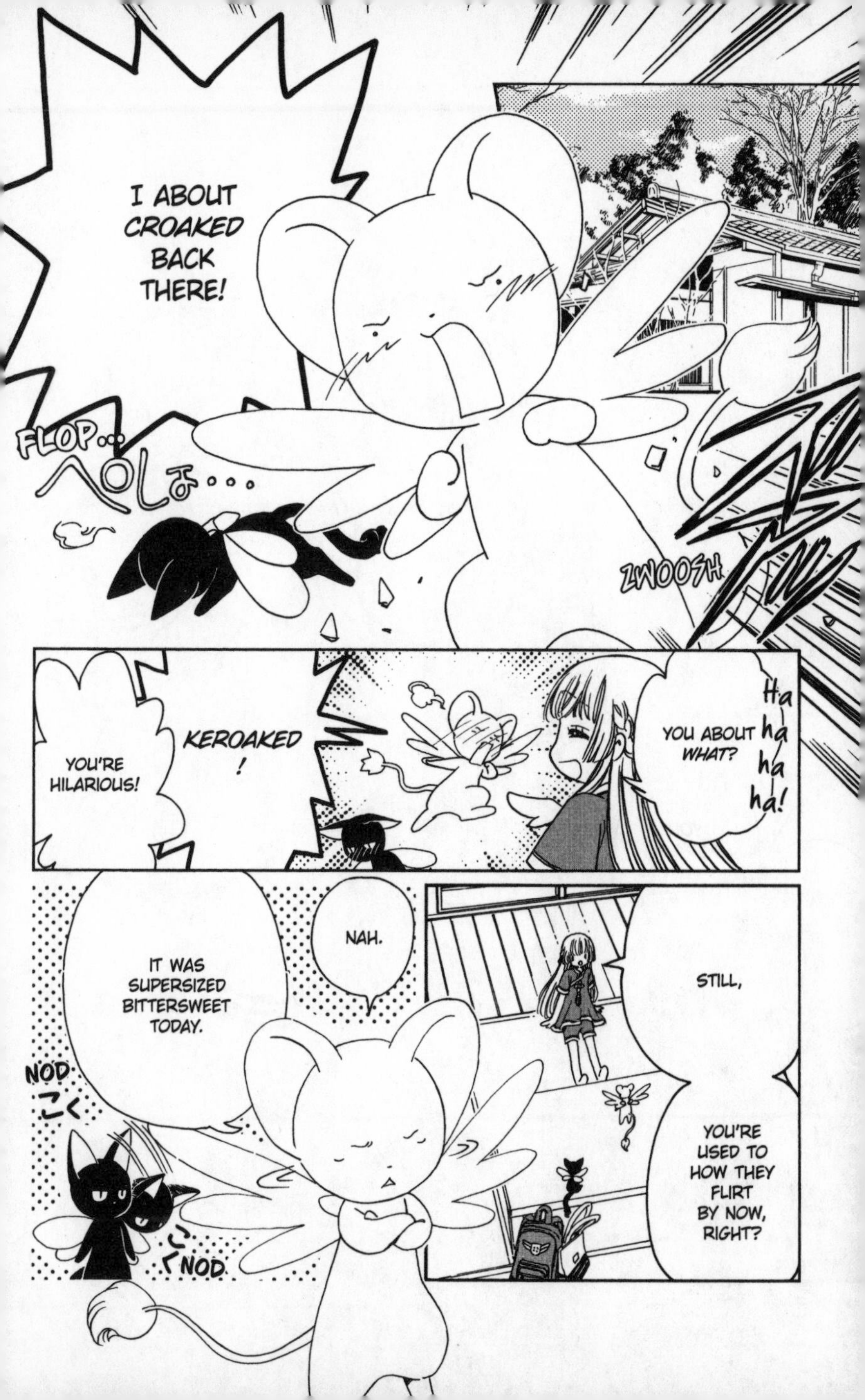
ZWOOSH
I ABOUT CROAKED BACK THERE!
FLOP...
ぺしょ...
Ha ha ha ha!
YOU ABOUT WHAT?
KEROAKED!
YOU'RE HILARIOUS!
STILL,
YOU'RE USED TO HOW THEY FLIRT BY NOW, RIGHT?
NAH.
IT WAS SUPERSIZED BITTERSWEET TODAY.
NOD
こく
こく
NOD

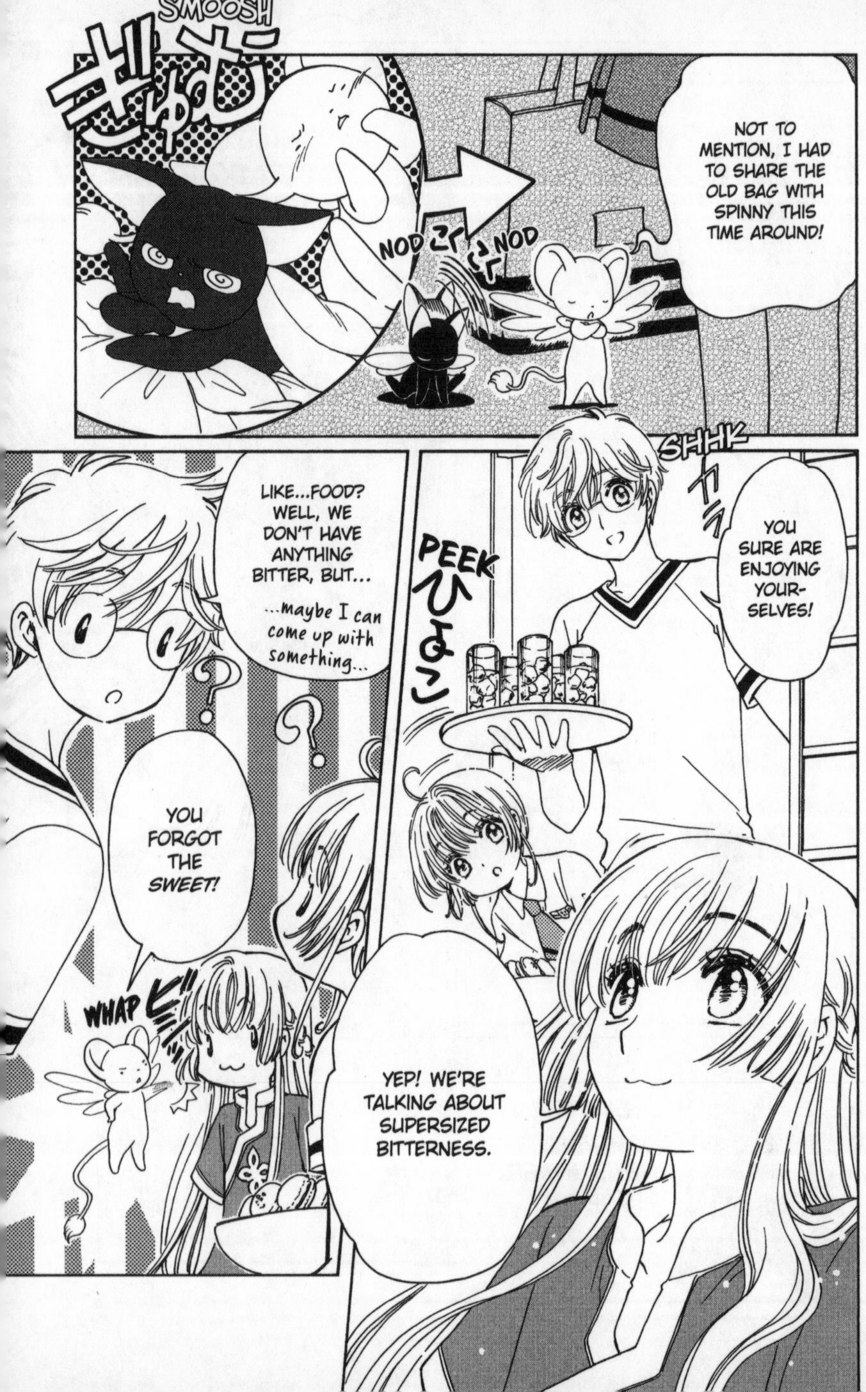

NOT TO MENTION, I HAD TO SHARE THE OLD BAG WITH SPINNY THIS TIME AROUND!
NOD NOD
SMOOSH
SHHK
YOU SURE ARE ENJOYING YOUR-SELVES!
PEEK
YEP! WE'RE TALKING ABOUT SUPERSIZED BITTERNESS.
LIKE...FOOD? WELL, WE DON'T HAVE ANYTHING BITTER, BUT...
...maybe I can come up with something...
YOU FORGOT THE SWEET!
WHAP

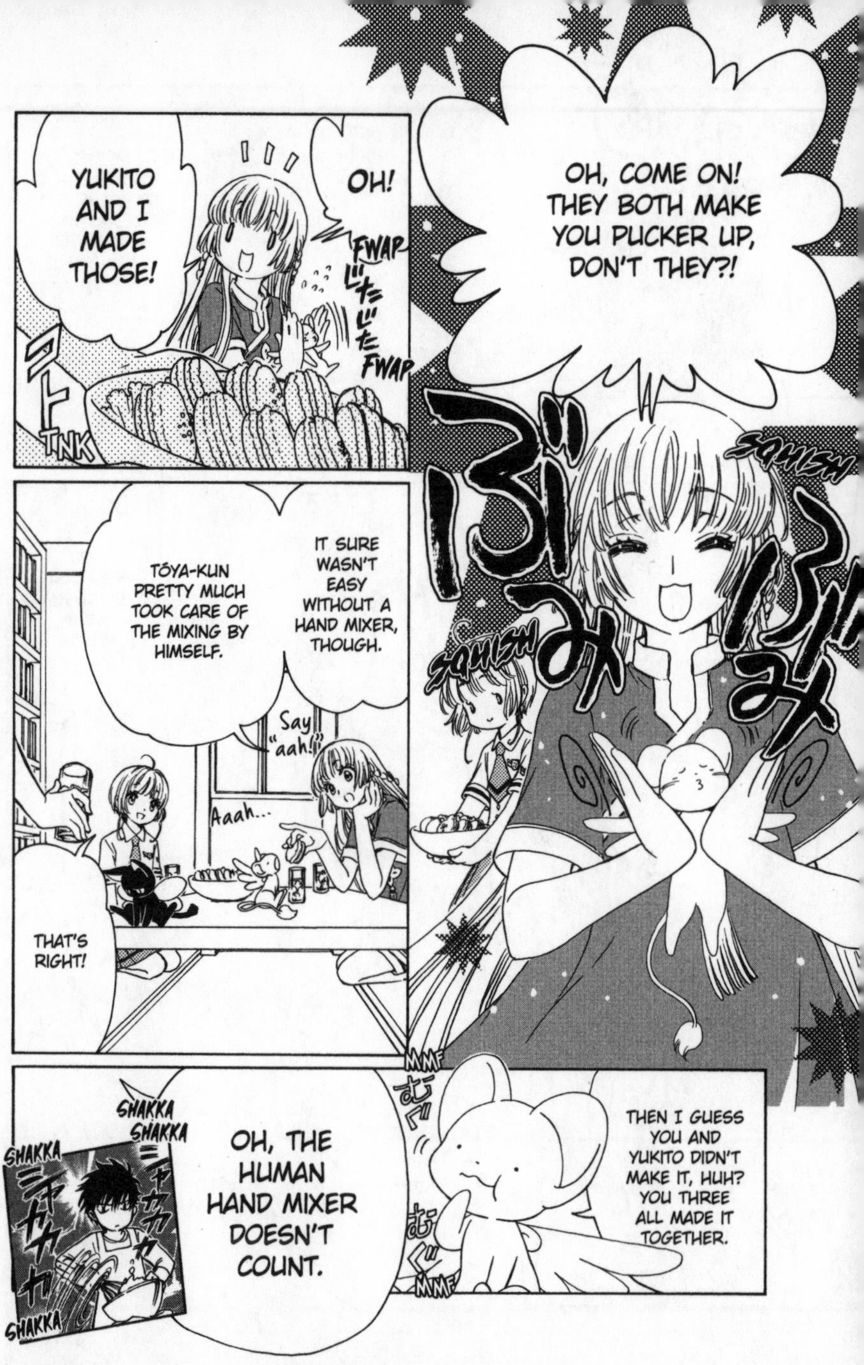
OH, COME ON! THEY BOTH MAKE YOU PUCKER UP, DON'T THEY?!
SQUISH
SQUISH
OH!
FWAP
FWAP
YUKITO AND I MADE THOSE!
TNK
IT SURE WASN'T EASY WITHOUT A HAND MIXER, THOUGH.
TŌYA-KUN PRETTY MUCH TOOK CARE OF THE MIXING BY HIMSELF.
Say "aah!"
Aaah...
THAT'S RIGHT!
THEN I GUESS YOU AND YUKITO DIDN'T MAKE IT, HUH? YOU THREE ALL MADE IT TOGETHER.
MMF
MMF
OH, THE HUMAN HAND MIXER DOESN'T COUNT.
SHAKKA
SHAKKA
SHAKKA
SHAKKA

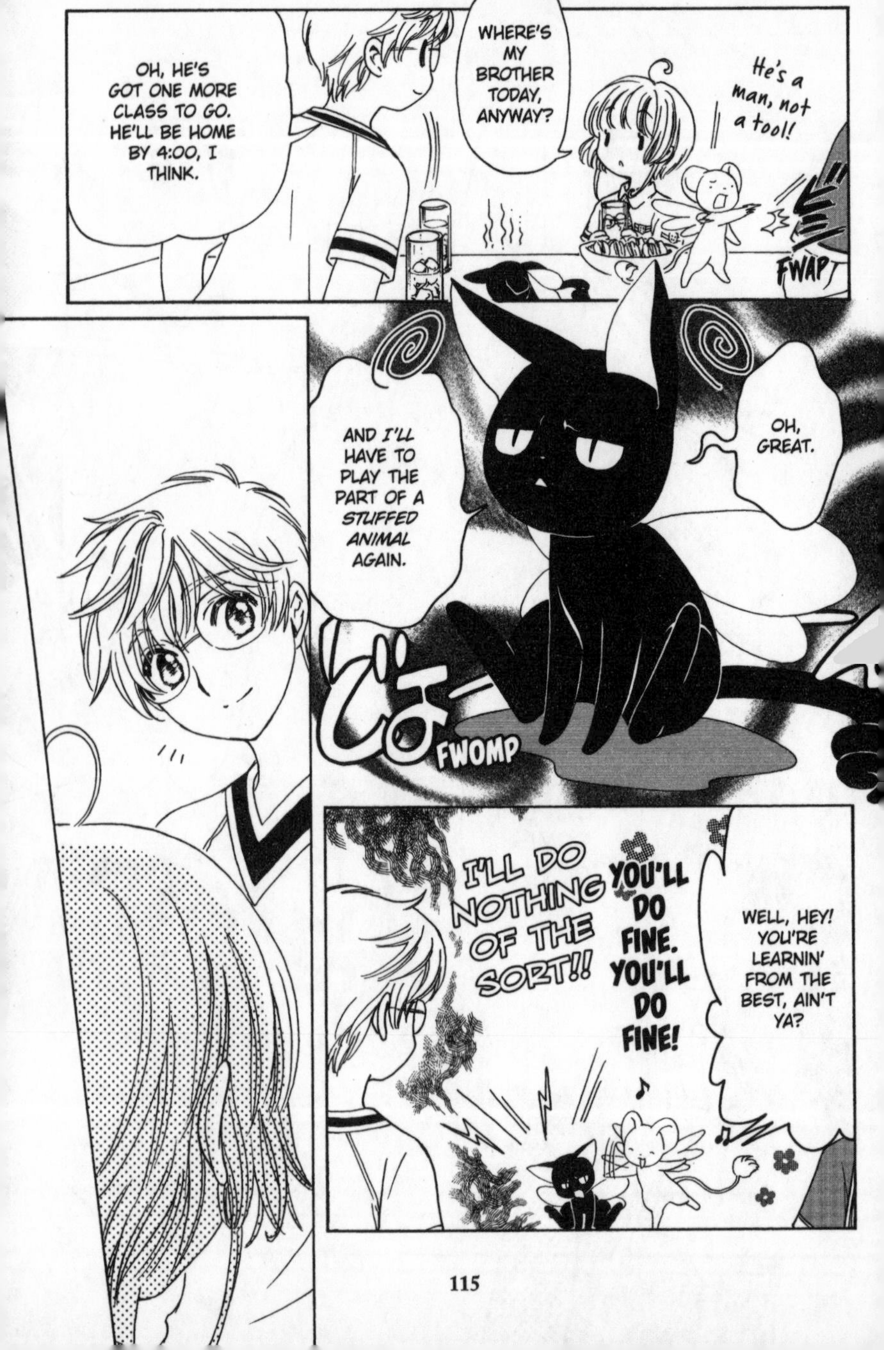
He's a man, not a tool!
FWAP
WHERE'S MY BROTHER TODAY, ANYWAY?
OH, HE'S GOT ONE MORE CLASS TO GO. HE'LL BE HOME BY 4:00, I THINK.
OH, GREAT.
AND I'LL HAVE TO PLAY THE PART OF A STUFFED ANIMAL AGAIN.
FWOMP
WELL, HEY! YOU'RE LEARNIN' FROM THE BEST, AIN'T YA?
YOU'LL DO FINE. YOU'LL DO FINE!
I'LL DO NOTHING OF THE SORT!!

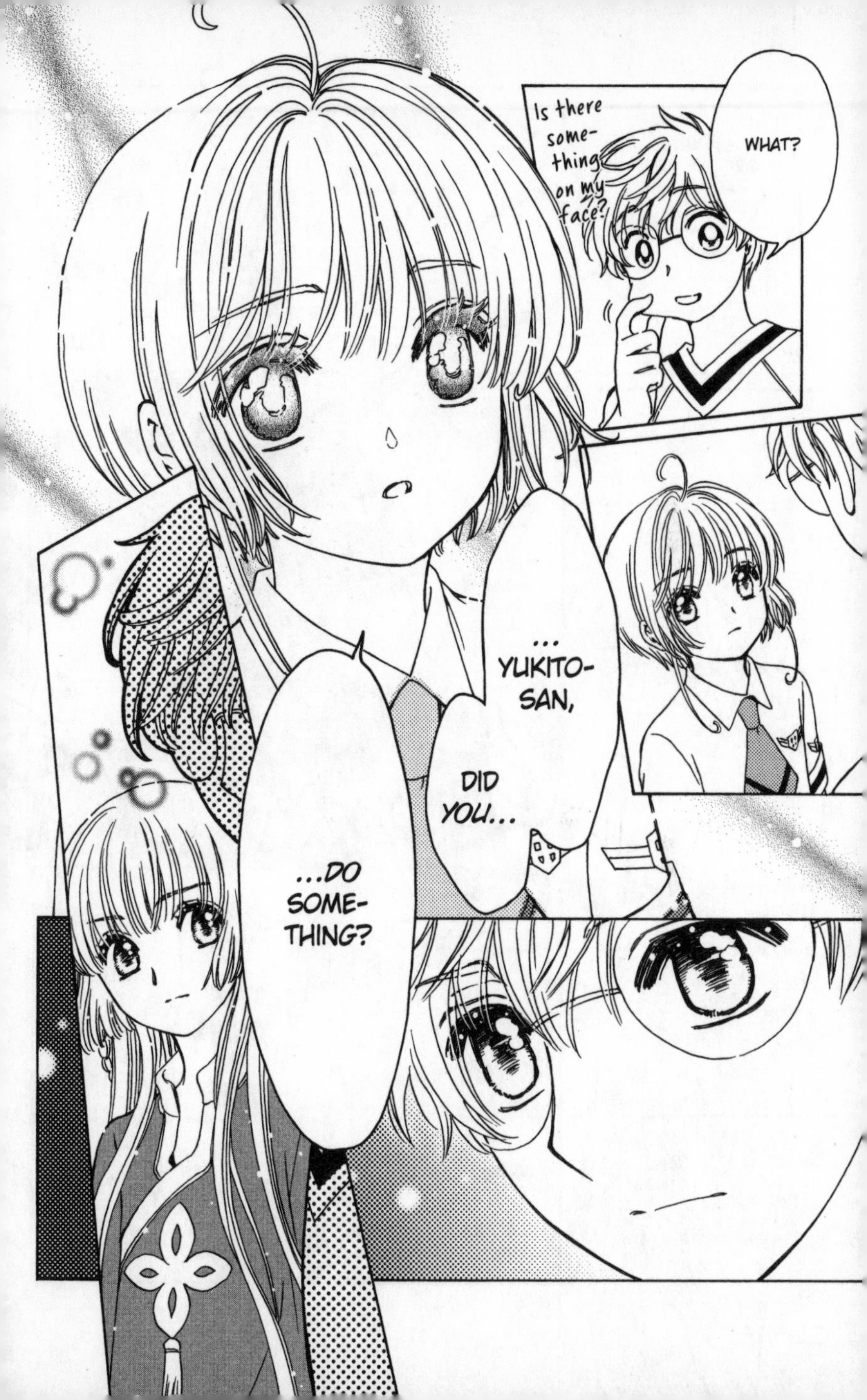

WHAT?
Is there something on my face?
...YUKITO-SAN,
DID YOU...
...DO SOMETHING?

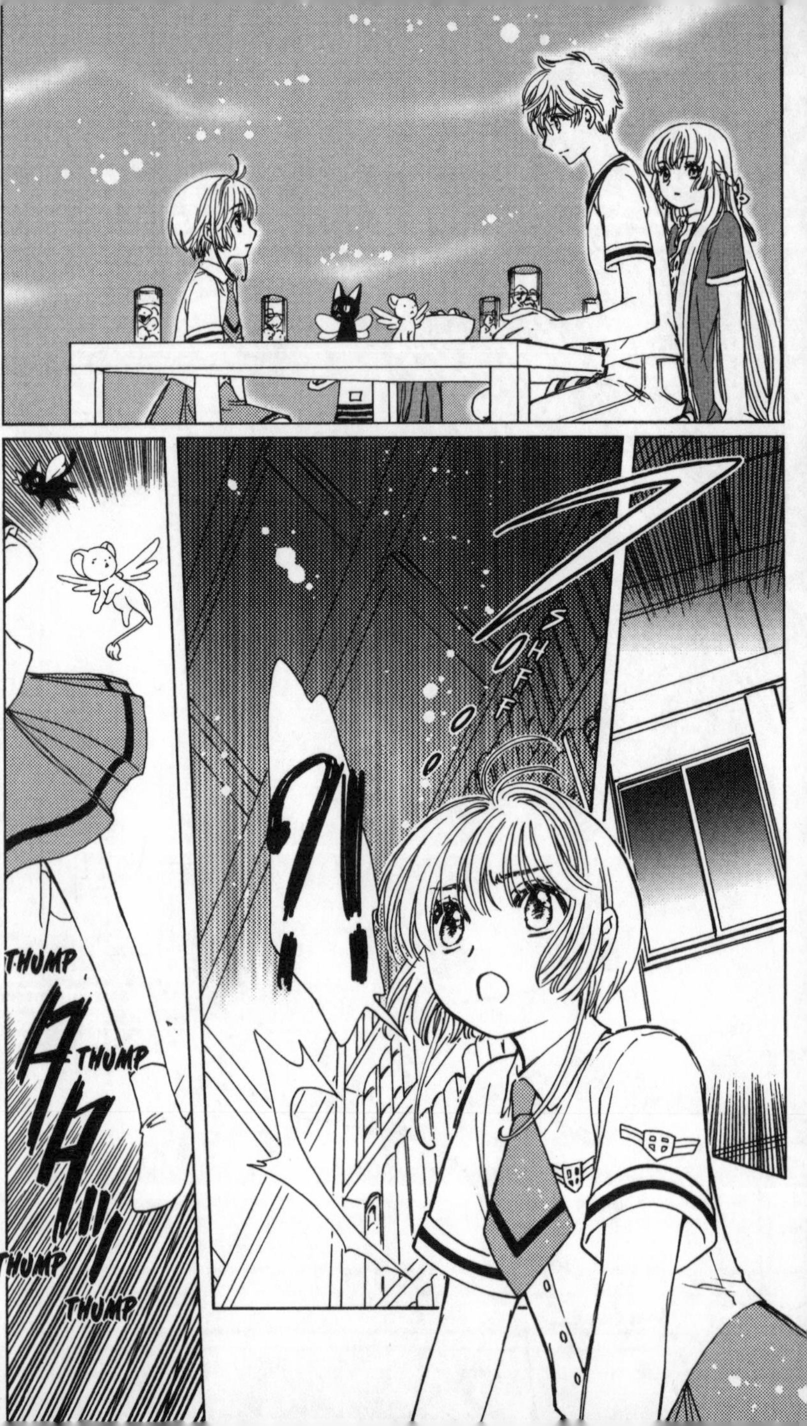
SHOFF
THUMP
THUMP
THUMP
THUMP

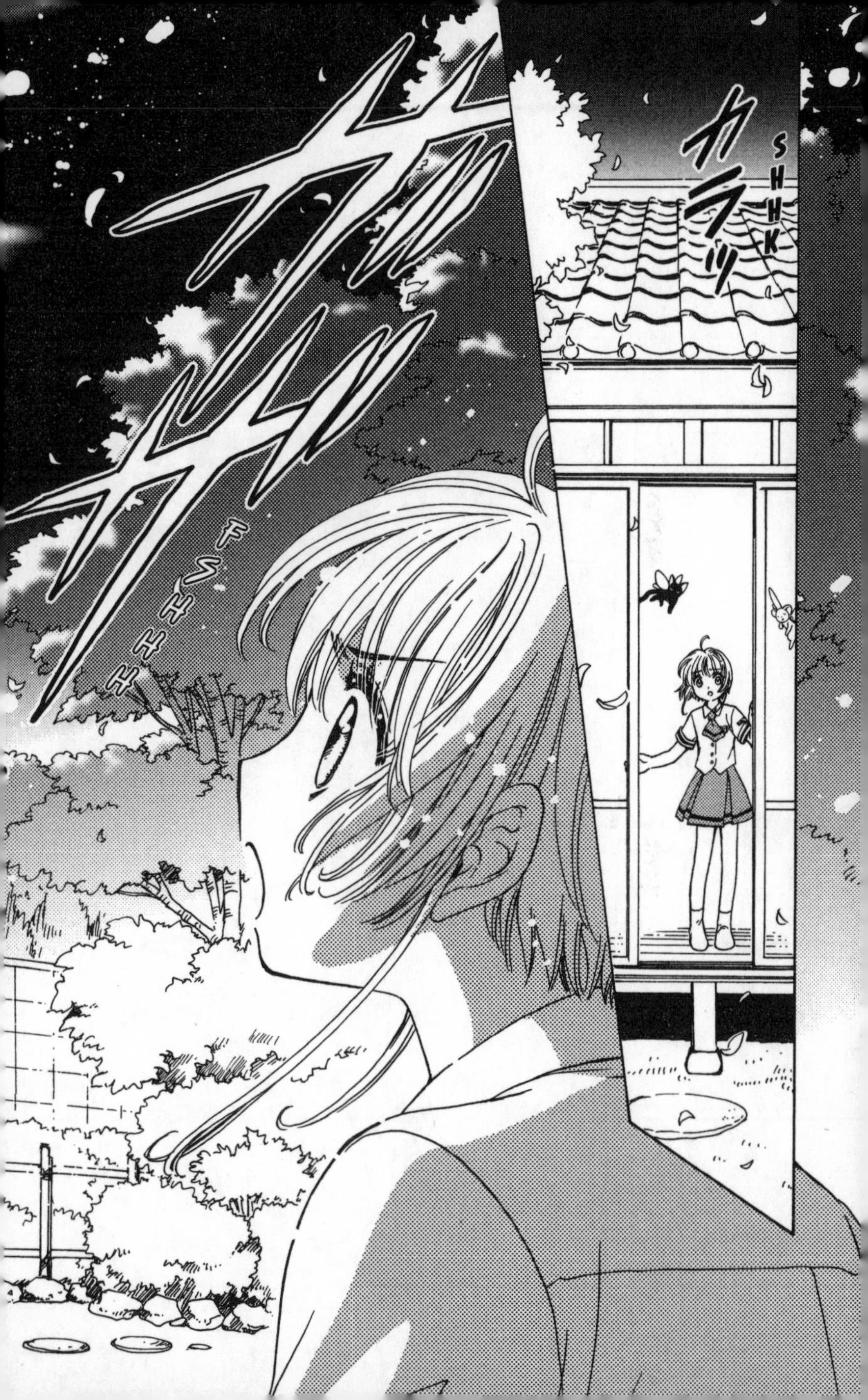
カラッ
SHHK
ザッ
FSHHHH

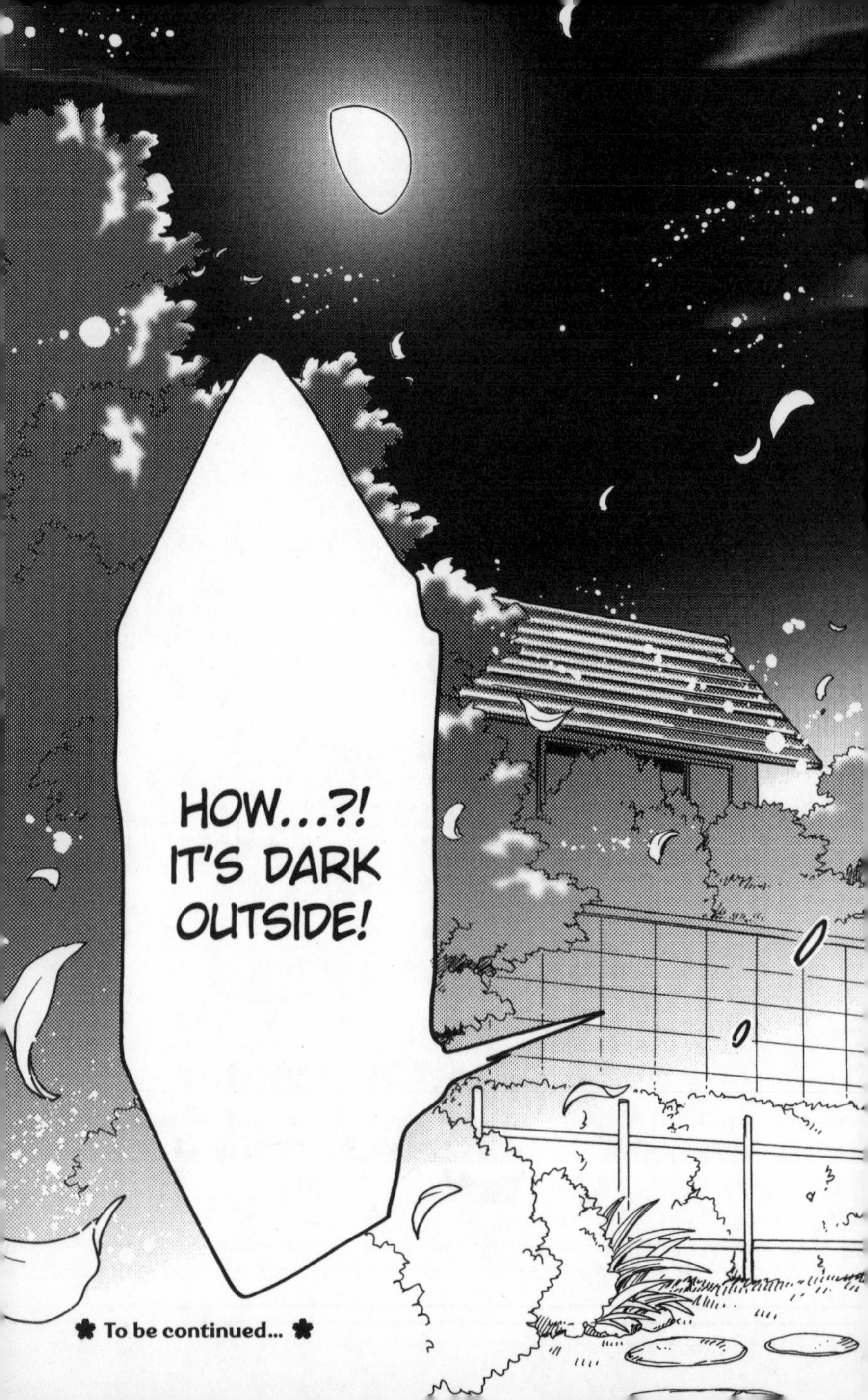
HOW...?! IT'S DARK OUTSIDE!

✿ To be continued... ✿

Cardcaptor
Sakura
CLEAR CARD

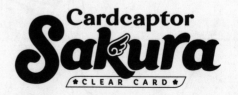

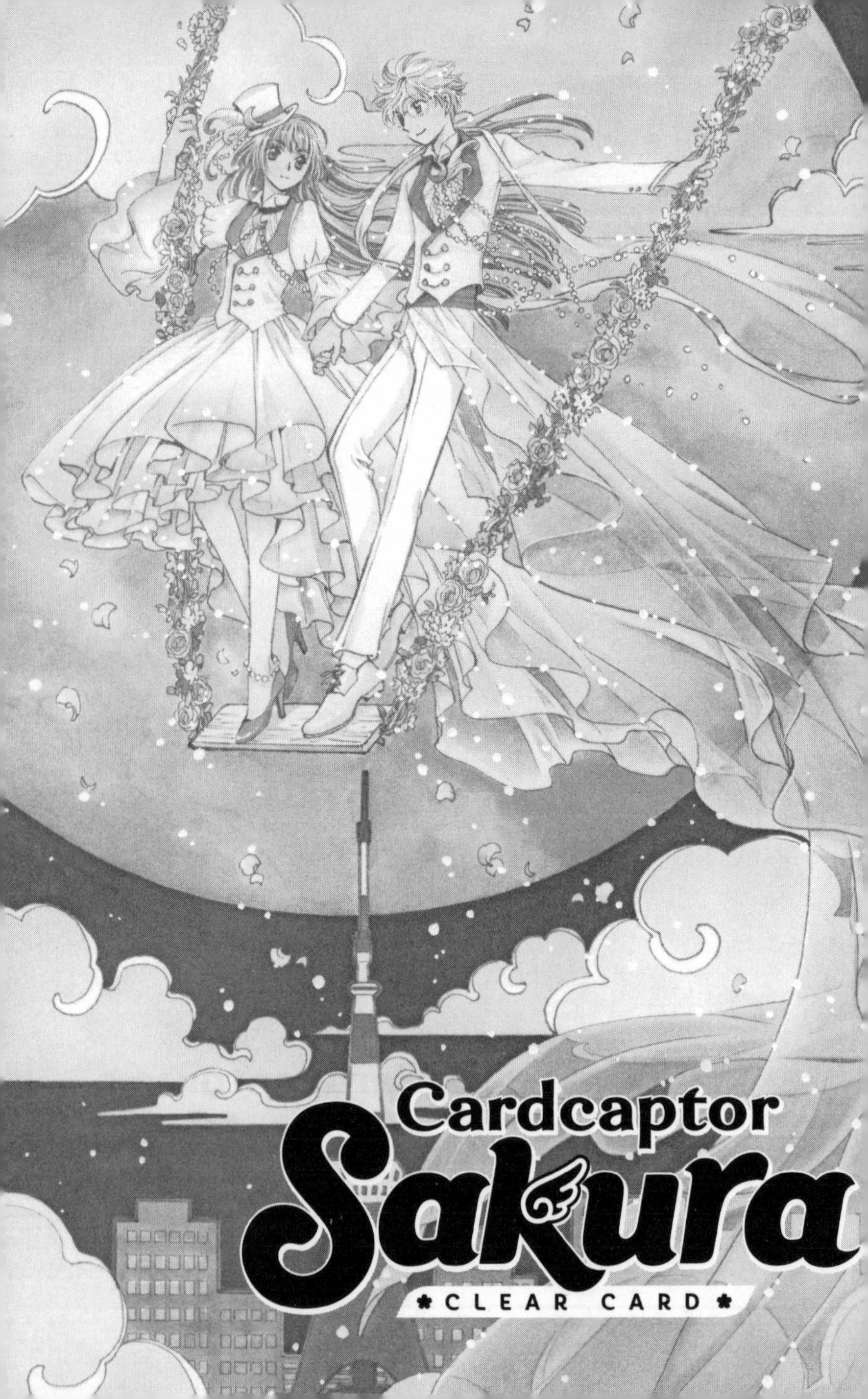
Cardcaptor
Sakura
CLEAR CARD

Cardcaptor Sakura

CLEAR CARD

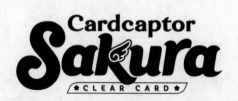

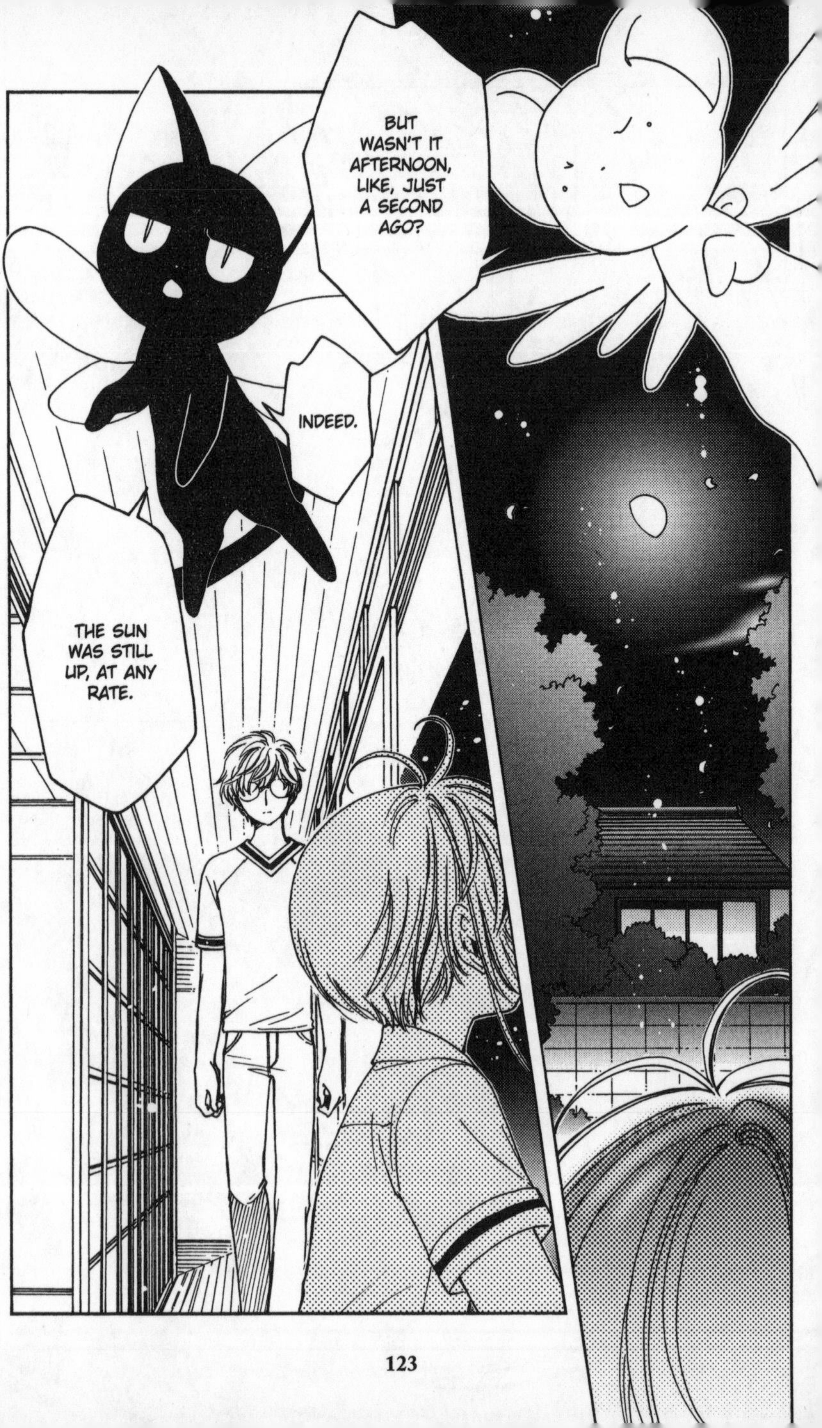
BUT WASN'T IT AFTERNOON, LIKE, JUST A SECOND AGO?
INDEED.
THE SUN WAS STILL UP, AT ANY RATE.

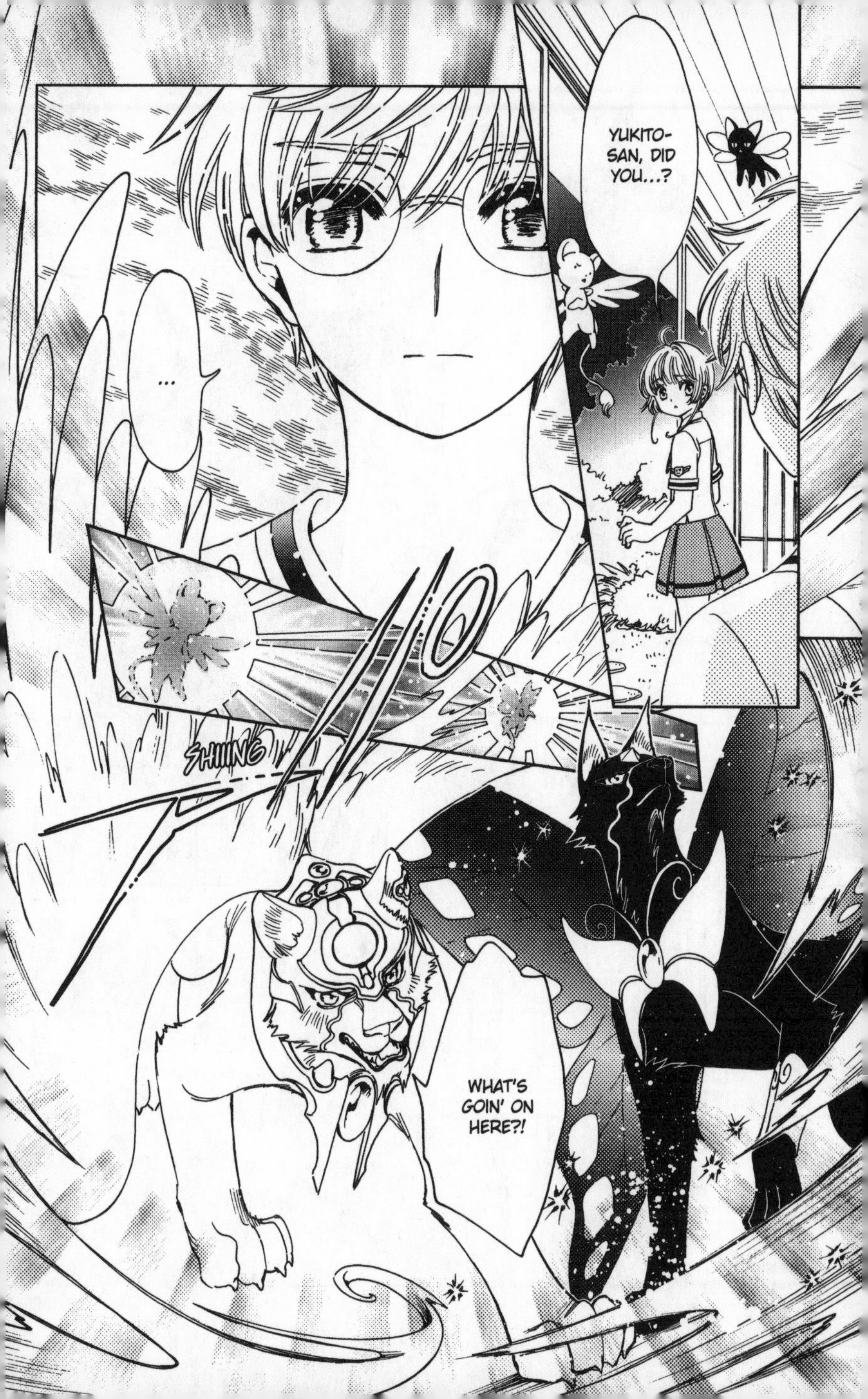
YUKITO-SAN, DID YOU...?
...
SHIIING
WHAT'S GOIN' ON HERE?!

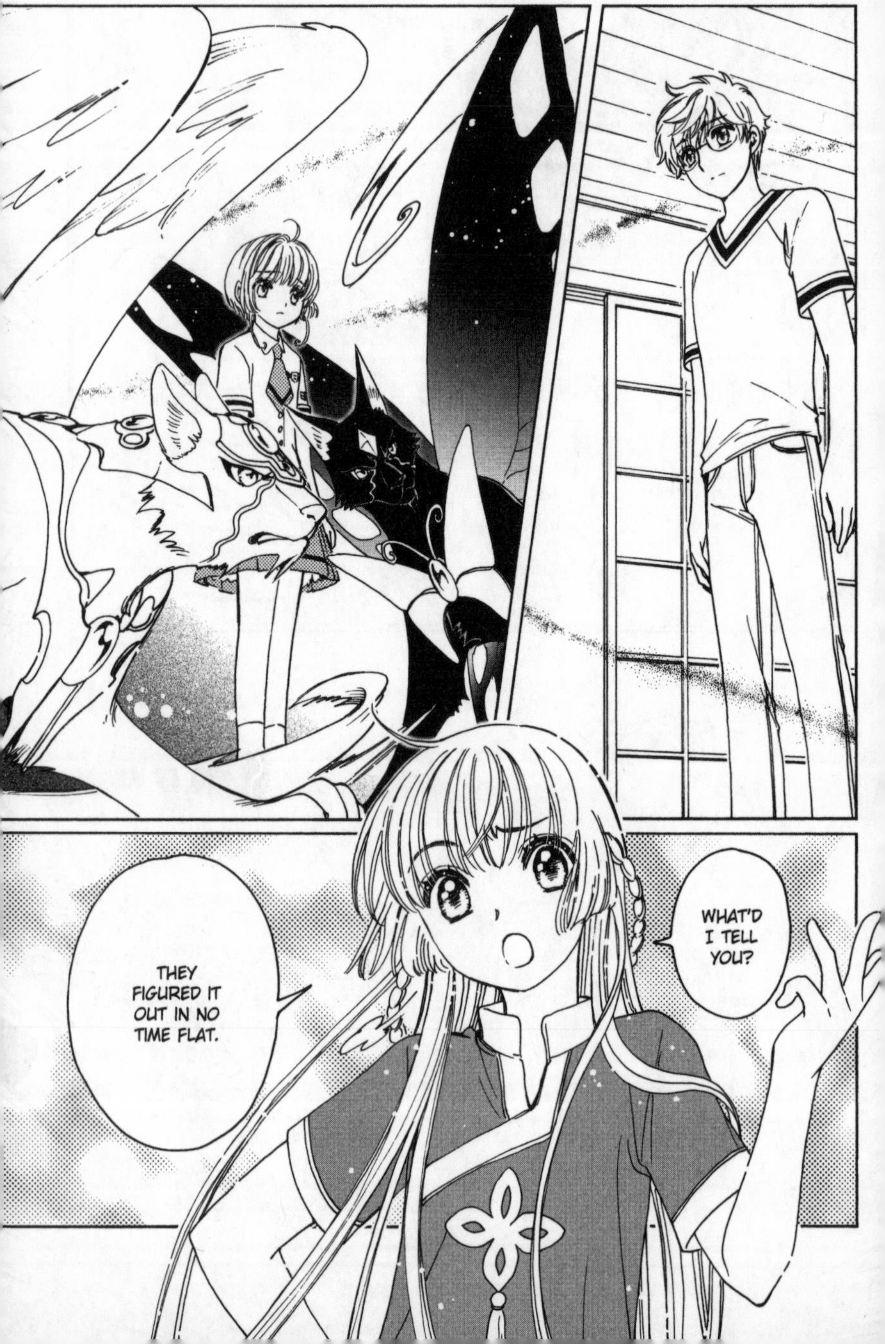
WHAT'D I TELL YOU?
THEY FIGURED IT OUT IN NO TIME FLAT.

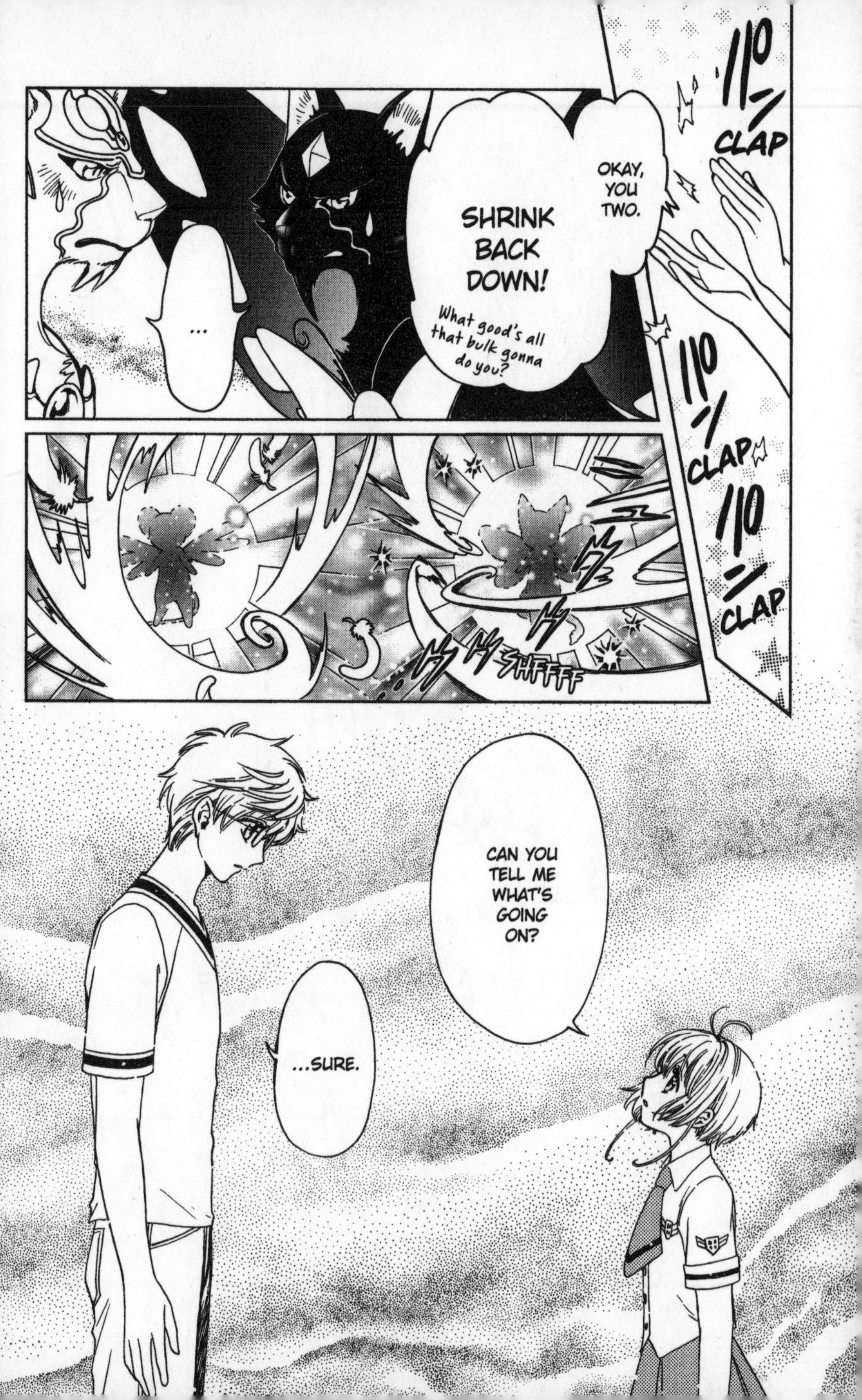
CLAP
CLAP
CLAP
OKAY, YOU TWO.
SHRINK BACK DOWN!
What good's all that bulk gonna do you?
...
SHFFFF
CAN YOU TELL ME WHAT'S GOING ON?
...SURE.

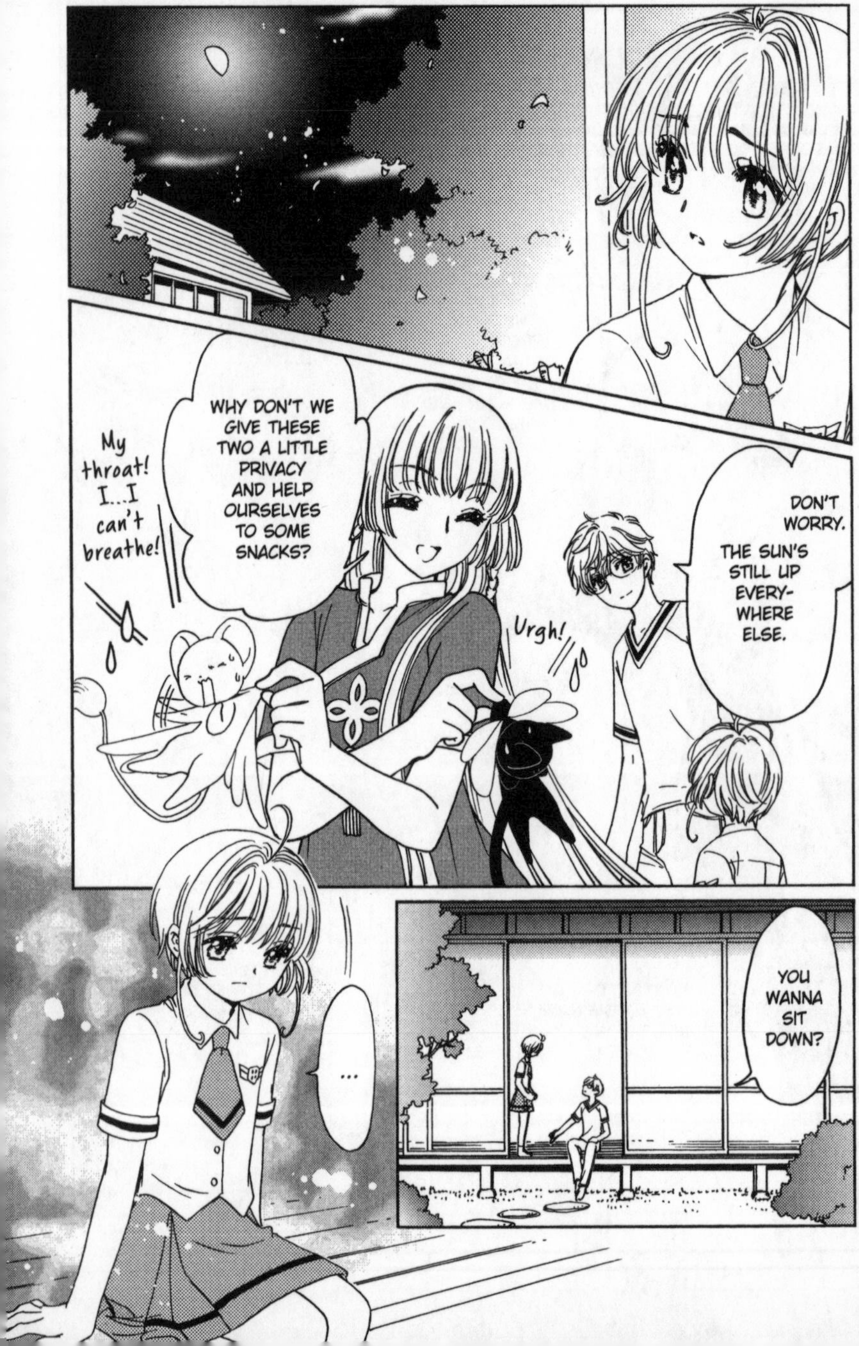
DON'T WORRY. THE SUN'S STILL UP EVERYWHERE ELSE.
WHY DON'T WE GIVE THESE TWO A LITTLE PRIVACY AND HELP OURSELVES TO SOME SNACKS?
My throat! I...I can't breathe!
Urgh!
YOU WANNA SIT DOWN?
...

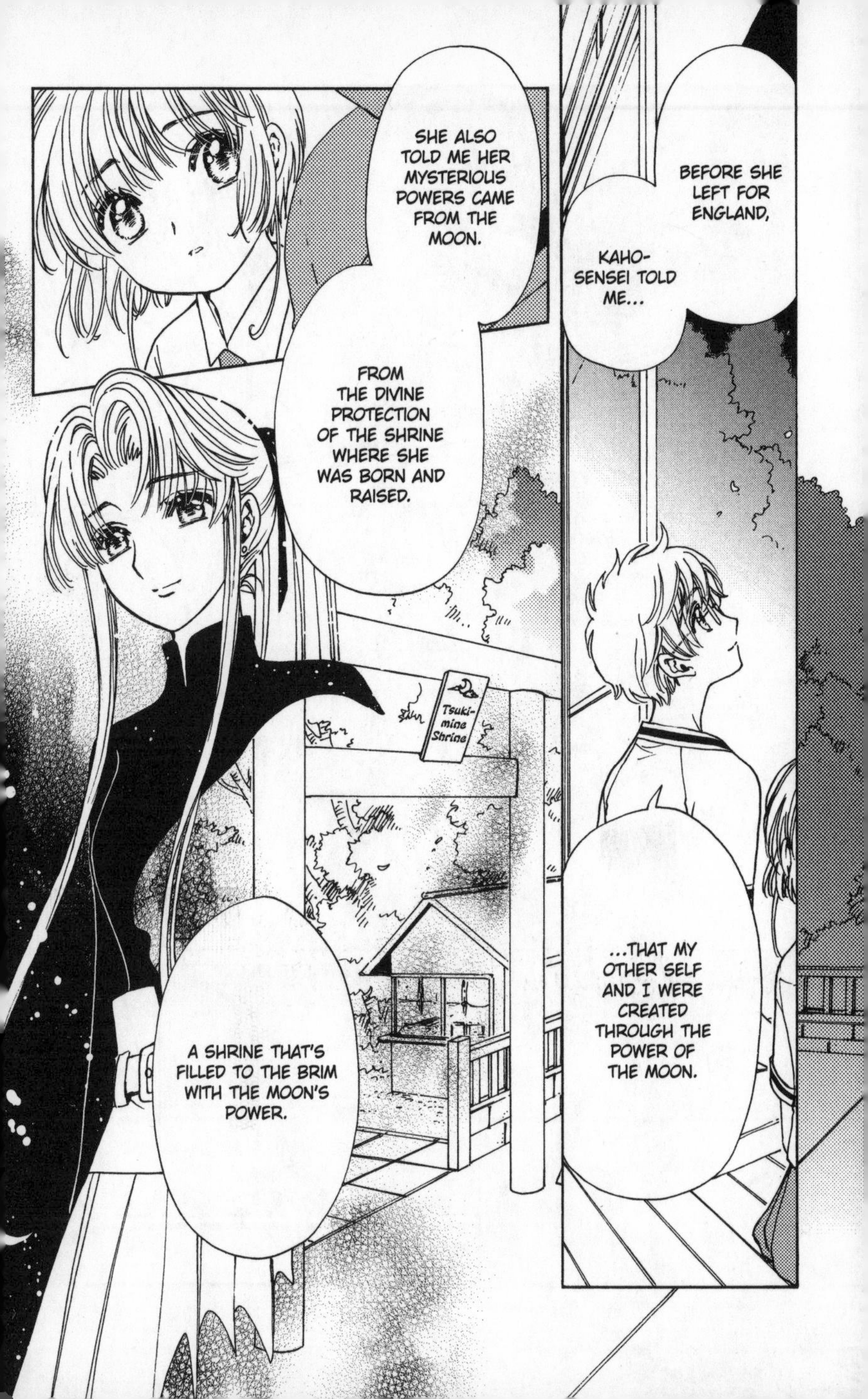
BEFORE SHE LEFT FOR ENGLAND,
KAHO-SENSEI TOLD ME...
...THAT MY OTHER SELF AND I WERE CREATED THROUGH THE POWER OF THE MOON.
SHE ALSO TOLD ME HER MYSTERIOUS POWERS CAME FROM THE MOON.
FROM THE DIVINE PROTECTION OF THE SHRINE WHERE SHE WAS BORN AND RAISED.
Tsukimine Shrine
A SHRINE THAT'S FILLED TO THE BRIM WITH THE MOON'S POWER.

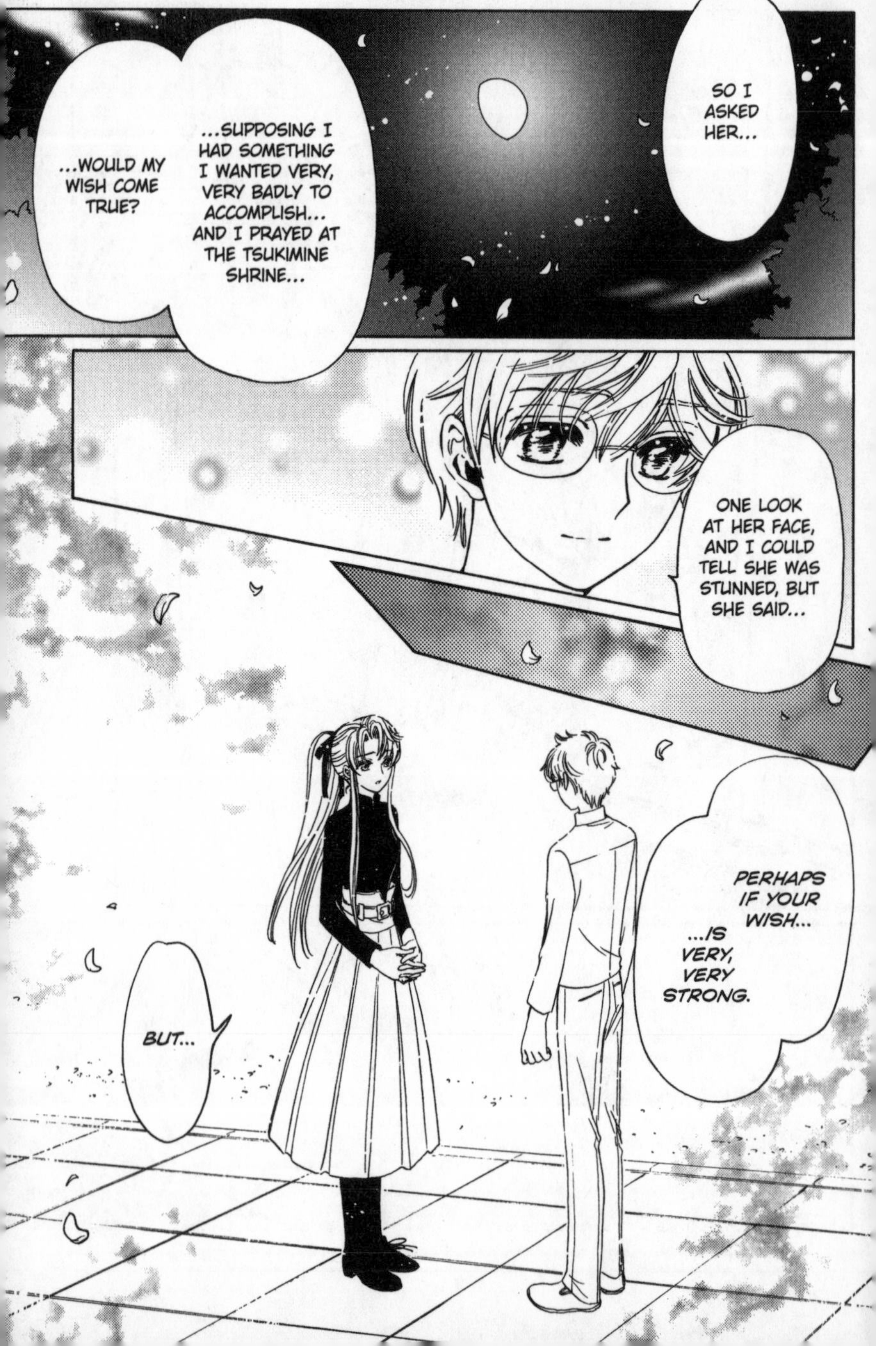
SO I ASKED HER...
...SUPPOSING I HAD SOMETHING I WANTED VERY, VERY BADLY TO ACCOMPLISH... AND I PRAYED AT THE TSUKIMINE SHRINE...
...WOULD MY WISH COME TRUE?
ONE LOOK AT HER FACE, AND I COULD TELL SHE WAS STUNNED, BUT SHE SAID...
PERHAPS IF YOUR WISH...
...IS VERY, VERY STRONG.
BUT...

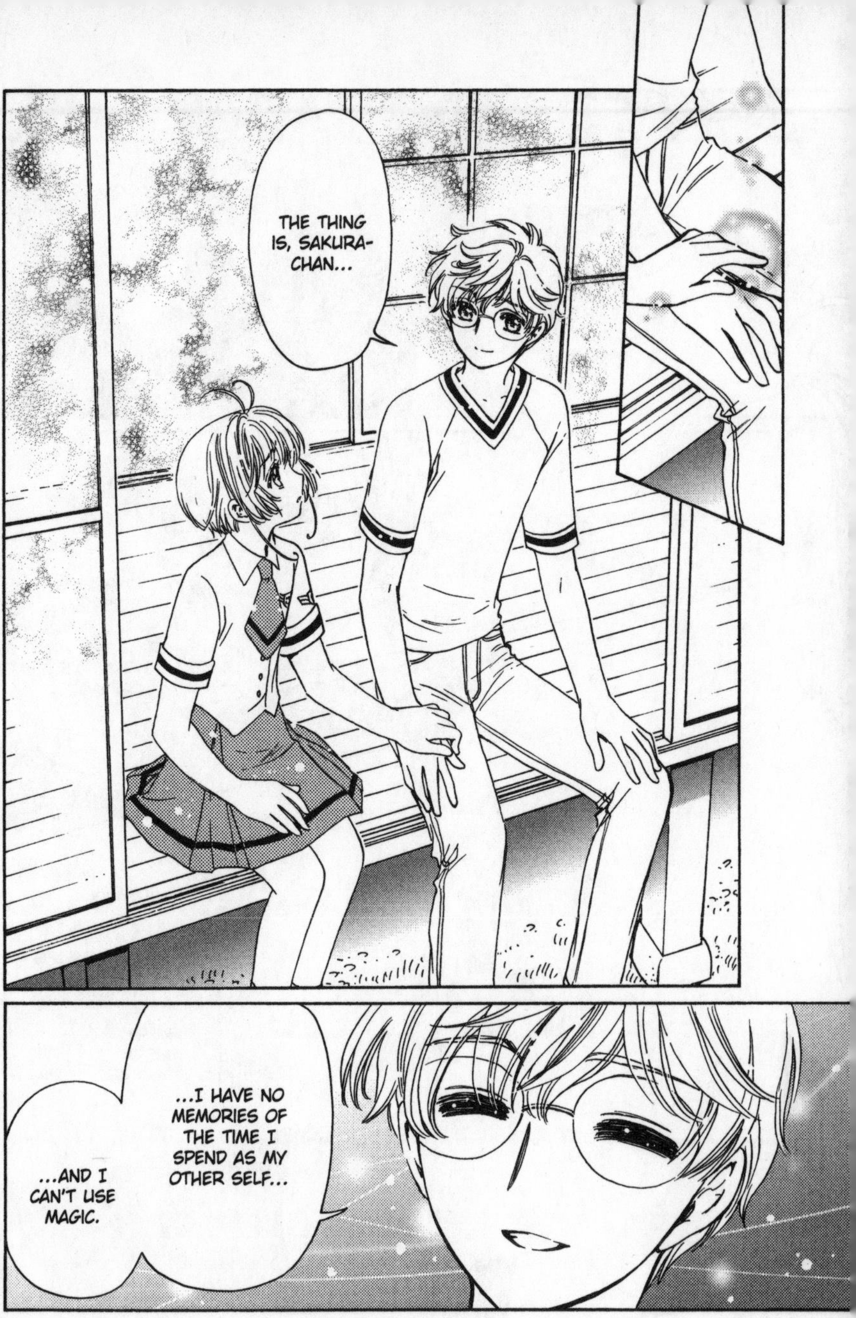
THE THING IS, SAKURA-CHAN...
...I HAVE NO MEMORIES OF THE TIME I SPEND AS MY OTHER SELF...
...AND I CAN'T USE MAGIC.

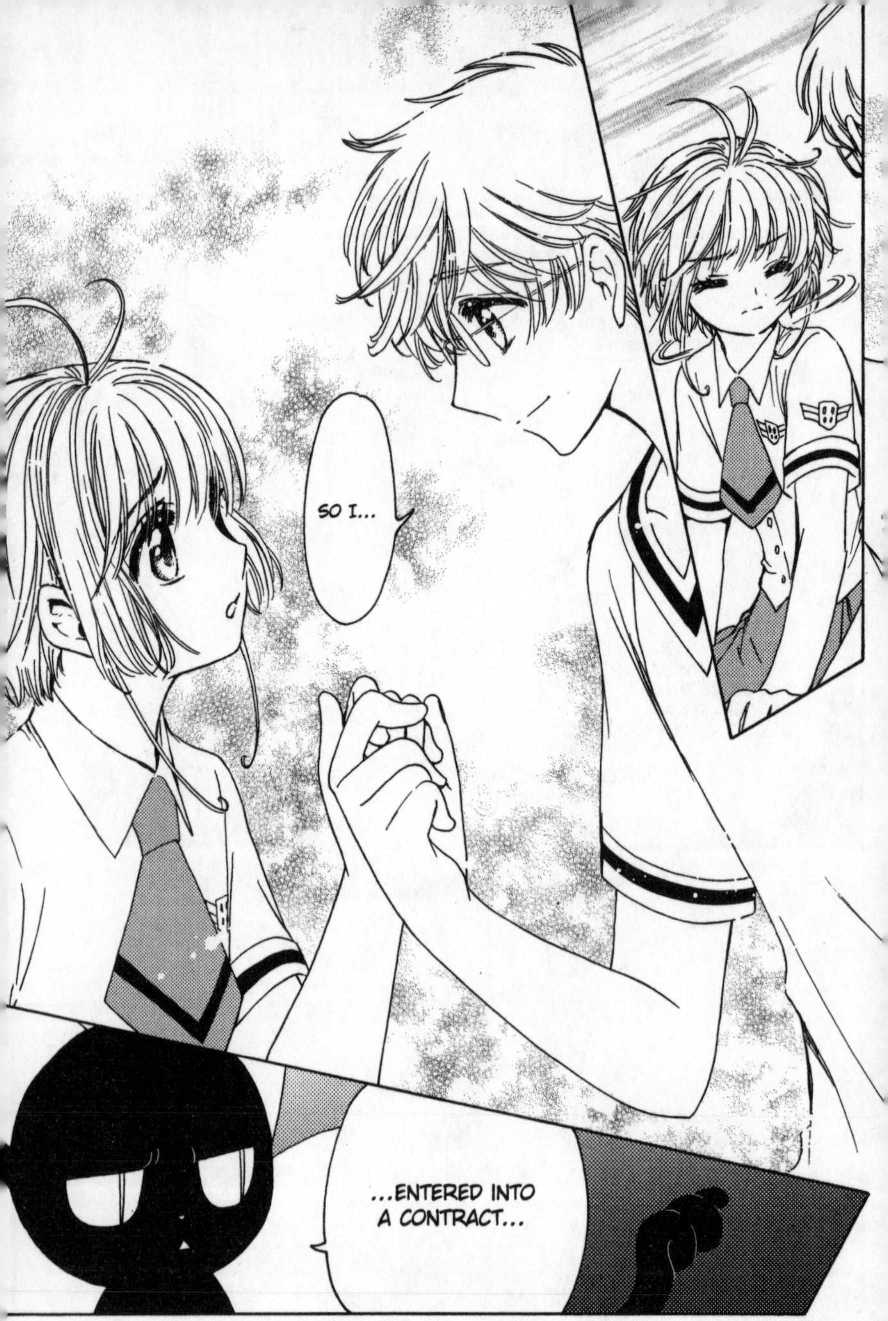
SO I...
...ENTERED INTO A CONTRACT...

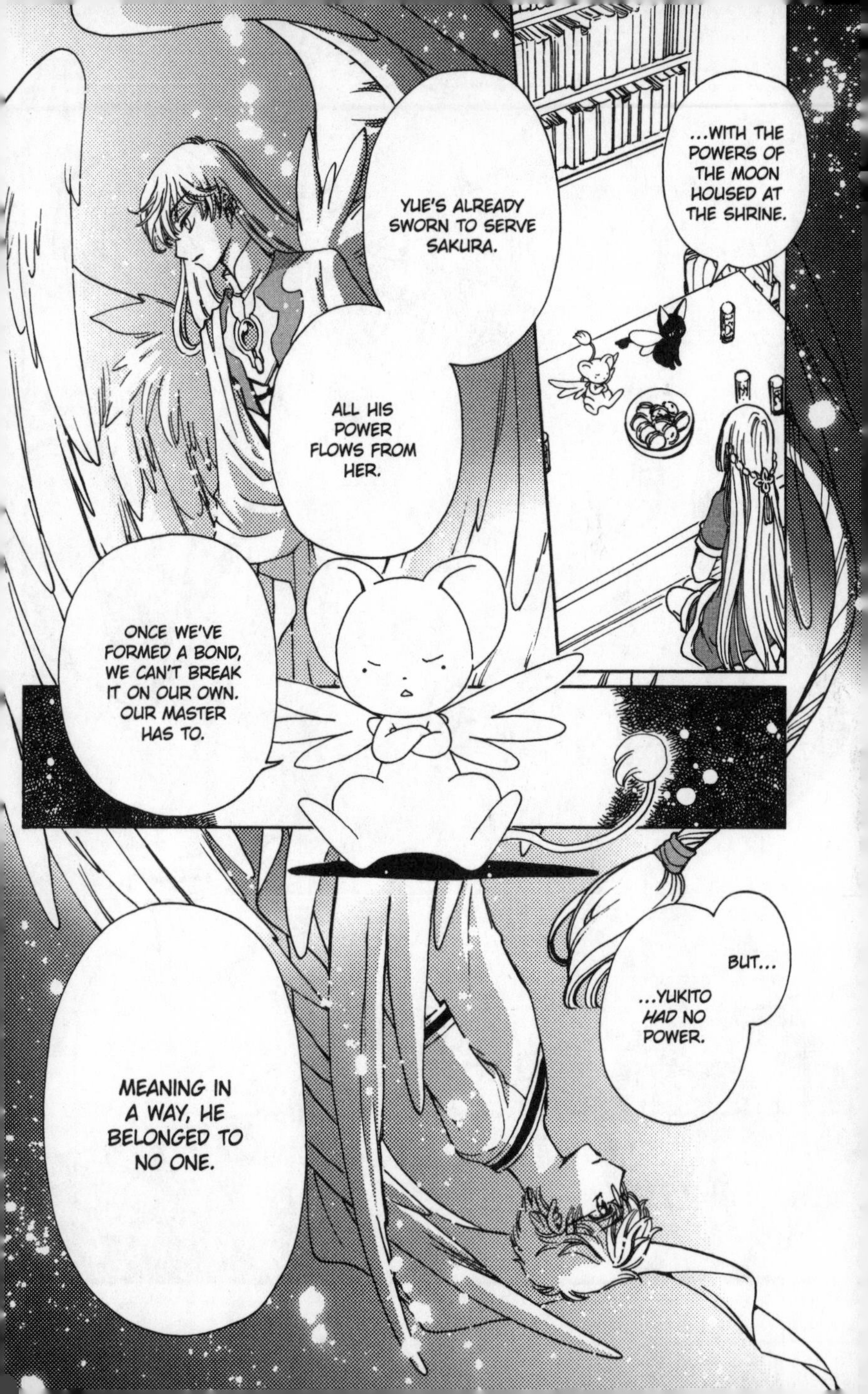
...WITH THE POWERS OF THE MOON HOUSED AT THE SHRINE.
YUE'S ALREADY SWORN TO SERVE SAKURA.
ALL HIS POWER FLOWS FROM HER.
ONCE WE'VE FORMED A BOND, WE CAN'T BREAK IT ON OUR OWN. OUR MASTER HAS TO.
BUT... ...YUKITO *HAD* NO POWER.
MEANING IN A WAY, HE BELONGED TO NO ONE.

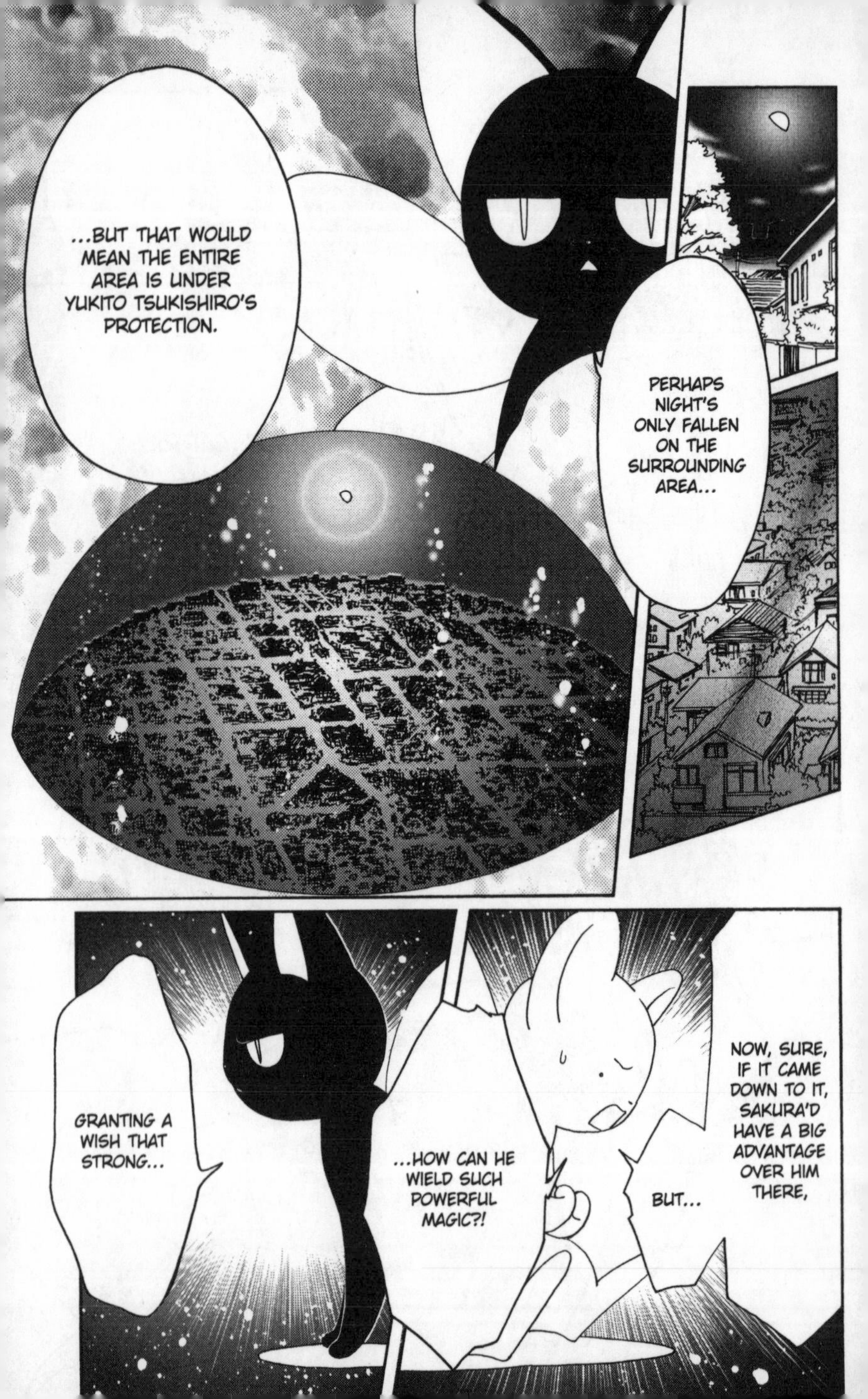
PERHAPS NIGHT'S ONLY FALLEN ON THE SURROUNDING AREA...
...BUT THAT WOULD MEAN THE ENTIRE AREA IS UNDER YUKITO TSUKISHIRO'S PROTECTION.
NOW, SURE, IF IT CAME DOWN TO IT, SAKURA'D HAVE A BIG ADVANTAGE OVER HIM THERE,
BUT...
...HOW CAN HE WIELD SUCH POWERFUL MAGIC?!
GRANTING A WISH THAT STRONG...

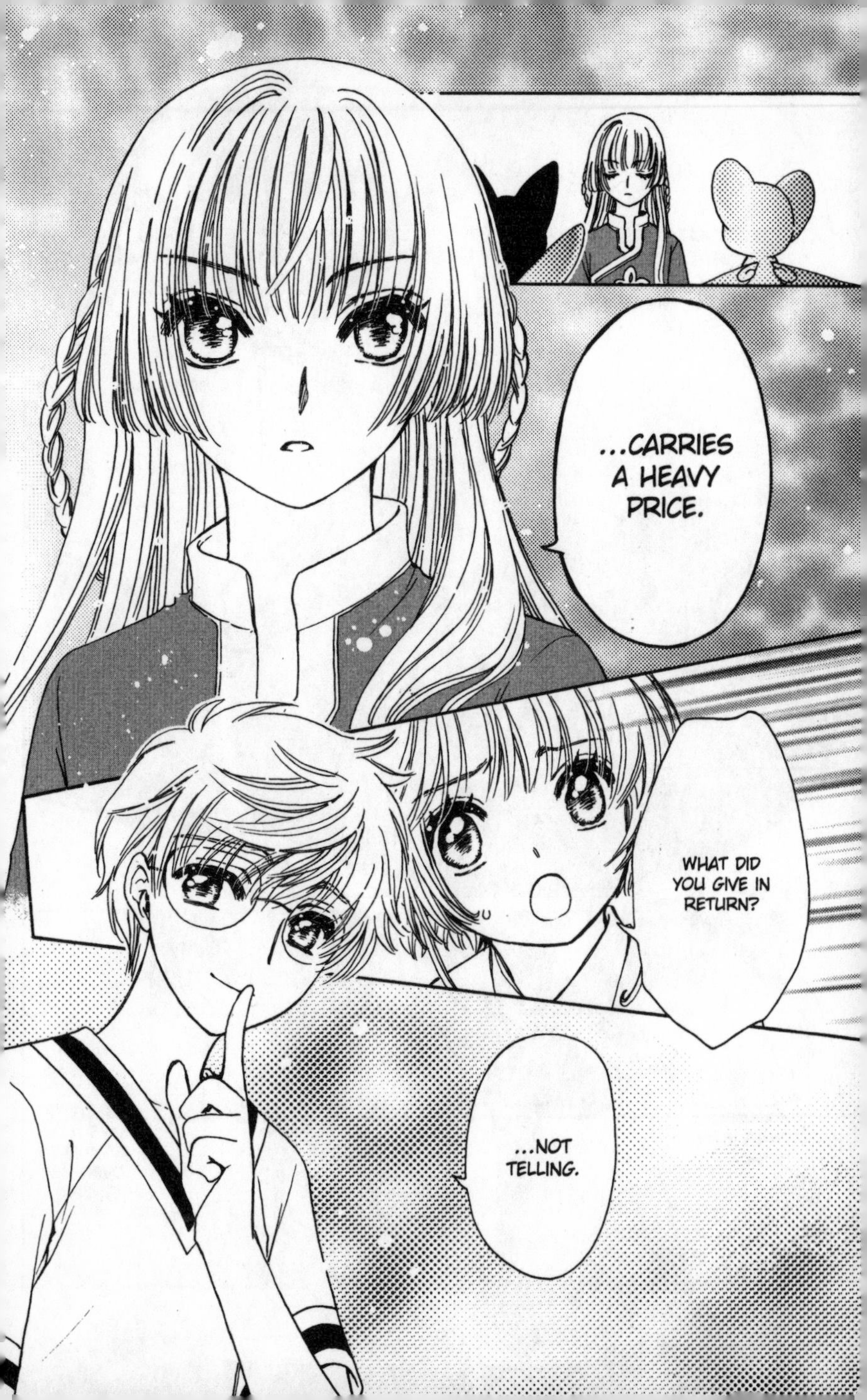
...CARRIES A HEAVY PRICE.
WHAT DID YOU GIVE IN RETURN?
...NOT TELLING.

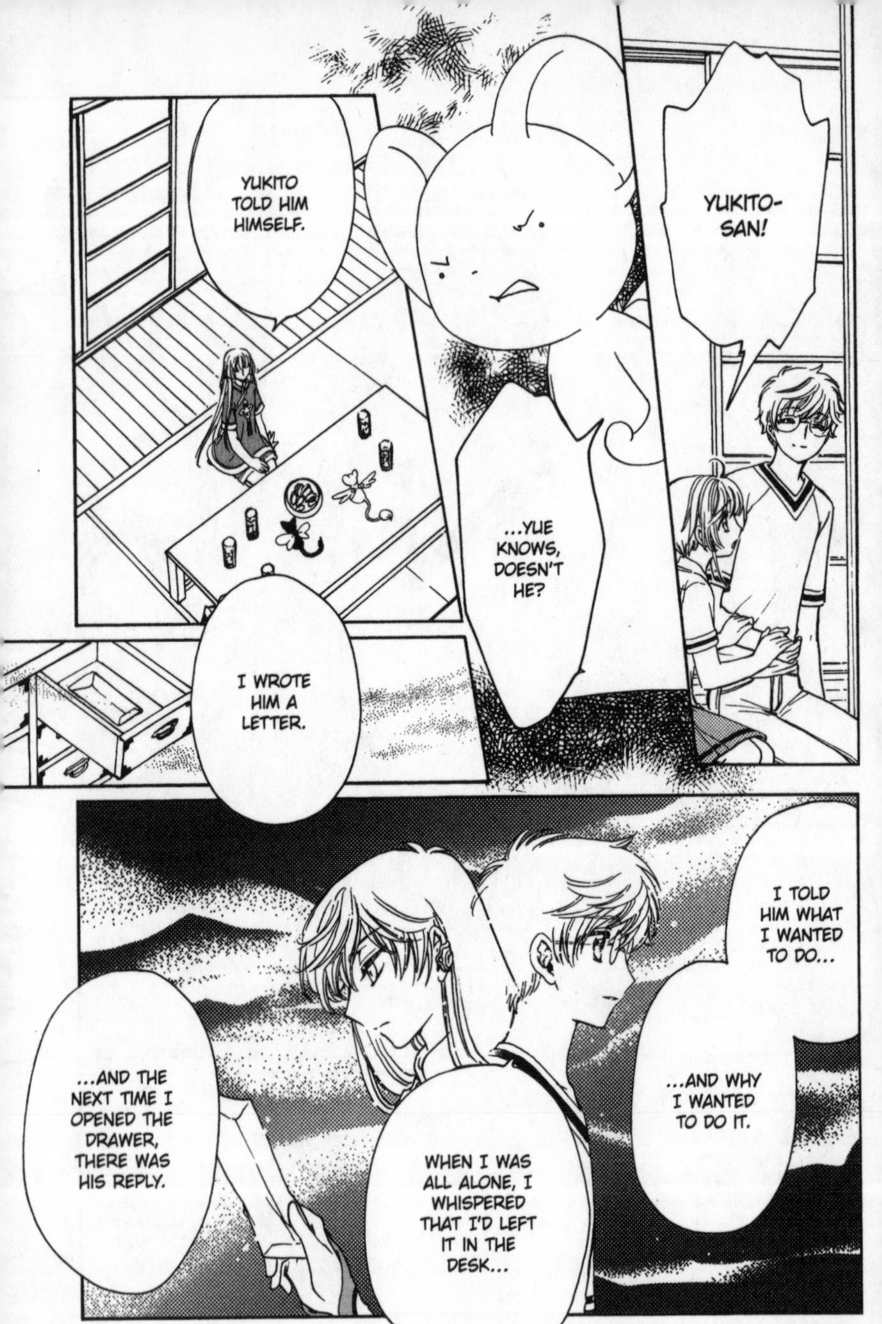
YUKITO-SAN!
...YUE KNOWS, DOESN'T HE?
YUKITO TOLD HIM HIMSELF.
I WROTE HIM A LETTER.
I TOLD HIM WHAT I WANTED TO DO...
...AND WHY I WANTED TO DO IT.
WHEN I WAS ALL ALONE, I WHISPERED THAT I'D LEFT IT IN THE DESK...
...AND THE NEXT TIME I OPENED THE DRAWER, THERE WAS HIS REPLY.

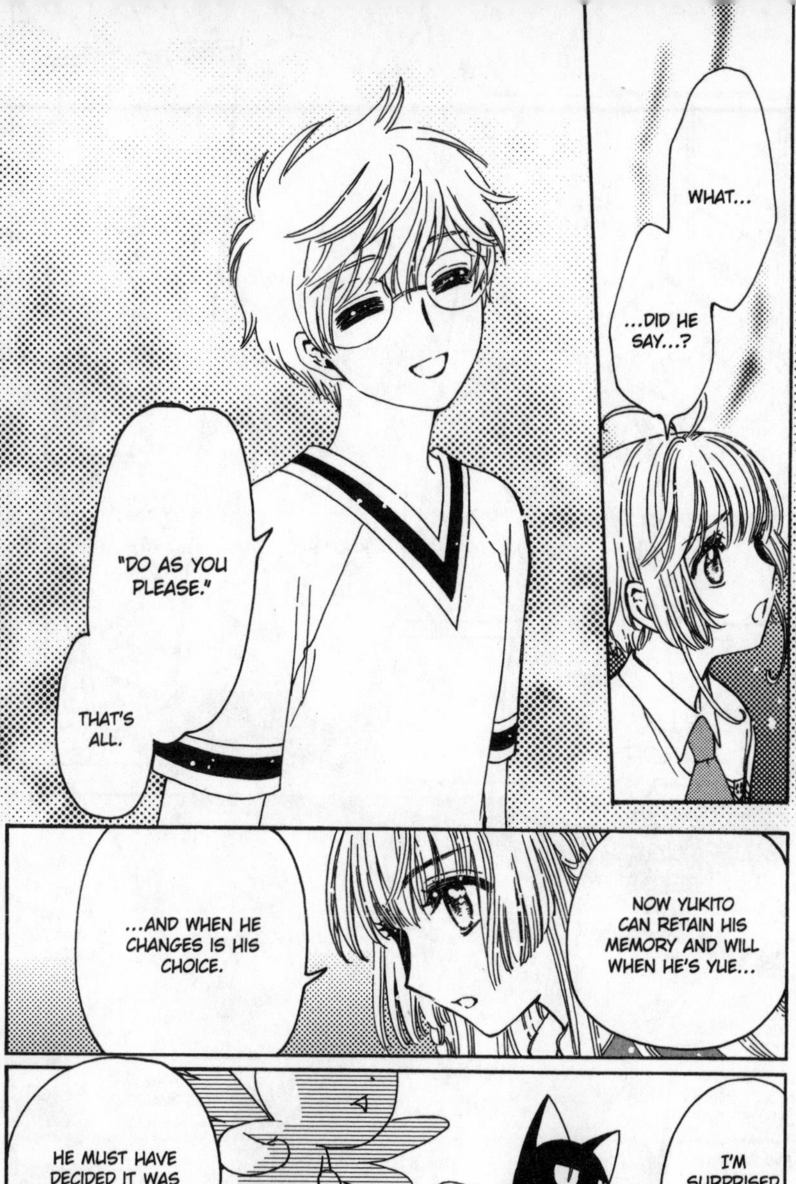
WHAT...
...DID HE SAY...?
"DO AS YOU PLEASE."
THAT'S ALL.
NOW YUKITO CAN RETAIN HIS MEMORY AND WILL WHEN HE'S YUE...
...AND WHEN HE CHANGES IS HIS CHOICE.
I'M SURPRISED YUE AGREED TO THAT!
HE MUST HAVE DECIDED IT WAS BEST FOR HIS MASTER...

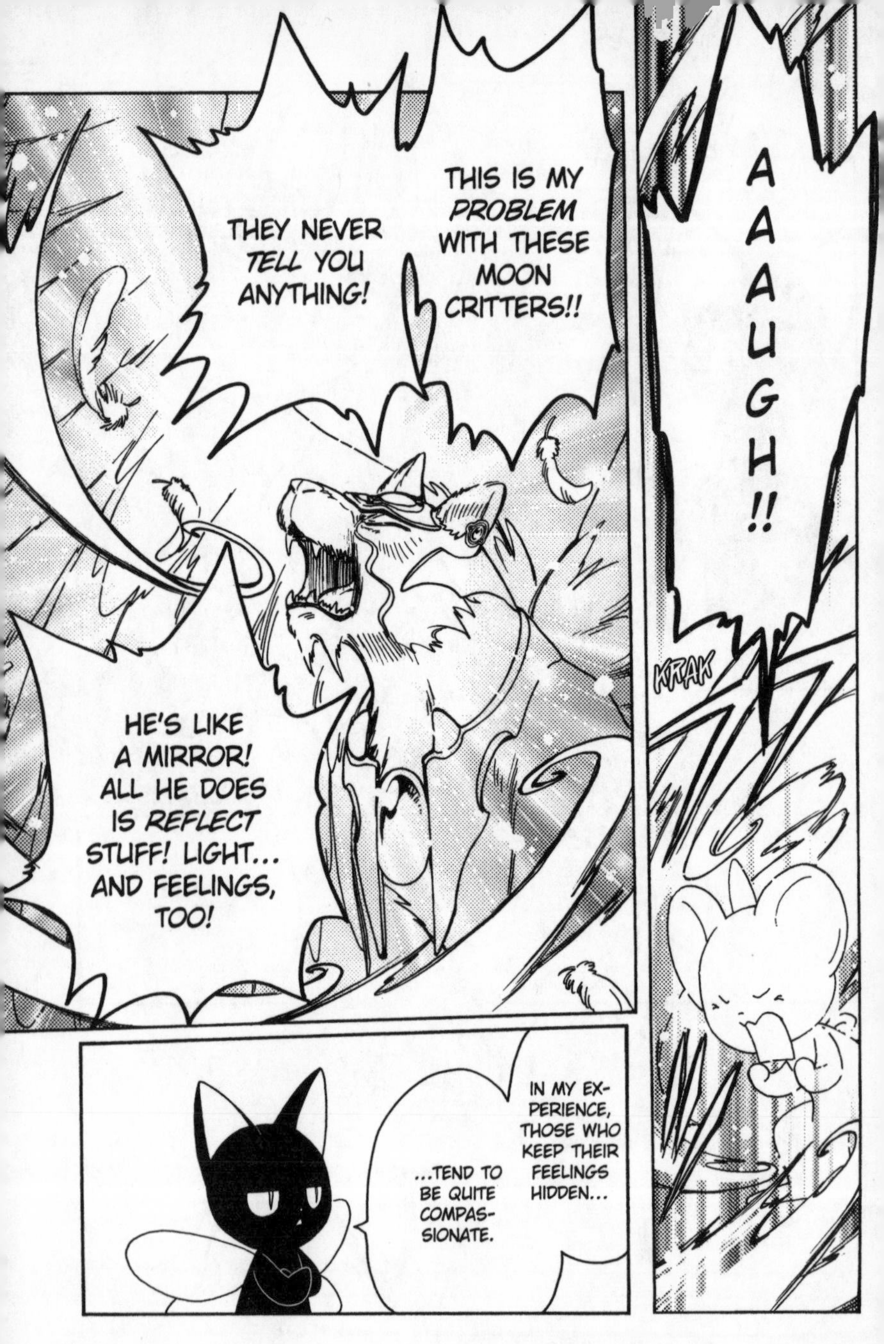
AAAUGH!!
KRAK
THIS IS MY PROBLEM WITH THESE MOON CRITTERS!!
THEY NEVER TELL YOU ANYTHING!
HE'S LIKE A MIRROR! ALL HE DOES IS REFLECT STUFF! LIGHT... AND FEELINGS, TOO!
IN MY EX-PERIENCE, THOSE WHO KEEP THEIR FEELINGS HIDDEN...
...TEND TO BE QUITE COMPAS-SIONATE.

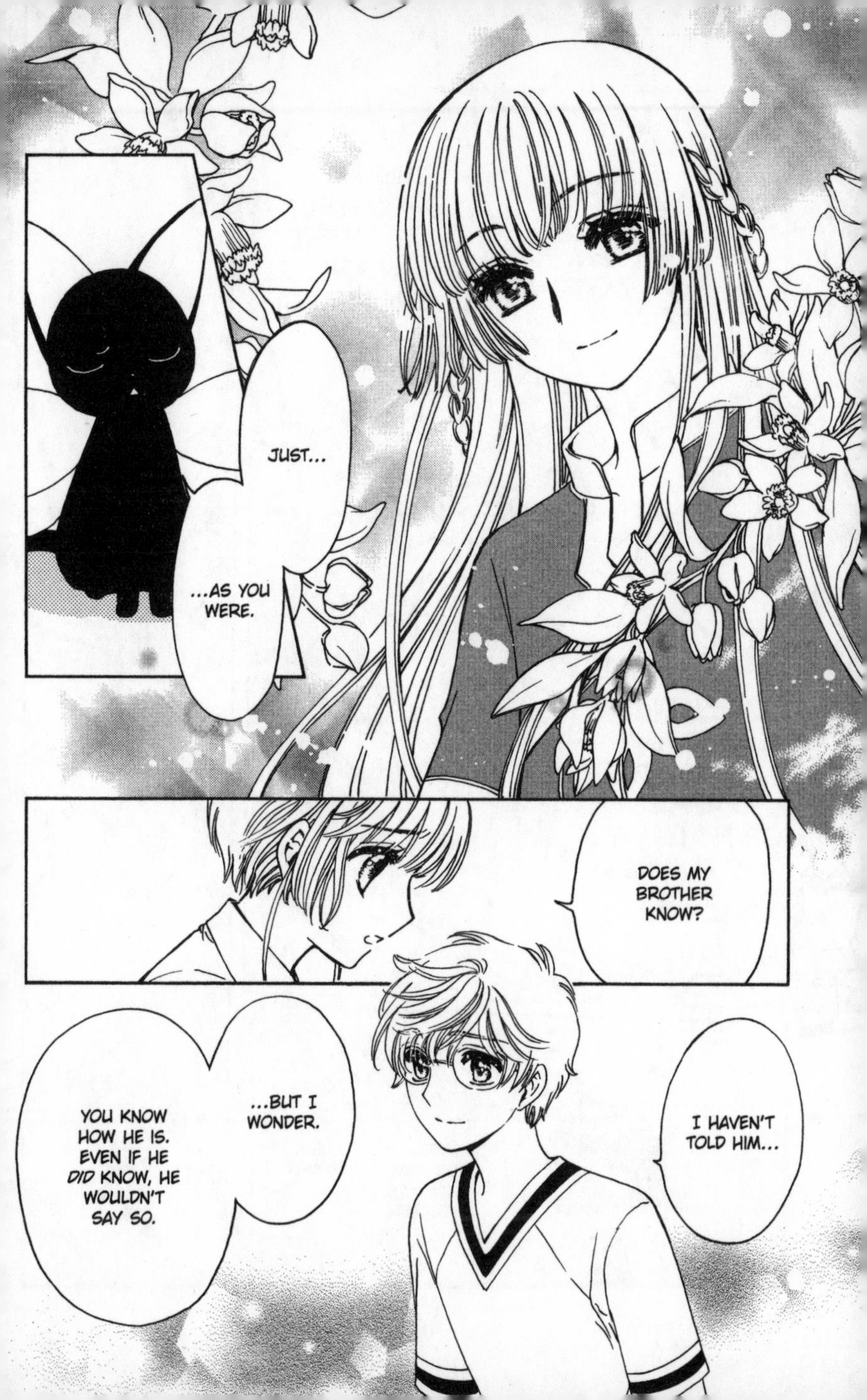
JUST...
...AS YOU WERE.
DOES MY BROTHER KNOW?
I HAVEN'T TOLD HIM...
...BUT I WONDER.
YOU KNOW HOW HE IS. EVEN IF HE *DID* KNOW, HE WOULDN'T SAY SO.

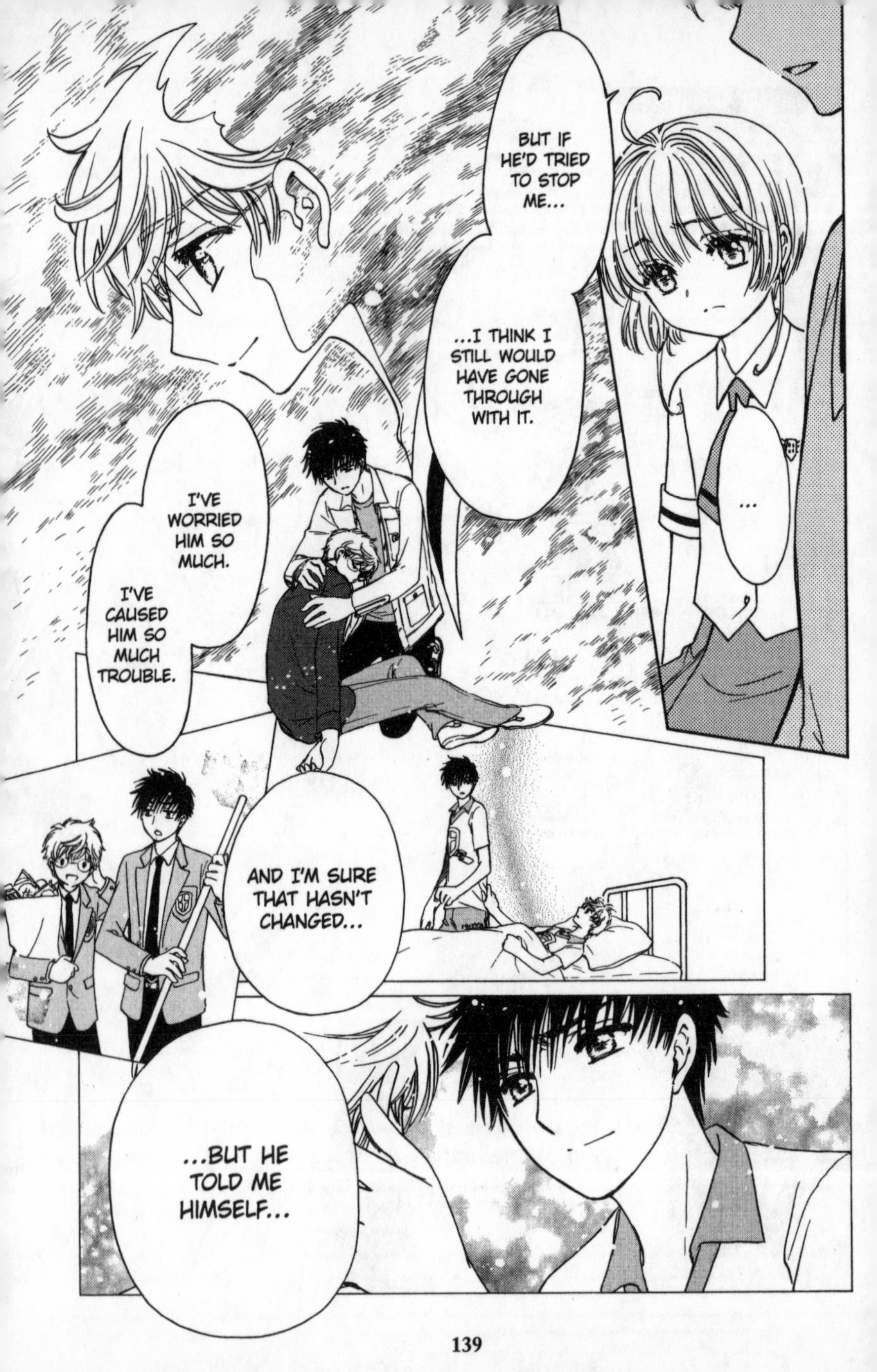
BUT IF HE'D TRIED TO STOP ME...
...I THINK I STILL WOULD HAVE GONE THROUGH WITH IT.
...
I'VE WORRIED HIM SO MUCH.
I'VE CAUSED HIM SO MUCH TROUBLE.
AND I'M SURE THAT HASN'T CHANGED...
...BUT HE TOLD ME HIMSELF...

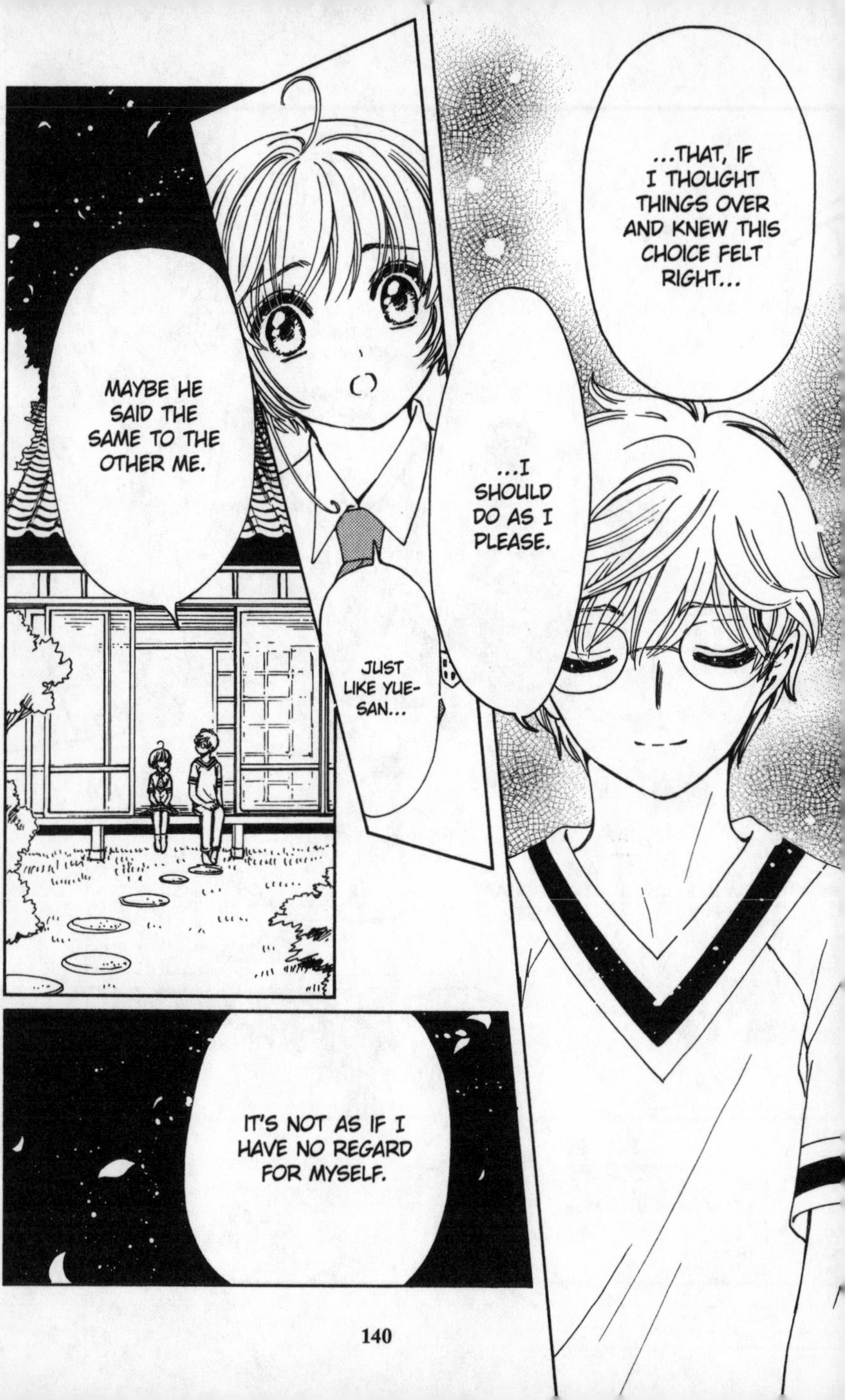
...THAT, IF I THOUGHT THINGS OVER AND KNEW THIS CHOICE FELT RIGHT...
...I SHOULD DO AS I PLEASE.
JUST LIKE YUE-SAN...
MAYBE HE SAID THE SAME TO THE OTHER ME.
IT'S NOT AS IF I HAVE NO REGARD FOR MYSELF.

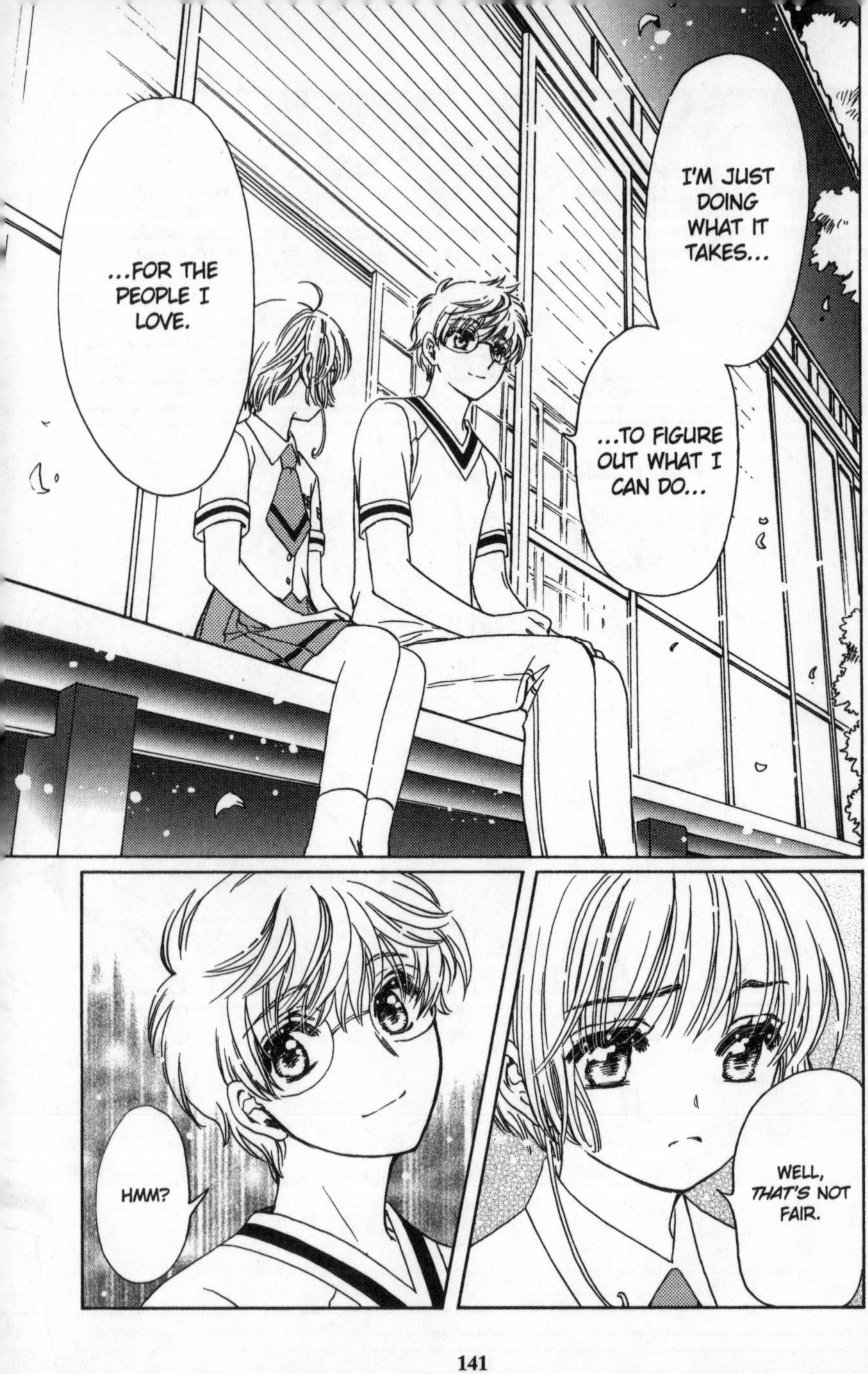
I'M JUST DOING WHAT IT TAKES...
...TO FIGURE OUT WHAT I CAN DO...
...FOR THE PEOPLE I LOVE.
WELL, *THAT'S* NOT FAIR.
HMM?

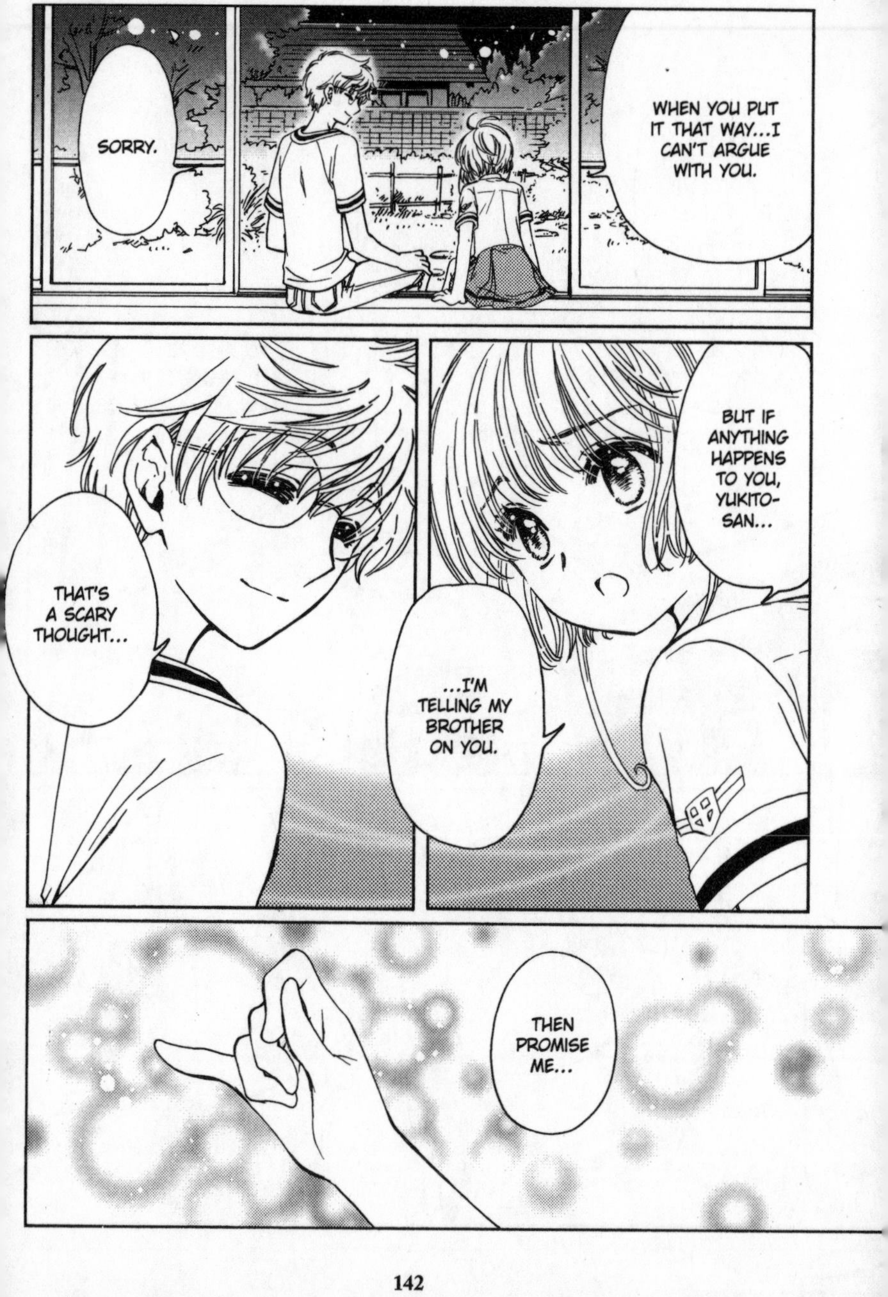
WHEN YOU PUT IT THAT WAY...I CAN'T ARGUE WITH YOU.
SORRY.
BUT IF ANYTHING HAPPENS TO YOU, YUKITO-SAN...
...I'M TELLING MY BROTHER ON YOU.
THAT'S A SCARY THOUGHT...
THEN PROMISE ME...

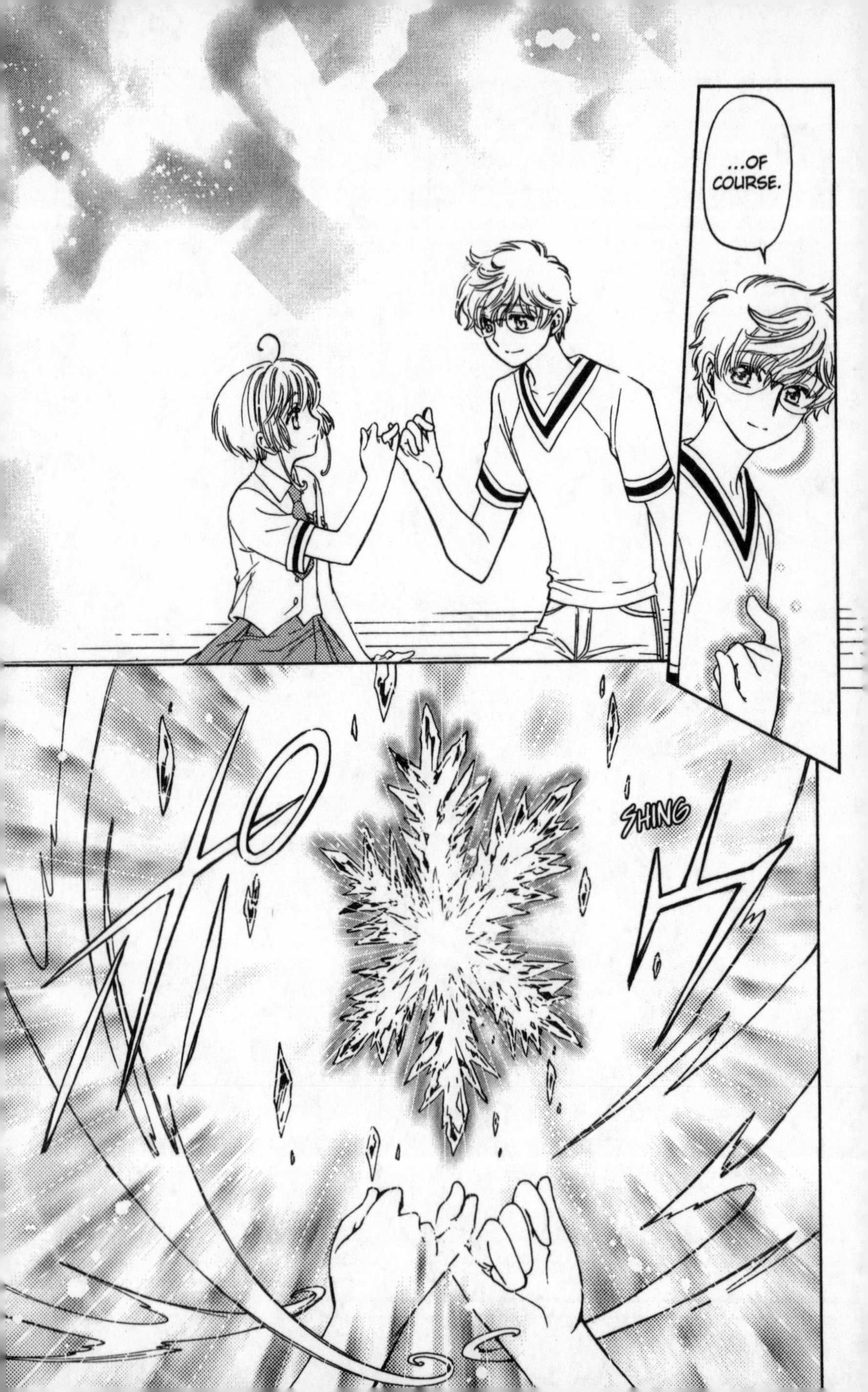
...OF COURSE.
SHING

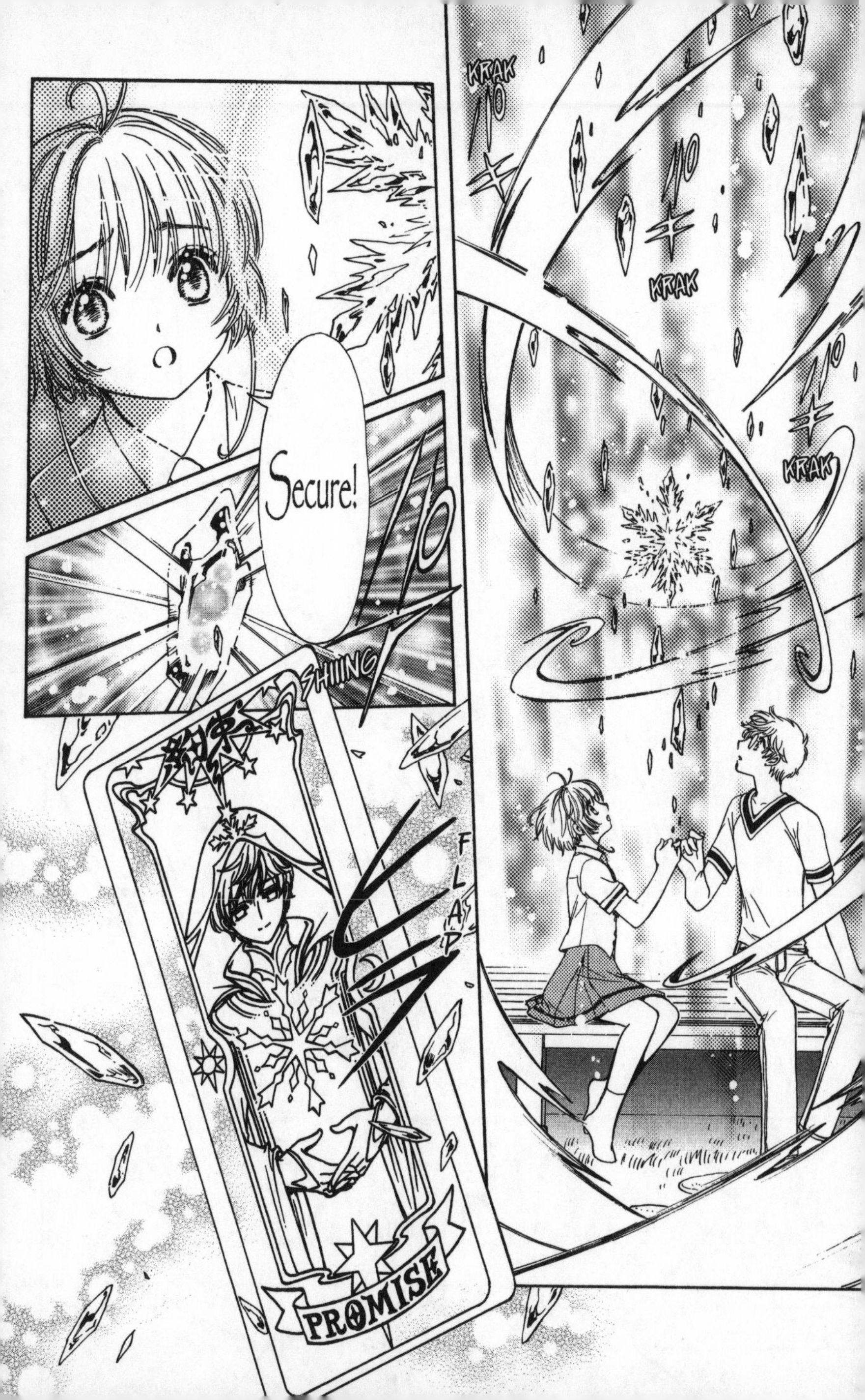
KRAK
KRAK
KRAK
Secure!
SHIING
FLAP
PROMISE

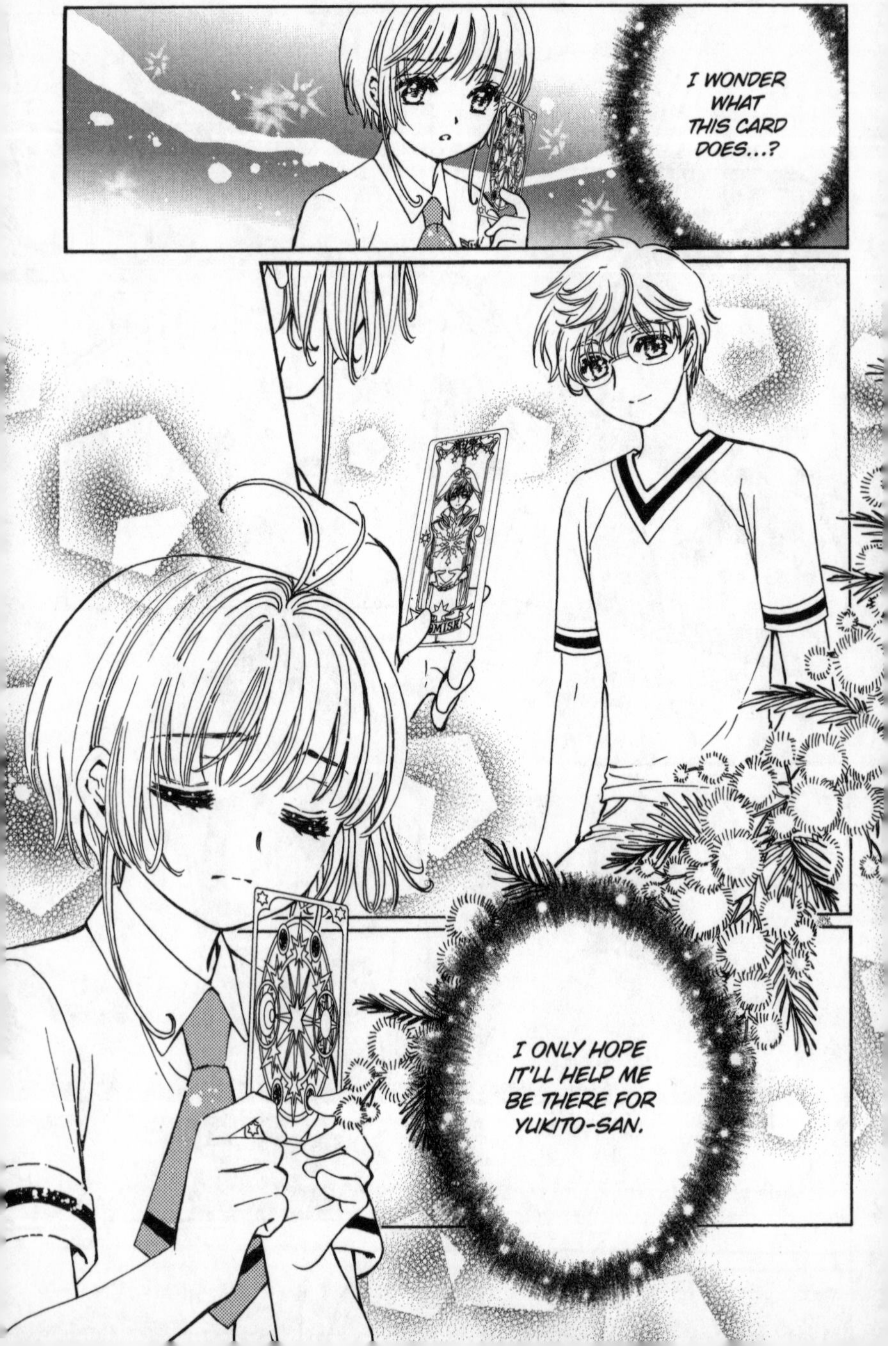
I WONDER WHAT THIS CARD DOES...?
I ONLY HOPE IT'LL HELP ME BE THERE FOR YUKITO-SAN.

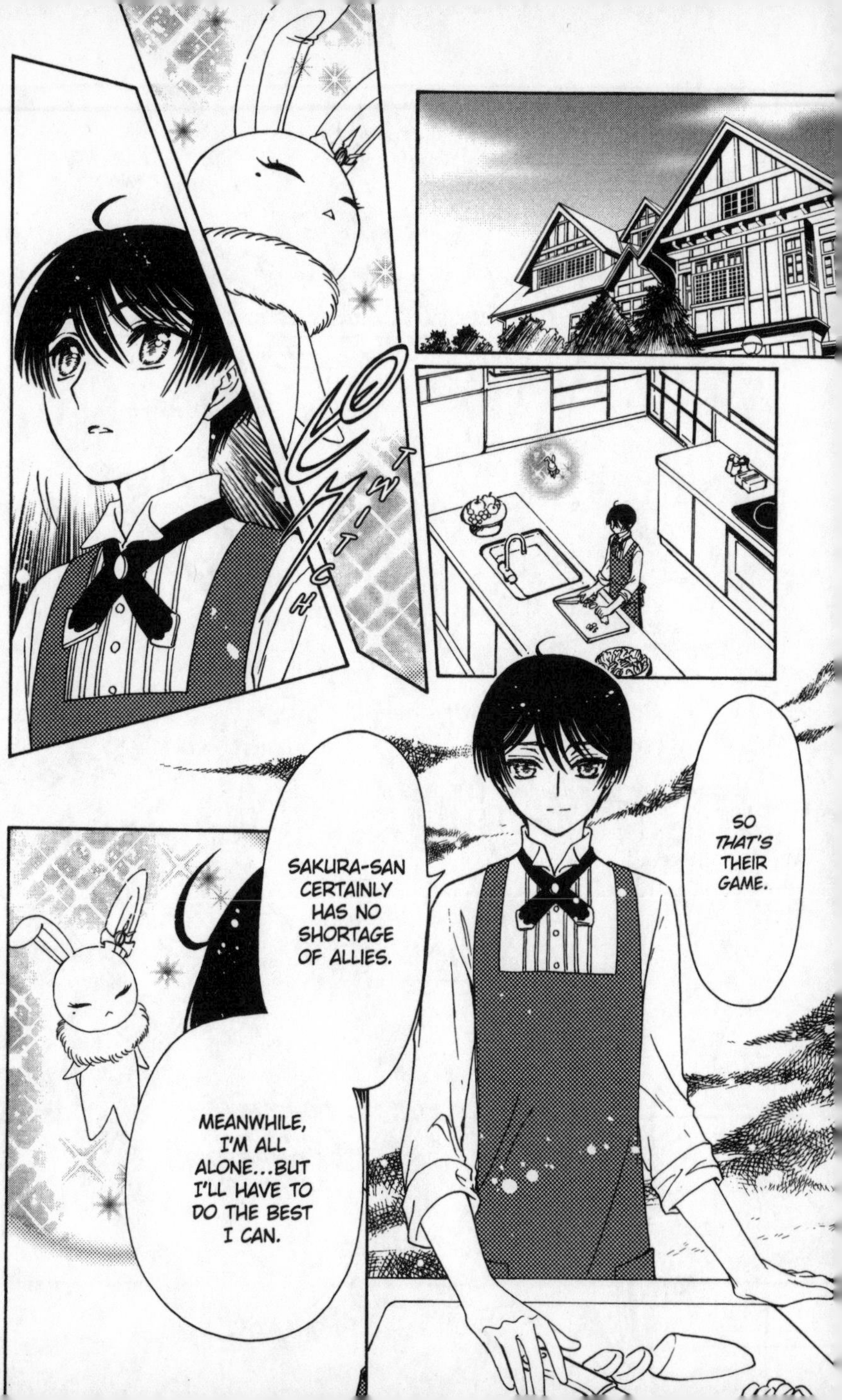
TWITCH
SO THAT'S THEIR GAME.
SAKURA-SAN CERTAINLY HAS NO SHORTAGE OF ALLIES.
MEANWHILE, I'M ALL ALONE...BUT I'LL HAVE TO DO THE BEST I CAN.

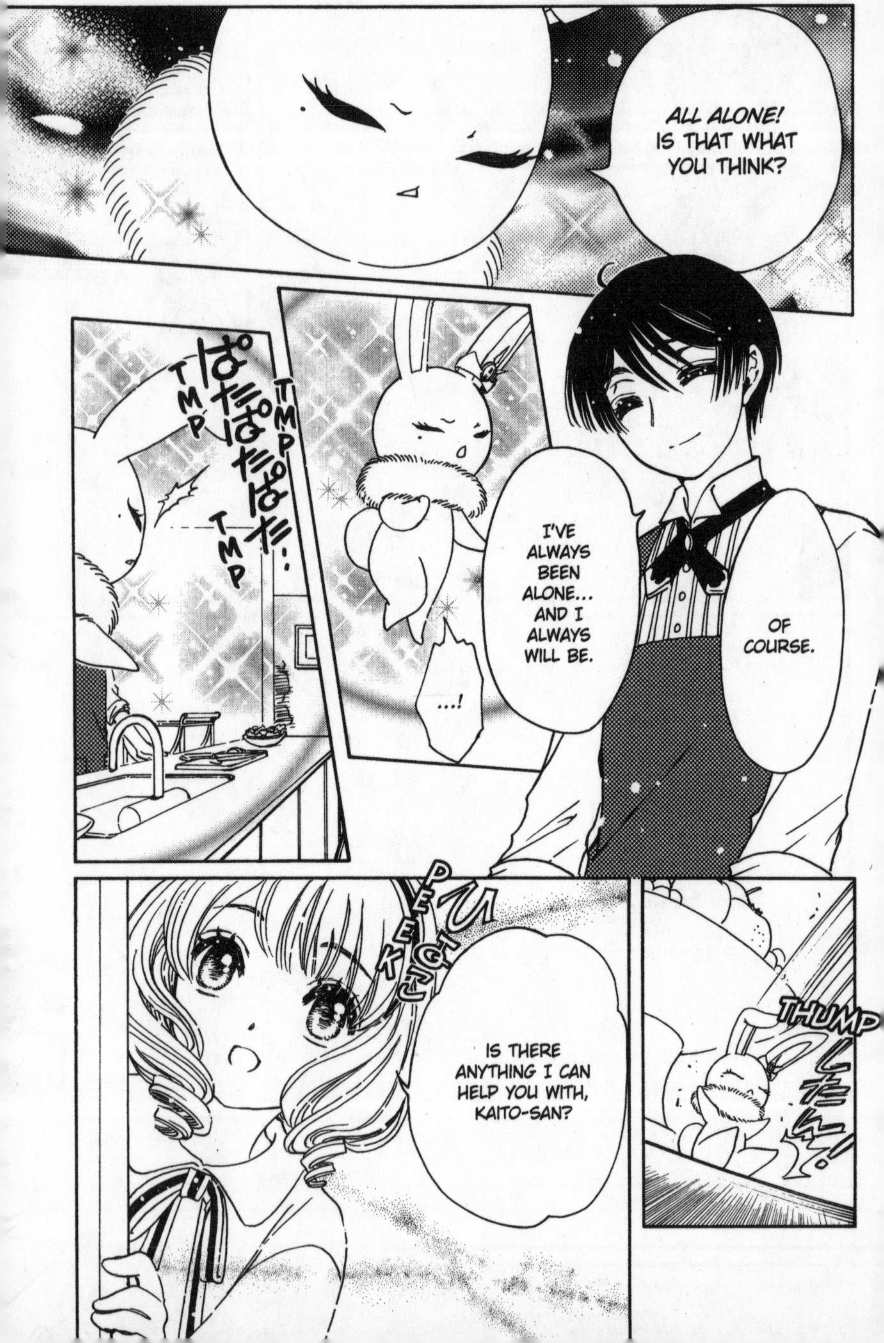
ALL ALONE! IS THAT WHAT YOU THINK?
OF COURSE.
I'VE ALWAYS BEEN ALONE... AND I ALWAYS WILL BE.
...!
TMP TMP TMP TMP
THUMP
PEEK
IS THERE ANYTHING I CAN HELP YOU WITH, KAITO-SAN?

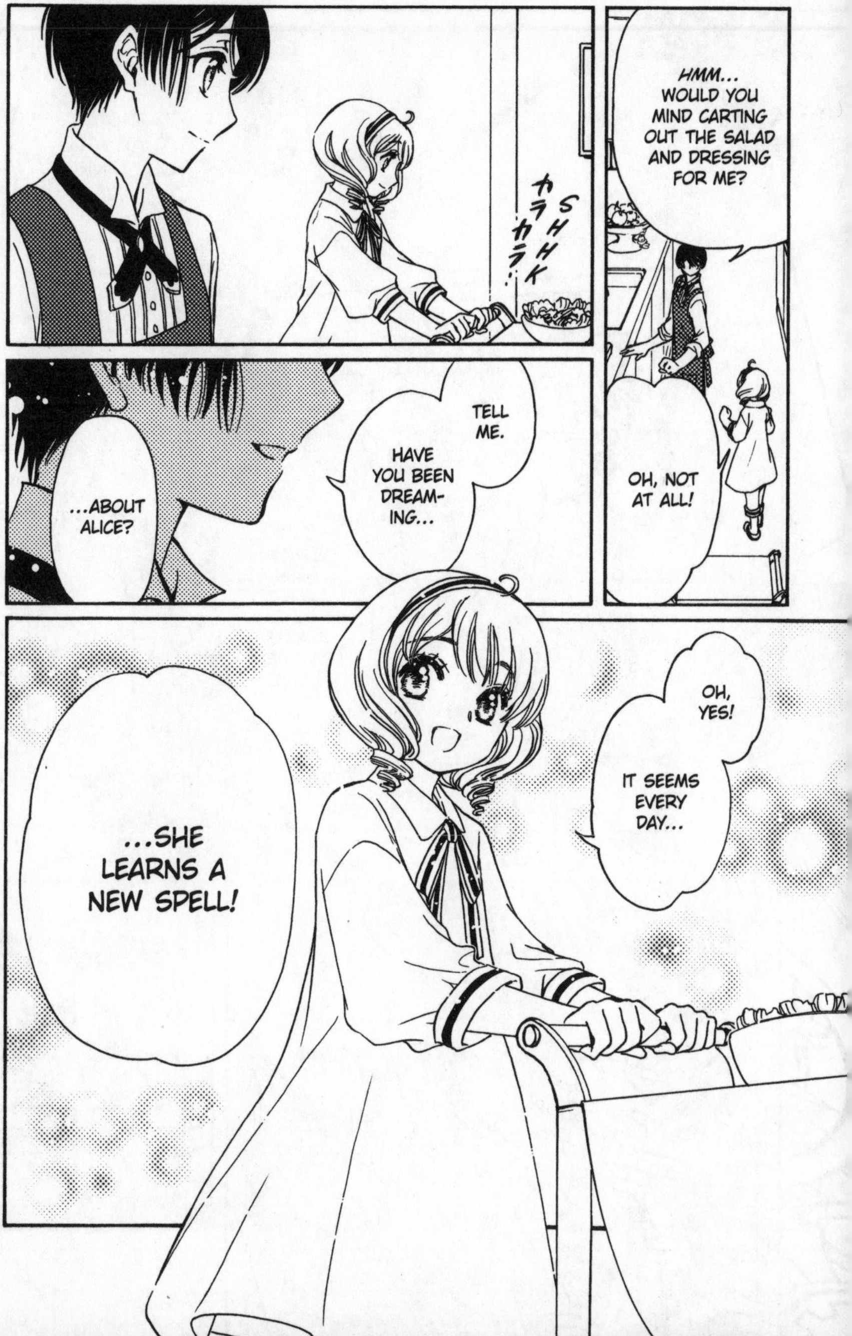
HMM... WOULD YOU MIND CARTING OUT THE SALAD AND DRESSING FOR ME?
OH, NOT AT ALL!
SHHK
カラカラ
TELL ME.
HAVE YOU BEEN DREAM-ING...
...ABOUT ALICE?
OH, YES!
IT SEEMS EVERY DAY...
...SHE LEARNS A NEW SPELL!

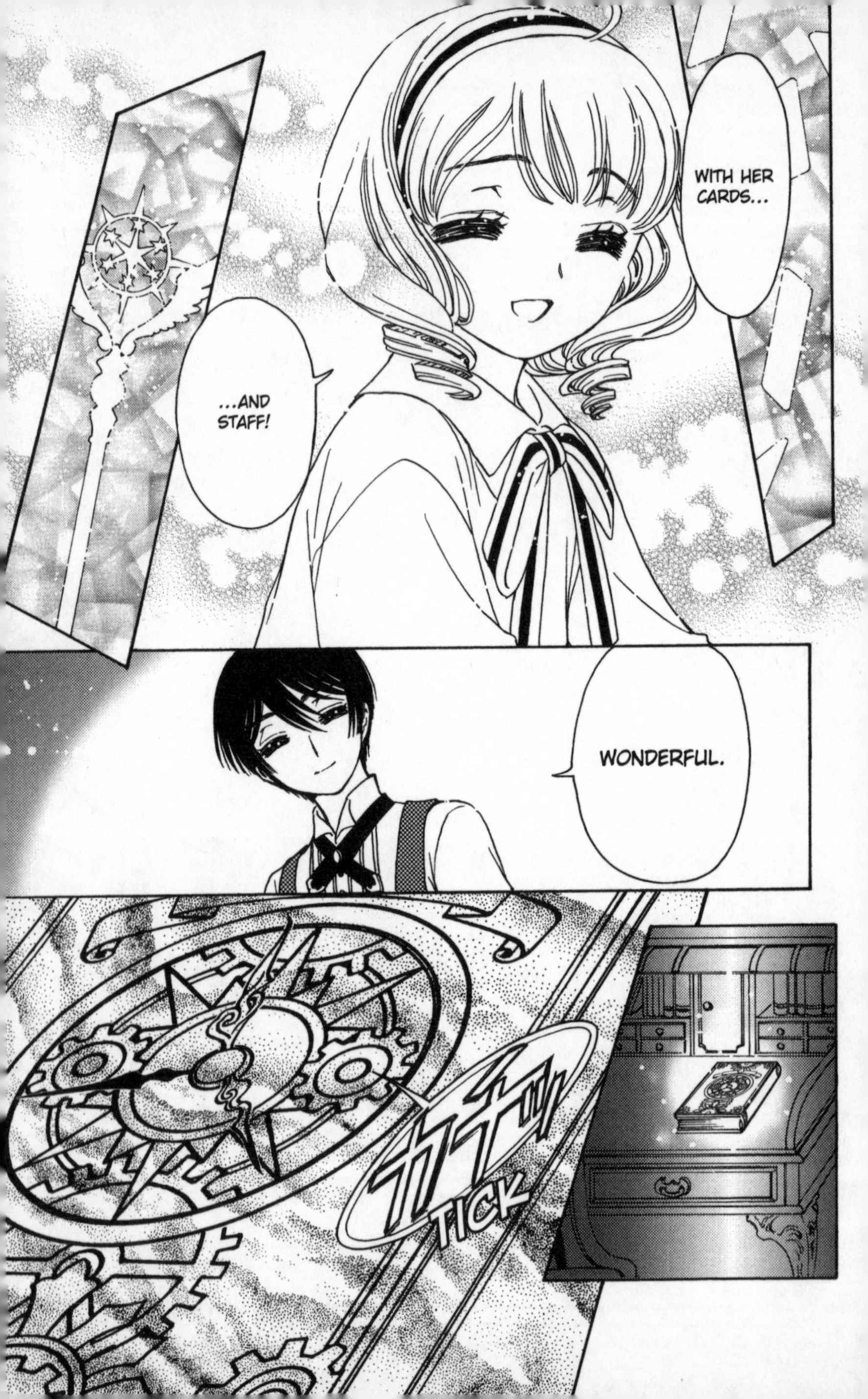
WITH HER CARDS...
...AND STAFF!
WONDERFUL.
カチッ
TICK

❀ Continued in Volume 10 ❀

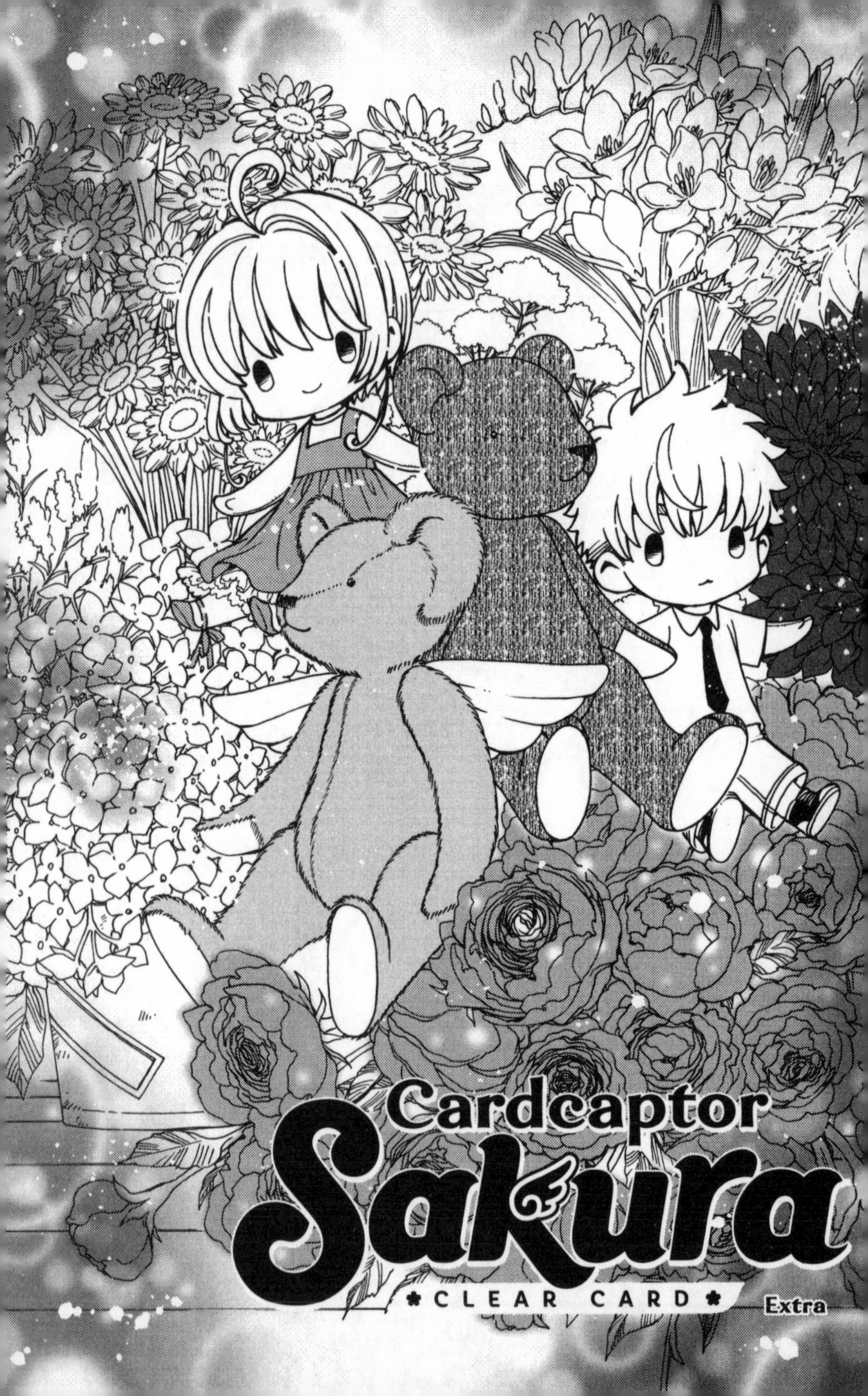
Cardcaptor
Sakura
CLEAR CARD
Extra

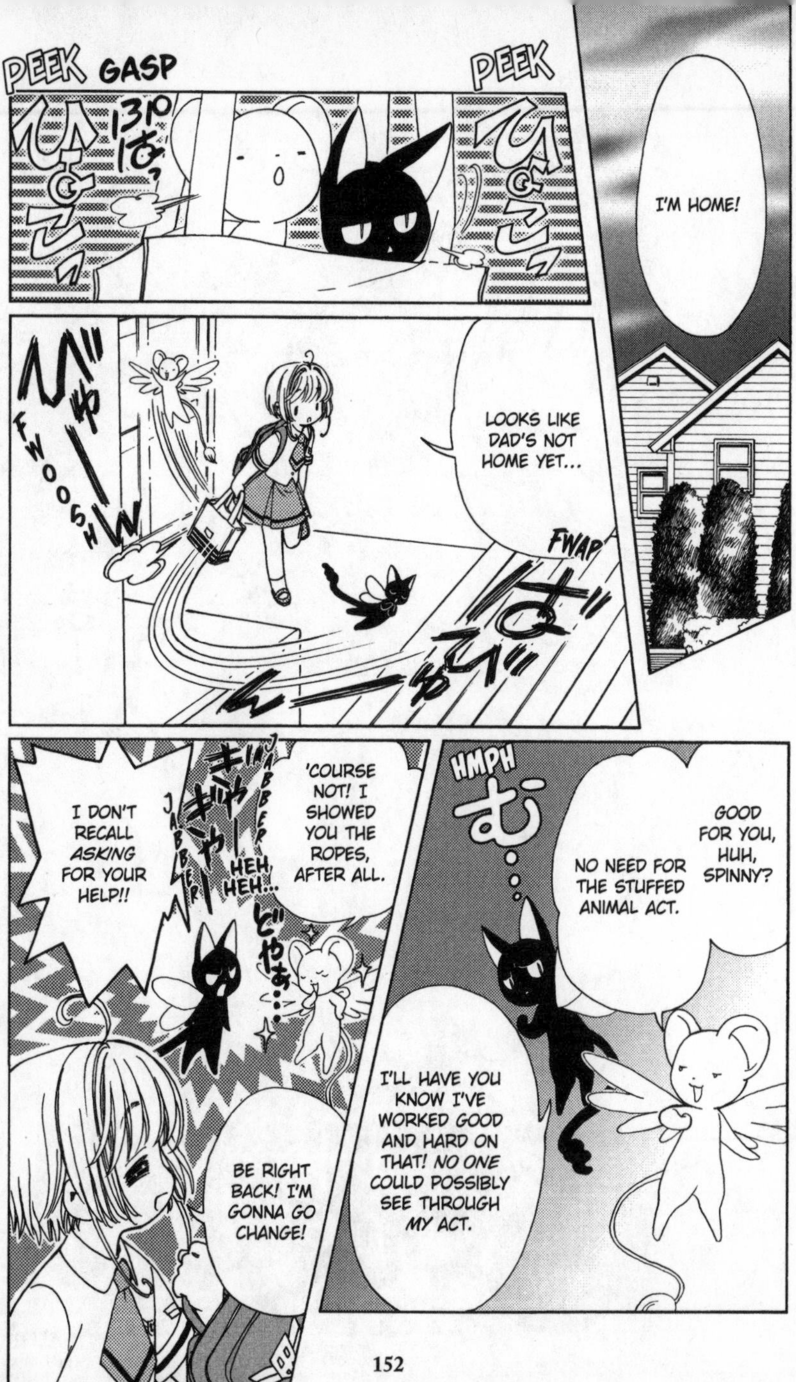

I'M HOME!
PEEK
GASP
PEEK
LOOKS LIKE DAD'S NOT HOME YET...
FWAP
FWOOSH
GOOD FOR YOU, HUH, SPINNY?
NO NEED FOR THE STUFFED ANIMAL ACT.
HMPH
I'LL HAVE YOU KNOW I'VE WORKED GOOD AND HARD ON THAT! *NO ONE* COULD POSSIBLY SEE THROUGH *MY* ACT.
'COURSE NOT! I SHOWED YOU THE ROPES, AFTER ALL.
JABBER
JABBER
HEH HEH...
I DON'T RECALL *ASKING* FOR YOUR HELP!!
BE RIGHT BACK! I'M GONNA GO CHANGE!

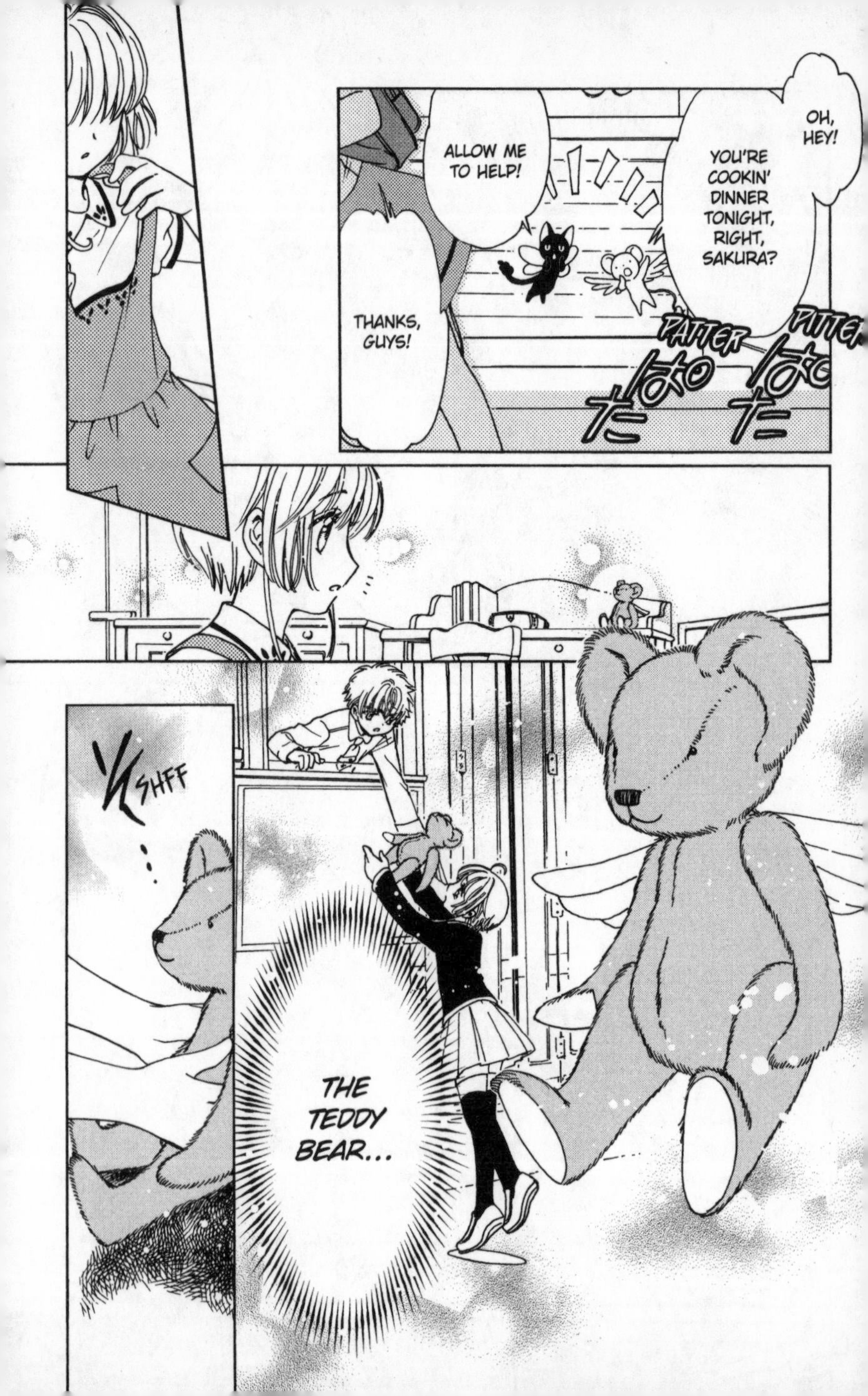

OH, HEY!
YOU'RE COOKIN' DINNER TONIGHT, RIGHT, SAKURA?
PITTER
ぱた
PATTER
ぱた
ALLOW ME TO HELP!
THANKS, GUYS!
SHFF
THE TEDDY BEAR...

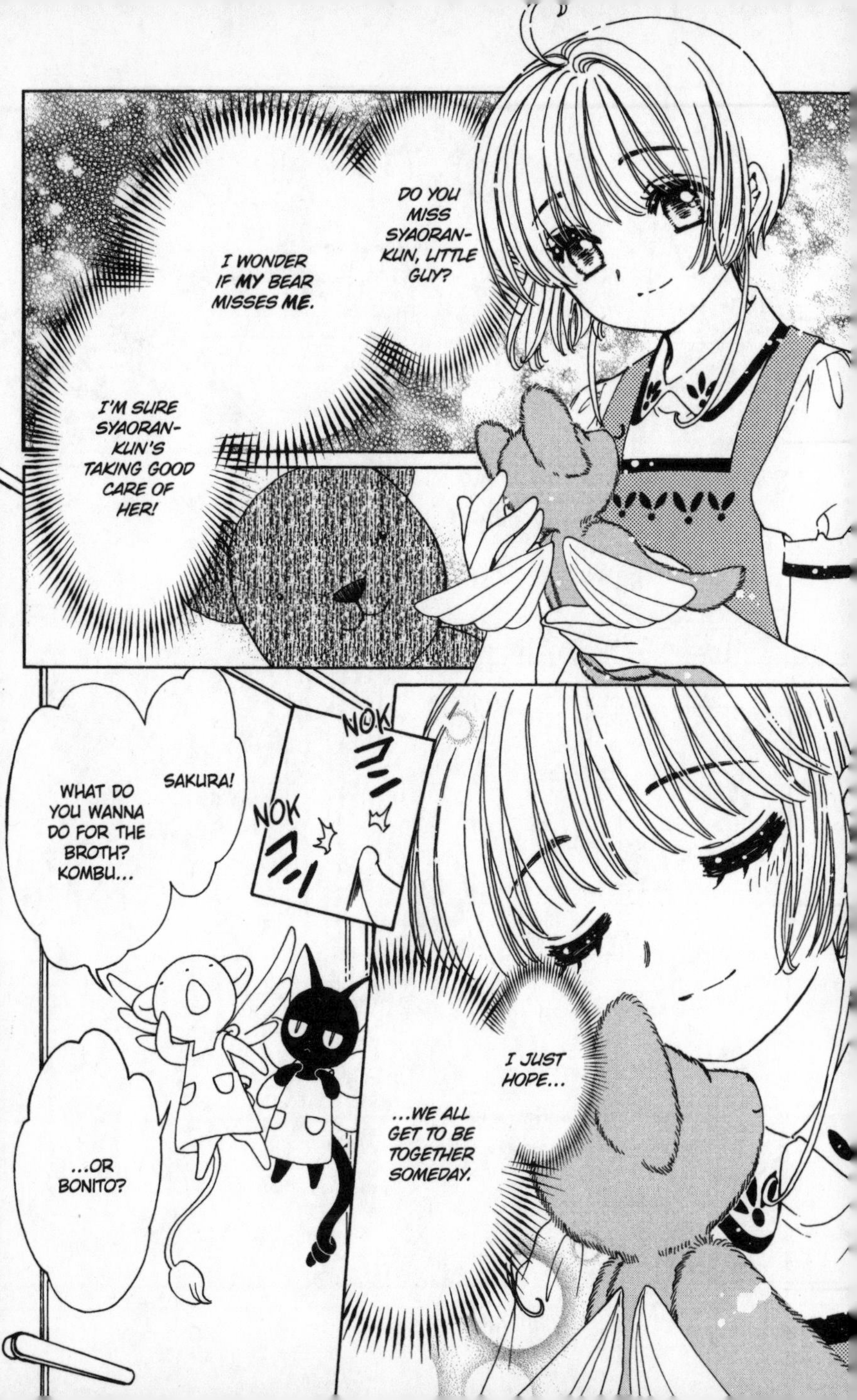
DO YOU MISS SYAORAN-KUN, LITTLE GUY?
I WONDER IF MY BEAR MISSES ME.
I'M SURE SYAORAN-KUN'S TAKING GOOD CARE OF HER!
I JUST HOPE...
...WE ALL GET TO BE TOGETHER SOMEDAY.
NOK
NOK
SAKURA!
WHAT DO YOU WANNA DO FOR THE BROTH? KOMBU...
...OR BONITO?

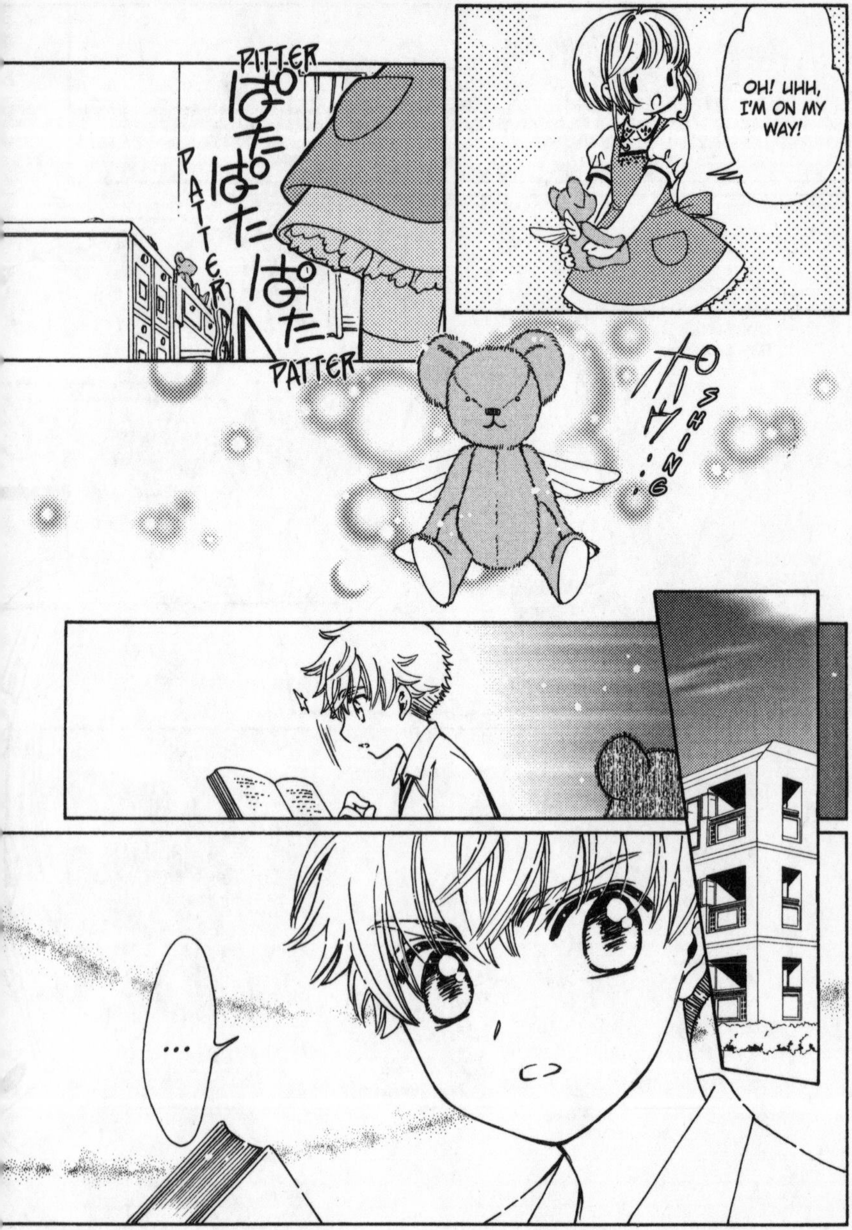
OH! UHH, I'M ON MY WAY!
PITTER
ぱたぱた
PATTER
ぱた
PATTER
ポワ…
SHING
...

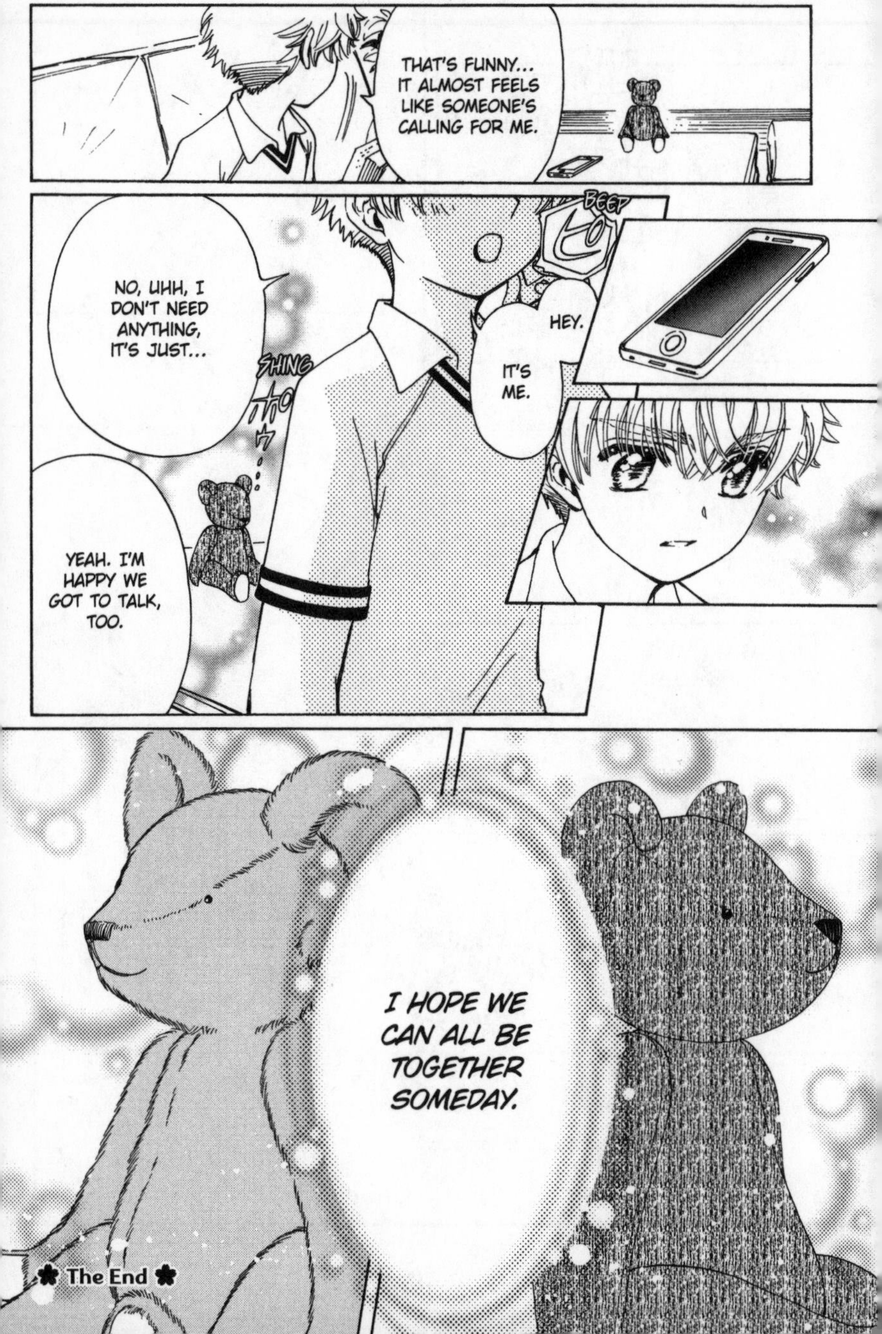
THAT'S FUNNY... IT ALMOST FEELS LIKE SOMEONE'S CALLING FOR ME.
BEEP
HEY.
IT'S ME.
NO, UHH, I DON'T NEED ANYTHING, IT'S JUST...
SHING
YEAH. I'M HAPPY WE GOT TO TALK, TOO.
I HOPE WE CAN ALL BE TOGETHER SOMEDAY.
The End

Cardcaptor Sakura

CLEAR CARD

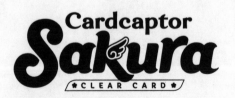

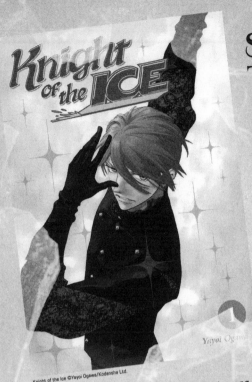

Knight of the Ice ©Yayoi Ogawa/Kodansha Ltd.

SKATING THRILLS AND ICY CHILLS WITH THIS NEW TINGLY ROMANCE SERIES!

A rom-com on ice, perfect for fans of *Princess Jellyfish* and *Wotakoi*. Kokoro is the talk of the figure-skating world, winning trophies and hearts. But little do they know... he's actually a huge nerd! From the beloved creator of *You're My Pet* (*Tramps Like Us*).

Chitose is a serious young woman, working for the health magazine *SASSO*. Or at least, she would be, if she wasn't constantly getting distracted by her childhood friend, international figure skating star Kokoro Kijinami! In the public eye and on the ice, Kokoro is a gallant, flawless knight, but behind his glittery costumes and breathtaking spins lies a secret: He's actually a hopelessly romantic otaku, who can only land his quad jumps when Chitose is on hand to recite a spell from his favorite magical girl anime!

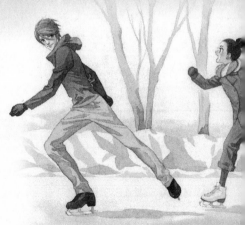

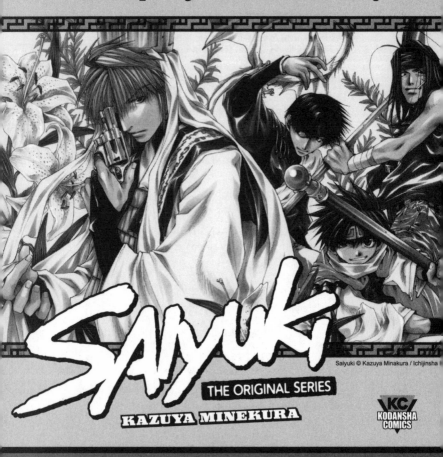

Cardcaptor Sakura: Clear Card volume 9 is a work of fiction. Names, characters, places, and incidents are the products of the author's imagination or are used fictitiously. Any resemblance to actual events, locales, or persons, living or dead, is entirely coincidental.

A Kodansha Comics Trade Paperback Original
Cardcaptor Sakura: Clear Card volume 9
copyright ©2020 CLAMP · ShigatsuTsuitachi CO.,LTD. / Kodansha Ltd.
English translation copyright ©2021 CLAMP · ShigatsuTsuitachi CO.,LTD. / Kodansha Ltd.

Published in the United States by Kodansha Comics, an imprint of Kodansha USA Publishing, LLC, New York.

Publication rights for this English edition arranged through Kodansha Ltd., Tokyo.

First published in Japan in 2020 by Kodansha Ltd., Tokyo, as Kaadokyaputaa Sakura Kuriakaado Hen volume 9.

ISBN 978-1-64651-033-7

Printed in the United States of America.

www.kodansha.us

9 8 7 6 5 4 3 2 1
Translation: Erin Procter
Lettering: Erika Terriquez
Editing: Kristin Osani
Kodansha Comics edition cover design: Phil Balsman

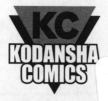

Publisher: Kiichiro Sugaw

Director of publishing services: Be
Associate director of operations: Ste
Publishing services associated managing editor: Madison Salters
Production managers: Emi Lotto, Angela Zurlo